Greenwich Council
Library & Information Service

IN HOUSE
QUALITY
SYSTEMS

Blackheath Library
Old Dover Road, SE3 7BT
020 8858 1131

Please return by the last date shown

27. SEP 04. 23 Oct		
	Thank You!	

To renew, please contact any Greenwich library

Issue: 02	Issue Date: 06.06.00	Ref: RM.RBL.LIS

A LICENCE TO PRINT MONEY

JAMIE REID

A LICENCE
TO PRINT
MONEY

MACMILLAN
LONDON

First published 1992 by
MACMILLAN LONDON LIMITED
a division of Pan Macmillan Publishers Limited
Cavaye Place London SW10 9PG
and Basingstoke

Associated companies in Auckland, Budapest, Dublin, Gaborone,
Harare, Hong Kong, Kampala, Kuala Lumpur, Lagos, Madras,
Manzini, Melbourne, Mexico City, Nairobi, New York, Singapore,
Sydney, Tokyo and Windhoek

ISBN 0-333-548043

A CIP catalogue for this book is available from
the British Library

Typeset by Florencetype, Kewstoke, Avon

Printed by Billing and Sons Ltd,
Worcester.

'Whether it is a good thing or not, the majority of people go racing not because of their love of horse flesh, not because it is a Sport of Kings, but because they want to bet.'

William Hill

'Now, Mr Bond. There are two gamblers . . . the man who lays the odds and the man who accepts them. The bookmaker and the punter. The casino and, if you like' – Mr Zographos's smile was sly with the 'shared secret' and proud with the right word – 'the suckers.'

From an unpublished James Bond story by Ian Fleming

This book is dedicated to the many betting and racing friends and associates whose touching faith in the punter's belief that 'losses are only lent' helped to make it all possible

Contents

A LICENCE
TO PRINT
MONEY

Introduction

The owner of a betting shop is prohibited by law from attempting to attract customers by directly encouraging people to gamble. They can advertise their phone line and results line services but the Betting and Gaming Act of 1961 insists that they may only cater for unstimulated demand. Cyril Stein, the chairman of Ladbrokes, the biggest and most powerful betting shop business in the world, has described his company as the Marks and Spencers of high-street betting. Yet no floor-to-ceiling plate-glass windows permit passing shoppers to gaze in at Cyril's wares and neither are his customers allowed even one solitary window through which to gaze at the world outside.

While it is considered all right for the Treasury to rake in some £467 million a year in betting duty and for punters to contribute over £37 million a year to the upkeep of the horse-racing industry, a fine hypocrisy continues to insist that what goes on inside betting offices should be hidden as far as possible from public view. Gambling can still not be considered an entirely respectable activity.

In hot summer months the law's insistence that betting shop doors must remain closed at all times can make life almost unbearable for those betting and working within. With no windows and, even in 1991, no shortage of cigarette fumes, the interiors can quickly become stale, stuffy and airless. Some shop managers open their doors and hang a beaded curtain over the entrance: air passes in and cigarette smoke, along with the tantalising sound of Tote dividends, greyhound racing at Monmore and horse-race commentaries from Kempton Park, drifts out. But 'nice' people passing by on the street cannot actually see ine possibly not so nice people inside.

Betting shops were banned altogether in Britain for over 100 years until 1961 during which time working-class punters were compelled to break the law to indulge in the generally harmless pleasure of placing a wager away from the racetrack. The Big Three betting-shop chains, Corals, Hills and in particular Ladbrokes, have pulled off a spectacular entrepreneurial triumph in taking this formerly illicit trade and turning it into a multi-million-pound leisure industry where the profits from betting on racing have been used to finance a whole range of other businesses from hotels to property development, casinos, bingo halls and do it yourself stores. Ladbrokes, once exclusive purveyors of betting to the aristocracy, were bought for £100,000 in 1957 by Cyril Stein's uncle Max Parker, himself one of our betting and bookmaking sons of Russian emigré parents. Today, Ladbrokes have a market value of over £2 billion.

That success has been made possible partly as a result of the company's own ruthless professionalism and commercial zeal and partly because, for all the continuing resistance of the Home Office, the British are a nation enthusiastically hooked on betting and gambling. Up to £10 million is bet off-course every day except Sunday when another piece of restrictive legislation continues to prevent either the opening of betting offices or the staging of race meetings with on-course cash betting. Yet bookmakers in general and not just off-course shop owners continue to be stigmatised by the rest of society and treated at best as akin to used-car and scrap-metal dealers and at worst refused entry to the Jockey Club and other ruling bodies of the racing establishment on the grounds that they are, well, not quite gentlemen.

A Licence To Print Money is not the work of a master professional gambler or betting pundit listing tips and advice for the ordinary punter. Anyone tempted to emulate the approach of some of its protagonists such as A. J. Kincaid would be embarking on a quick if enjoyable path to ruin. (And I should add that some of the characters, horses and situations described here, principally in the Cheltenham, Brighton and Redcar chapters, have been deliberately changed or disguised in order, as they said about the Gay Future affair, to protect the guilty.) The book is a personal, prejudiced and idiosyncratic account: part history, part evocation, part argument and part dramatisation. It acknowledges the debate raging between bookmaking and racing interests over what portion of the profits generated by betting on racing should go towards the financial viability of racing itself, but it accepts no obligation to come up with an all-embracing solution to that problem or, even, to accord racing the normally benevolent dispensation that it has come to expect. It is written out of a passionate love for the Turf but also from an equal enthusiasm for betting and gambling and an unashamed preference for the style and personalities of 'the ring'. It believes that Britain is emphatically a bookmaking culture and that bookies and punters are connected to one another by symbiotic mutual dependency. It is only with a bookmaker that the punter has the exhilarating possibility of being able to beat the market.

There is all the difference in the world between the big, modern, corporate betting-shop chains and the old-fashioned risk-taking rails bookies but that should be a reason to challenge the former and encourage the latter, not to drive them all out of racing altogether. A racecourse without a bookmaker would be about as exciting and atmospheric as a gymkhana without a beer tent.

I should like to thank everyone at Macmillan who has worked on the book and in particular my editor Roland Philipps for his inexhaustible patience and wise advice and Hazel Orme for her painstaking grammatical assistance. I should also like to thank Paul Mathieu for permitting me to draw on material covered in detail in his fascinating study *The Druids Lodge Confederacy*, which has already become an acknowledged classic on one of the most intriguing episodes of betting and racing history. I am especially grateful to Richard Thomas, for sharing with me his invaluable knowledge of bookmaking, and to the late Larry Lyons, formerly of the *Cork Examiner*, who pieced together so many of the details of the Gay Future story. Finally I must thank Cat Ledger without whose different but equally invaluable support there would have been no book.

CHAPTER ONE

A Three Day Party

WE WERE trapped within the kill-zone of a foul-smelling hamburger van that was situated towards the rear of the oldest remaining part of the Members' Enclosure at Cheltenham. The nauseous, rancid stench of burnt onions, and cheap, out of a box, frozenly nasty hamburger patties was stinging our nostrils and watering our eyes. And even amid the drunken babel of hundreds of laughing, talking and singing voices we still seemed able to hear every squelch of the plastic ketchup and mustard bottles as they splattered their contents wide onto reddening booze-inflamed cheeks and blue-and-caramel-coloured velvet-collar coat lapels.

We were not customers for these unsavoury examples of salmonella in a bun. We were simply trying to get a drink in the Kerstin bar next door. Such was the frenzied demand for refreshment from all four corners of the track that this same malodorous outdoor kiosk, not instantly visible unless you knew where to look, had become the only public drinking hole on the course where it was still remotely possible to get served within sixty minutes. There were plenty of other hamburger vans. There was a rash of fast-food pimples dotted right round the track. But some years before the racecourse manager Mr Edward Gillespie, a small crisp man with a dashing line in cavalry twill trousers and Viyella check shirts, had seen fit to preside over the destruction of the one surviving bar with any character and atmosphere in which there had been the reasonable expectation of being able to buy a round between races. Apparently not content with the plastic and overcrowded facilities in the first-floor section of the main stand, Mr Gillespie and his board had given the order to bulldoze the old Arkle bar too to make way for a windowless low-ceilinged construction with the same name but less than half the personality. Here, the wretchedest drinkers were now squeezed and compressed, one on top of another, like replica casualties in a rush-hour train crash. Leaving the likes of us with no alternative other than to take our chances in this little fume-ridden outdoor stockade with its own security guards standing at the gate – not to keep others out but to keep us in – and with its own miniature Fort Apache fence with half-drunk plastic cups of bubbly and Scotch ranged along the rim.

But what on earth had got into us, myself and others? Like that intrepid punter A. J. Kincaid, the racing correspondent and form book specialist John Moynahan, Major Tom, the bookmaker's man, and a young Surrey motor dealer and unlicensed bookie with Spanish connections and the mysterious and confusing nickname of Cheltenham Tony? What had possessed us to put up with these execrable conditions? To spend good money, not just today, which was the third and final leg of the ordeal, but for the two previous days, just to be able to stand idiotically shoulder to shoulder in this absurd spot?

The first and most obvious answer was that we were all completely and certifiably insane. Bereft of all judgement, intellect and taste. But there was also, quite seriously and truthfully, a nobler motivation, a deeper imperative for our madness. This was the National Hunt Festival. The most impassioned, the most competitive and the most spectacularly hedonistic of horse-racing's big shebangs, comprising, along with the four days of Royal Ascot each June, the World Poker Championships of racetrack gambling.

It would probably be fair to say that the great majority of the ordinary non-racing public, the twice-a-year Grand National and Derby Day punters, are not really aware of the mystique of Cheltenham. They know a little bit about Epsom, Newmarket and Ascot. They may even be familiar with the glamorous and engrossing events that take place in Louisville, Kentucky, on the first weekend in May and in Melbourne, Australia, on the first Tuesday of November. Yet they do not generally understand that, as far as the true believers in the horse-playing community in both Britain and Ireland are concerned, none of these other meetings, however distinguished and exciting they may be, can ever quite compare with the three-day gathering that assembles in the Cotswolds each March.

Flat-racing has numerous festivals throughout the season. The professionals, the addicts and the serious freeloaders can move on every few weeks from Chester to York to Epsom to Ascot to Newmarket to Goodwood back to York and so on. Jump-racing builds towards the Mecca of Cheltenham all winter long. Nine of the eighteen contests are championship events. All of the top steeplechasers and hurdlers from both Britain and Ireland take part, and the speculation as to who will come out on top in their respective divisions begins at the end of the previous October and, come Cheltenham, reaches a pitch of sustained intensity rarely equalled on the level. To be a great name in National Hunt racing you have to prove that you can win at Cheltenham and because all the great names in jumping have won there, many of them like Arkle, Mill House, Dawn Run, Persian War, Sea Pigeon and Night Nurse running their hearts out at successive Festivals, contributes a timeless sense of history and emotion to each Gold Cup meeting. Desert Orchid's owners showed how much they respected that tradition when they allowed the grey to take his chance in the 1989 Cheltenham Gold Cup even though heavy rain and snow had turned the conditions dramatically against him. And that he managed to prevail, albeit narrowly, winning for only the second time in his life around a left-handed track, was a glorious if corny vindication of the Cheltenham spirit.

If the racing is in the championship class then the Prestbury Park racecourse is a fitting arena for such momentous struggles. The stands may be predominantly ugly and modern, lacking in either grace or style, and in March they are backed up by a small army of corporate-entertainment chalets and sponsors' marquees. Yet the racetrack itself is set in an exhilarating natural amphitheatre overlooked by the long imposing line of the Cotswold Hills. The two wide galloping circuits are not fenced in or bounded by a suburban railway line or reclaimed gravel pit as at Sandown and Kempton. The downhill gallop on the far side, as the horses stream away out into the country, gives way to a left-handed uphill climb which leads on to the farthest point on the course. It is here that battle is invariably and thrillingly joined. There is then a dramatic downhill sweep towards the third last jump and then another left-handed turn into the straight, which is where many races have been won or lost. And even after the final obstacle, there is still the long, stamina-sapping uphill climb to the winning post.

Cheltenham, though, is not only about racing. It is also about betting. The stories of the big Festival touches, the ones that were landed and the ones that went astray, are truly the stuff of which gambling legends are made. All the big players attend, as well as thousands of smaller-scale enthusiasts. It is extremely difficult, and a major challenge to the punters' skill, consistently to show a profit over the week because the competition is so intense. But the strength of the market, due to there being so much money circulating, means that good horses with serious winning chances will often start at much better prices than you will encounter at a normal run-of-the-mill race meeting.

Generally speaking, up to 95 per cent of all betting on horse-racing takes place off-course, some of it through telephone credit-account wagering but most of it through the nation's 9,300 or so licensed betting shops. Yet it is the on-course market, strong at Cheltenham and Royal Ascot but notoriously weak for the rest of the time, that sets the odds or starting prices at which most off-course bets, unless agreed otherwise, are settled.

The starting prices or SPs are the official odds at which the horses in a race are returned. The responsibility for collating them is in the hands of starting-price reporters working for the Press Association and the racing trade papers. They, or their staff and assistants, move around the betting ring before every horserace at every race meeting throughout the year. They base their SPs on the final show of odds available before the 'off', which means the moment when the starting stalls crash open if it's a flatrace or the moment when the starter's tapes go up if it's a steeplechase or hurdle race. (Starting stalls are used on the flat as with so many races being run over short distances, it is vital to ensure that all the runners get an even break. There are no races over fences and hurdles of less than two miles in distance so stalls would make a negligible difference.)

At the typical Monday and Tuesday meetings at places like Nottingham and Wolverhampton, on-course attendance will often amount to little more than a thousand paying spectators with hardly a big spender among them. At meetings like these it takes only a couple of four- or sometimes even three-figure bets to see the odds of a fancied horse contract dramatically. It is not unusual for these £500 and £1,000 wagers to be placed not by individual gamblers but by on-course representatives of the Big Three off-course betting shop chains: Ladbrokes, Coral and Hills. The Big Three regularly, and quite legally, hedge money into the racecourse betting pool but not simply to 'lay off' or cover liabilities they may have incurred as a result of the specific bets of certain of their off-track customers. They also act to contract starting prices and reduce across the board the likely pay-out they will have to make to their betting-shop clientele.

At meetings like the Cheltenham Festival, where the daily attendance rises to over 44,000 and there is no shortage of high-rolling gamblers in the crowd, it takes much larger sums of money to be bet before a horse's odds seriously shorten up and it is therefore much harder for the Big Three to dominate. At Cheltenham the leading on-course bookies will be prepared to accept numerous four- and five-figure bets for the most fancied horses because they know that, with so much more money and custom around than usual, they should still have every opportunity to balance their books on each contest and, hopefully, be able to show a profit on the three days of Festival trading.

This situation, whereby the Big Hitters are both present and able to 'get on', is also to the advantage of the smaller punters. They may not want to back the 'jolly' or the market leader that the insiders are piling into but they will find that other horses in each race (and at Cheltenham almost all the races have fields well into double figures), can be backed at remarkably generous odds – due once again to the overall sums of money circulating. Given that this is the Festival with all the prestige – and matching levels of prize money – these horses will often be far from nonentities but animals coming into the meeting with serious form credentials of their own. And, as any study of past Festival results regularly shows, the fixture offers plenty of value betting opportunities at odds of between 5–1 and 14–1 *if* you are wise enough and patient enough to look for them.

It is always happily accepted that the Irish love to bet but the British, for all the residue of Victorian and puritanical influences in the national character, are also enthusiastically partial to a gamble. Some £10 million is bet off-course every day and household gambling losses of £2.6 billion are posted annually. Ladbrokes estimate that the combined turnover in the nation's betting offices during the three days of Cheltenham – much of it admittedly the same money going round and round – is in the region of £75 million. The precise on-course figure is not available because although some individual bookies will reveal their margins, if asked, the on-course bookmakers do not collectively disclose the details.

What can be said about the trackside wagering is that most of it is wild, reckless and obsessive, with stories of sensational triumphs and defeats spreading rapidly like exaggerated reports of wartime engagements. But if one thing distinguishes the British and Irish punters from the greater number of their counterparts in America and France it is that they tend to identify with their horses far more, regarding them as familiar and even sympathetic characters rather than as the mechanical objects of their wagering. Animated discussions of a horse's record and potential, of trainers, jockeyship and form will invariably be taking place in every bar and enclosure on the course at meetings like Cheltenham or York. But on all except the vintage big-race days the turfistes and rail-birds at Longchamp and Gulfstream Park seem to be engaged in a strictly numerical game of chance and not a lot more. At the same time, neither the occasional nor the compulsive punters head for the racetrack and the betting ring simply to try to beat the form book or to partake in an ascetic or religious rite. They go there to enjoy themselves. The pleasure principle is an integral and essential part of the gamble. And, unlike some other race meetings that have tried arbitrarily to add the word festival to their sometimes decidedly unfestive occasions, Cheltenham is an authentic three day party that appeals to all types and classes of punter – pallid urban sophisticates as well as hard-riding hunting men and women from the shires. For many of those present the celebrations go on night and day with but a few hours' break for sleep. The local service industries do their best to pump up the race-goers' buccaneering approach to money, and hotel rooms as far away as Bristol and Birmingham change hands for two or three hundred pounds a night, while country-house hotels in the Gloucestershire environs charge up to £60 a head without wine for their Gold Cup night dinners. And, not to be outdone, those ever-popular characters the racecourse caterers require £37.50 for frankly unremarkable bottles of champagne.

With its annual position one week before the spring equinox the Festival is sometimes blessed with glorious mild almost high-summer weather when coats come off, spirits soar and money gravitates towards the fast-ground horses. In other years the weather will lash out with a last vicious turn of winter, bringing driving rain, high winds, hail, sleet and even snow to Prestbury Park. That is when only the bravest horses excel, the racing takes on an epic quality and the wild siege-like atmosphere renders everyone present drenched, drunk and mesmerised with excitement.

It was to participate once again in this annual passionate outburst of sporting, gambling and bacchanalian revelry that Kincaid, Moynahan, Tony, the Major and myself had made our way back to Prestbury Park. Like all experienced punters and festival-goers, we had gone there expecting to bet, to lose, to shake our heads and to talk about our losers (and perhaps occasionally about our winners) and, in particular, to reflect on our so nearly inspired judgement, the absurd callousness of fate and the eternally obvious and optimistic reasons to expect imminent success, in the next, the very next race on the card. And, since the action on the track at Cheltenham pauses every thirty-five minutes or so, there is only one possible way to fortify oneself for more of the demented behaviour that the Festival demands. You have to drink. And as by this final stage of this final afternoon no badge on Kincaid's, Moynahan's, Tony's or my own lapel deemed us worthy of admittance to a grandiloquent private box – and the hampers of tuck and bottles of splash therein – and as Major Tom, who had done the rounds of the Turf Club tent and the more exclusive bookmakers' suites, was not prepared to vouch for us in these carpeted acreages, we had no alternative but to embrace the delights of the 'temporary outdoor refreshment facility' where the barmen and women, whey-faced unemployed kids from Newport and Cardiff, were dressed up by the caterers in bow-ties, striped aprons and straw boaters rather like imitation butchers' boys and girls in some cosy Edwardian serial.

Up at the front, A. J. Kincaid was endeavouring to battle his way back through the throng, clutching several bottles and armfuls of plastic cups. For some reason he had chosen to wear a black Basque beret on his head although one suspected that he imagined it was an Irish priest's cap and would therefore be considered appropriate for the occasion. His trenchcoat was crumpled and muddy. He looked as if he was about to lose his glasses and his cigarette had burnt low, but he navigated his way determinedly onwards – for this was, after all, to be a celebration. Kincaid had struck in the last, the sixteenth race of the meeting. In the sixteenth out of eighteen Festival events he had finally backed a winner. And who was to say that winners could not be backed at handsome prices in the next and then the last race as well? He perched one of the bottles of vintage Bollinger on top of an adjacent dustbin and plastic cups were handed round. Kincaid popped the cork of the other bottle and in that peculiarly drunk, inane and oh-so-friendly

11

language of the racecourse we all drank a toast to his health, generosity and sagacious judgement.

'Gentlemen.'

'My dear chap.'

'My dear chap.'

'Many congratulations.'

'My first of the meeting.'

'And two races still to go.'

'I'm doubling up on this favourite in the next.'

'But, of course.'

'But, naturally.'

'Here's to it.'

'Here's to the favourite in the next.'

'Here's to them all.'

'And here's to the bookies.'

'To the old enemy.'

'Here's to them. And God bring us that one big winner.'

Cheltenham Tony reached swiftly for bottle number two as the rest of us turned pathetically to the scrunched-up pages of our green plastic-covered Chaseform Notebooks, to our mangled copies of the *Racing Post* and the *Sporting Life* and to the now almost illegible, cautiously analytical comments in the Timeform racecard. What possible help did we expect to find there? In what subterranean and self-deluding corner of our minds did we imagine that we were remotely capable, at this eleventh hour, of backing a winner ourselves? Of making sense of horse-racing's arbitrary puzzle? Of heading into the ring with even the slenderest chance of outsmarting sober, hard and guileful bookies, who had most likely been memorising probabilities, odds, form and inside stable information in antiseptic hotel rooms since dawn – if not for the whole night, the whole week and the whole month before? We were all members of the daftest soft-touch fraternity in existence. Punters. Hopeless, compulsive and invariably losing punters. British punters. Who, on all the available evidence, will put up with almost any amount of overpriced, overcrowded, second-rate discomfort as long as they can get a scent of the action, an opportunity to bet, a share in the orgasm.

Against all the odds, at this moment anyway, we were defiantly and incomprehensibly happy. Happy to be almost broke. Or happy suddenly to have a few hundred quid in readies in our pockets and to be a grand up on the scorecard with Heathorns and

Hills. One of us was happy not to be in an office. One of us was happy not to be in jail. One of us was happy not to be in a shopping mall or marital home. Oh yes, I'm afraid that some punters are spectacularly, and probably quite nauseatingly, chauvinistic and, indeed, some gamblers would say that for them no sexual experience can ever quite match the trembling, intoxicating thrill of an across-the-board accumulator or short-head touch. Most of all, though, as connoisseurs will understand, we were happy just to be there in that place (even *that* place) at that time, seeming to other more timid and circumspect souls like swanky and virile fellows. Positive players at the Big Casino. Downing our fizz, dicing with chance and batting the cigarette smoke out of our eyes. We must have looked pretty damned impressive.

Of course, we weren't the only punch-drunk group, the only ragged band of punters trying to keep up appearances on Cheltenham racecourse during the closing stages of this Thursday afternoon. Beyond the serving area and the whey-faced straw-hatted kids and the lines of clamouring drinkers were a set of picture windows giving us a superb, not to say laughable, in all honesty embarrassing, view of one of the least desirable so-called private boxes on the whole racecourse. It was inhabited by toffs of the old (not to mention the sadly impoverished or even downright mean) school holed up rather desperately in this ancient (perhaps soon-to-be-demolished) part of the stand to avoid having to rub shoulders with the *hoi polloi* and *nouveaux* in the new stand. That awfully ugly new stand whose front boxes do, rather unfortunately, happen to offer a superb view of the racing but which do cost a teeny bit of dough, not to say considerably more than the average ex-Colonel or retired MFH is any longer capable of coughing up.

The older women were wearing their Robin Hood or chorister's hats, the chaps were in black bowlers and country tweeds worn with large trouser turn-ups. Comforted only by the odd rock-hard sausage roll or glass of sherry and trying, in spite of the rest of us riff-raff and louts, punters and drinkers gazing rudely in through their exclusive window panes, still to seem like toffs of yore, their gamble being the notion that if they studiously ignored our gaze and carried on talking loudly – as if they were all at a typical car boot picnic at the Heythrop point-to-point – one would continue to be impressed by them even in their otherwise patently reduced circumstances.

'Wasn't Dessie simply marvellous?'

'Simply marvellous.'

'Super Dessie.'

'Super Des.'

'So courageous.'

'So brave.'

'Such a trooper.'

'Such fun.' Pause. 'But he didn't win, darling, did he?'

'Oh, I know. But wasn't he simply marvellous?'

One rheumy-eyed old boy, a former Cavalry Club chum of a bowler-hatted steward, was not joining in this inconsequential chatter. Neither was he impressed by the wretchedly stale cakes and the indifferent port. He was standing on his own at one end of the box, scrutinising his racecard, fingering his moustache and whistling a regimental air. The ordinary spectator may have thought that he was just another clueless old pensioner without a handle on the game. But they would have been wrong. He was, in his own way, entirely conversant with the dominant obsession, as the Major, who predictably happened to know the occupants of the box, assured us all afterwards. Even at that moment he was contemplating a gamble, a stroke as daring in its context as our friend Kincaid's four-figure plans to increase his winnings from the last. Can I, should I, dare I, the old stager was thinking, risk five pounds each way on the favourite? Not with those rather intimidating bookmakers, naturally, but with those nice, polite and unthreatening ladies who work behind the windows of the Tote.

A flurry of rubbish, blown across the track by the breeze, preceded the horses as they came out onto the course before the next. Turning our coat collars up against the wind, we fought our way up the hill behind the stand towards the bookies. Somewhere away to my left I thought I glimpsed out of a corner of my eye . . . a great and famous man. None other than the racing and gambling legend J. P. McManus. John. The Kid. The Sundance Kid from Killmallock, Co. Limerick. A name to whisper with awe. A bookmaker, yes, very much a bookie, but much more than that. A major punter, a professional, a player. A man with a reputation for outrageously cool, measured and high-stakes touches. A Fast Eddie Felson and an Amarillo Slim. Now, if you were to meet him for the first time you might express some surprise at his renown. You would encounter a forty-one-year-old, five-and-a-half foot, teetotal Irishman with three children and a loving wife. He would talk to you in an unfailingly courteous and soft-spoken manner, modestly eschewing his reputation, and you would go away suspecting him of possessing all the menace and danger of an altarboy on a Friday night outing to the Wimpy Bar. But you should never under-estimate J. P. or over-romanticise him – and he would not expect you to. For if you were to get involved with him in any kind of bookmaker-punter gambling transaction, he would make it his professional business to know the up and down side of your every move. Which is why the likes of Kincaid, Moynahan, the Major, myself and many others all talk of him in such respectful and reverential tones.

Did he not clear some quarter of a million pounds when his own horse, Mister Donovan, took the first race on the second day, 17 March, St Patrick's Day, of the 1982 Cheltenham Festival? How much was his share of the phenomenal three hundred grand gamble on Forgive 'n' Forget in the Coral Golden Hurdle Final twelve months later? And did he once play backgammon for three consecutive days and nights against the intrepid Charles Benson, formerly 'The Scout' of the *Daily Express*? Starting in Robert Sangster's house on the Isle of Man, continuing in the helicopter on the way to Ayr races, then in the Turnberry Hotel, then in the helicopter back again and once more in the house on the island. Was Benson not at one point well clear of his field until he, unfortunately though understandably, had to resort to alcoholic refreshment to maintain his energy? Did the Kid refuse everything bar the odd glass of milk and occasional soft drink? Did he win in the end . . . naturally? But who is going to ask him about it now and why should he tell? It's a tacky and ignorant journalist who expects a professional punter to reveal the innermost details of his staking plans. For what claim has an interfering writer and his paper or book on the secrets of a gambler's heart?

Back on the ground at the rear of the stand at Prestbury Park, a caterer's van suddenly plunged towards us, scattering dithering and deliberating punters in its wake. When we looked round again McManus was lost and gone. Disappeared in his sleek cashmere into the lift and away up into a private box beyond. Would he dream of taking a drink, I wondered, even so much as one nonalcoholic orange juice, in the Kerstin bar next door to the burnt onions and the hamburger van? Not a chance, by jinks. And by such criteria are the true winners from the rest divided.

CHAPTER TWO

Playing the Horses

THE RACETRACK at Cheltenham may be a spectacular battleground but for the three days of the Festival it is only one of two equally important fields of combat. The other is the betting ring. On average there is at least one equine fatality at every National Hunt Festival meeting. Blood can be spilt in the betting market every half-hour. You would almost never sense or see these things on an ordinary Monday at Folkestone but on the really big days at a premier track, like Cheltenham or Ascot, the tension is palpable. An intense and pervasive combination of greed, bravura, excitement and fear.

One of the more arcane customs of the British Turf decrees that the bookmakers, vulgar tradesmen that they are, cannot set up their pitches in the socially clean air of the Members' Enclosure. They have to be corralled in the ring or Tattersalls' Enclosure next door (so called because it was originally to Tattersalls' auction rooms in Newmarket that eighteenth-century gentlemen punters went to settle their bets).

The first bookmakers were the characters with pencils and books in which to record wagers who turned up on Newmarket Heath whenever gentlemen gathered to race their thoroughbreds and a crowd came to watch. To begin with, betting on horse-racing had mainly been confined to private sweepstakes between the individual owners. Once the numbers of spectators began to increase and move beyond the owners' immediate coterie of friends and associates, there was an obvious opening for enterprising outside individuals to step in and offer a set of prices to all parties.

The underlying principle of betting is that there are two sides to the odds: on the left the stake put up by the bookmaker and on the right that put up by the punter. By convention it is the bookie who offers or 'lays' the odds and the punter who quantifies the unit of the bet, be it £5, £50, £500 or whatever. The bookmaker acts as stakeholder holding both stakes until after the race is decided. Odds are always stated in a manner whereby both sides can be given in whole numbers so fractions such as $1\frac{1}{4}$, $1\frac{1}{2}$ and $1\frac{3}{4}$ translate into 5–4, 6–4 and 7–4. (Alas, the old fractions like 100–6 and 100–8 were rounded down to 16–1 and 12–1 many years ago.) Odds which truly reflect a horse's chance would be called 'fair' but the bookmaking industry is understandably intent not simply on paying its expenses but on making a profit and the odds offered on a racecourse or in a betting shop are all to some degree 'unfair' or 'over round' to allow an element of profit to pertain.

Laying unfair odds is the operating basis on which all commercial betting is structured but there is a crucial difference between slot machines or roulette wheels and a sporting event. In the former category the proper mathematical odds can be calculated almost exactly but horse- and greyhound-racing, like football, tennis and golf, remain a matter of opinion with room for errors and differences of view on both sides.

Up until the early nineteenth century it was believed that to show a profit on sporting contests like boxing and racing, the professional odds makers always had to have a superior knowledge of form or access to inside information or both. Then the layers realised that as long as the overall set of odds included a margin of profit, and as long as all the contestants could be offered in various proportions, it wasn't strictly necessary to know the true or fair chances of each individual participant. The bookmakers' profits started to flow once they put this principle into effect.

Let us imagine you have a two-horse race between Pendil and The Dikler. No matter their relative chances, a profit is bound to accrue to the layer if he can find two people, one willing to put a 'monkey' or £500 on Pendil at 4–5 and one willing to place a similar amount on The Dikler at the same price. Whichever of them wins, the bookie will have taken £1,000 in stake money but will only have to pay out £900 in winnings leaving him with a profit of £100. A more realistic trading scenario might involve six punters wanting to back Pendil and four wanting to back The Dikler, all prepared to wager £100. The bookie obviously has to offer different odds reflecting the differing level of demand so he prices up Pendil at

1–2 and The Dikler at 5–4. If Pendil wins the layer faces a pay-out of £300-worth of winnings plus £600 in stake money but as he's taken £1,000 on the whole race he still shows a profit of £100. If The Dikler triumphs he has to pay £500-worth of winnings and £400-worth of stake money. Again he shows a profit of £100.

Most racecourse betting situations will, of course, be vastly more complicated because of larger fields, many more punters and a wide range of stakes. Imperfections will inevitably arise. Some winners will be more profitable than others and sometimes a race will leave a bookie out of pocket, but as long as the overall odds contain a margin of profit and as long as the layers continue to make a reasonably informed and skilful guess as to what proportions their customers will want to bet in on the different runners, they ought *theoretically* to be assured of some long-term gain no matter which horse wins or what its true or fair odds should have been.

To understand precisely how the bookmakers compile their odds, and therefore what notional profit should accrue to them from each set of prices, you have to remember that they work according to a percentage-chance table of nought to a hundred. On this scale nought technically equals no chance, and one hundred equals a certainty. If all odds were fair then the total of these percentage chances would be exactly a hundred, but, in practice, the total will nearly always exceed that number. This excess is called the over-round, and the greater the over-round the greater the margin of potential profit for the bookie.

On 5 July 1990 seven runners went to post for a five-furlong two-year-old selling race at Haydock Park. Their odds with one bookmaker, with the approximate percentage chance in brackets, were: 5–2 (29 per cent), 7–2 (22 per cent), 4–1 (20 per cent), 6–1 (14 per cent), 7–1 (13 per cent), 8–1 (11 per cent), and 12–1 (8 per cent) making a total of 117 which means that the over-round figure was 17, giving the bookmaker a potential profit of 14.5 per cent on turnover or 17/117ths, providing he was able to lay all the runners according to the odds percentages. On the same day a nine-runner seven-furlong two-year-old race at Sandown had an over-round of only 9, technically representing a better betting proposition while a twenty-runner £35,000 mile-and-a-quarter handicap on the same card had an over-round of over 40 representing an extremely bad betting proposition.

The punter who makes a habit of regularly checking the

over-round and confining his bets to when it is lower than average should, theoretically, be able to improve his returns because the point of percentage chances is that they provide some means of checking the credibility of any set of odds. From time to time situations arise when the boards bookmakers are betting 'over-broke', meaning that in their efforts to persuade the public to get involved they may be offering a set of odds on a race which, at a certain point, at the best prices being offered, will comprise a total of percentage chances that add up to less than a hundred. In these circumstances it is possible to back every horse in the race and be sure of making a profit and the really numerate and perceptive punter who studies odds carefully enough may occasionally be able to avail themselves of this luxury.

Since 1961 there have been two equally legitimate and equally accessible branches of the betting and bookmaking industry: on-course and off-course. There are different types of bookmakers within each branch and in each sphere the punters have a choice (unlike their counterparts in Europe or most states in America) of betting either with the bookies or with the Tote.

Off-course betting is mainly the preserve of the Big Three multiple betting-shop chains (William Hill, Ladbrokes and Coral) who hold 45 per cent of the licences and control roughly 60 per cent of off-track turnover. There is a second division of chain firms such as Stanley Leisure and Surrey Racing and also some 4,000 independently owned shops run by small bookmakers who may own anything between one and forty shops each.

Betting-shop punters can try their luck with a wide variety of different wagers, the most common being the standard win-only and each-way bets. An each-way bet means that you are backing your horse or greyhound to win *and* to be placed, so therefore you must hand the bookmaker double the stake. A £5 each-way bet accordingly costs £10 to place and so on. If your selection wins, you get paid out on both parts of your bet as well as getting your stake back. If your selection is placed, you get back your place stake money and a proportion of the win odds. There is no place-betting on races with four runners or less. In fields of five to seven, the bookmakers pay out a quarter the odds a place on the first two only; in races of eight runners or more they pay out a fifth the odds the first three. In horse-racing handicaps they pay out a quarter the odds a place the first three on fields of twelve to fifteen and a quarter the odds the first four if there are sixteen runners or over.

Off-course punters are particularly attracted to accumulator bets such as doubles, trebles and Yankees which hold out the tantalising possibility of a bumper pay-out for only a small stake. In a basic accumulator, such as a treble, the winnings and stake money from each leg automatically go on to the next leg but if any of the three legs is a loser, the whole bet goes down. A Yankee is a multiple bet of four selections in four different races; it consists of six doubles, four trebles and one four-timer, making eleven bets in all. Therefore a £1 Yankee actually costs £11 to place. If any part of the Yankee comes up, the punter receives some return. If the whole bet comes up, and if the selections are not all odds-on favourites, there is the theoretical chance of a life-changing six-figure pay-out. The odds on these accumulator bets, like the odds against a big win on the pools, are actually stacked heavily in the bookmaker's favour. A treble consisting of three one-in-four chances has only an overall one-in-thirty-six chance of succeeding but the slender prospect of fabulous riches continues to propel countless off-course TV-watching armchair punters into their local Ladbrokes office each Saturday afternoon.

Off-course betting also includes credit-account wagering with independent bookmakers, who may not have any betting shops but who, like the Big Three themselves, have on-course representation. Most credit betting is day of the race but it also includes ante-post betting which means backing your selections several days, weeks or even months before the race in the hope that the odds you are getting will be considerably better than the eventual starting price. These days you don't even need an account to bet by phone with some firms as they will also accept bets up to a certain limit with Switch cards and Building Society debit cards. An increasingly popular form of credit-account betting, at least for the more discriminating high-stakes punter, is with one of the firms of financial or index bookmakers that have flourished in the City since the mid-1980s. Index betting, which brings to bookmaking the parlance of the markets, involves the punters in 'buying' or 'selling' at certain levels and has proved particularly popular in the booming area of sports betting such as on the 1990 World Cup soccer competition in Italy and on the 1991 Rugby World Cup in Britain.

Half-way through the second round of the rugby tournament, IG Index, run by Old Etonian former merchant banker Stuart Wheeler, quoted a points spread of 1340–90 for the total number of points that would be scored in the competition. If you fancied that the bookmaker's estimate was too low and that the total points scored would be in excess of 1390 then you would have wanted to 'buy' that index. If your judgement turned out to be correct then your profit would have been however many points by which the 1390 figure was exceeded, multiplied by your stake. If, on the other hand, you had believed that even 1340 points would not be scored, you would have wanted to 'sell' the IG Index quotation and that would have meant, providing you were right, that however many points by which the total number fell short you would have made that figure multiplied by your stake. If, in either instance, you had got your Index figures wrong then your loss would have been your stake money multiplied by the number of points by which you were out.

Index betting is a quintessentially modern and off-course form of bookmaking. On-course bookmaking, the oldest and most traditional side of the business, is still officially split between two distinct areas: the boards bookies and the rails bookies. In practice, at all except the biggest meetings the distinction between the two is becoming increasingly blurred.

The boards bookmakers, who bet only in cash, are the conventional bookmaking figures: the men you see standing on upturned boxes and crates and shouting the odds. They trade from allotted pitches in the ring, a pitch being the place where they are allowed to set up their 'joint' or the equipment that they need to lay bets. The names of the contestants in each race are displayed on a sheet attached to a board and the bookies adjust each horse's price with chalk in response to the fluctuating movements of the market once betting exchanges get under way. A large satchel, hanging from the front of each joint, is used to salt away the bookie's takings and it is into these satchels that the layers reach when they have to pay out winning bets.

Boards bookmakers deal mainly in straightforward win- and each-way betting although one or two bookies in the ring will always offer bets without the favourite. This means that for gambling purposes they take the likely market leader out of the race and form a new market around the remaining runners. The punter wins if their selection either finishes first past the post or second to the favourite but the re-formed odds will not be as generous as they would have been if the favourite were being taken on in a full market.

Boards bookmakers also bet in the second ring or Silver Ring, the cheapest enclosure on the racecourse and the one furthest away from the centre of the action. The volume of money bet in the Silver Ring and the size of individual wagers is rarely much beyond the loose change level and few bookmakers can afford to contemplate an annual winter holiday in Barbados if they are confined for long to this marketplace.

The rails bookmakers, like the firm for whom Major Tom is the chief public-relations representative, are the independent credit bookmakers and the on-course representatives of the Big Three. They will nearly all take bets in cash as long as the sums are not derisory (and at poorly attended meetings that is often how some of them do their best business) but nominally their main trade is on the book with well-known clients or 'faces', a face being a shrewd and regular punter with close connections to a particular trainer or stable. The rails operators get their name from the position they adopt along the railings separating the Members' Enclosure from Tatts. They might as well be called the Members' bookies as most of their customers come from that section of the crowd. Like the boards men they have to stay on the Tattersalls' side of the divide although they are not allowed to put up a board to advertise their prices as it might interfere with the Members' sightlines. By tradition the toffs, swells and supposedly better-off punters simply stroll across the lawn to strike a wager discreetly with the layer of their choice without having to worry about money or having to rub shoulders with the *canaille* in the pit next door.

It is at the big festival and weekend race meetings that the independent rails bookmakers come into their own. All the really serious betting at fixtures like Cheltenham and Royal Ascot, the £20,000, £30,000 and £50,000 win bets and the high stakes straight and reverse forecasts (where you have to name the first two animals home) takes place not in cash but on credit along the rails.

When it comes to laying off their liabilities with one another, which means placing bets with other bookmakers on horses for whom they have taken substantial sums to cover themselves against loss and balance their books, the course bookies rely on no modern high-technology information system. They are still dependent on the unique, age-old and essentially private language of the tic-tac men. Tic-tac is the name for a kind of code or semaphore of hand and arm signals used to receive and send messages. It takes many years to master the nuances of the tic-tac vocabulary and not surprisingly most operatives are born into the game and have inherited their knowledge and skill from previous generations. The tic-tac men and occasionally women stand up on stools at one end of the ring, high up above the punters and bookies. Their rapid sign language, often preceded by a shrill whistle to attract a layer's attention, sometimes shunts huge sums of money around the ring, from pitch to pitch, in a matter of seconds.

The most important difference between betting on-course and off-course is that you pay no tax on racecourse bets whereas off-course bets are subject to a 10 per cent deduction. The tax can be paid when you place your wager, which is obviously the cheapest way to do it, or you can have it deducted from your winnings if there are any. The betting tax and the chance – which only exists on-course – to shop around in search of the best price, are the two most persuasive, though by no means the only, reasons always to obey John McCririck's injunction and, 'Come racing, come racing,' providing you have the time, money and opportunity to do so.

British punters do not have to deal with the bookmakers. They have the option of betting with the Tote. The Horserace Totalisator Board to give it its full name, traces its history back to 1928 when Parliament decided to set up a publicly run pool-betting system to generate money to support racing. The word 'tote' comes from the adding machines that were originally used to count and register the tickets sold, a process conducted today much more rapidly by computer. The current Tote Board was set up in 1961 in the same year that off-course cash betting with bookmakers was officially legalised. Today's Tote is split into three different sections: a small off-course betting-shop subsidiary, a large credit-betting division and a monopoly of on-course pool betting. In pool betting all the stake money wagered enters a pool and, after the operators have taken out their deductions to cover their overheads and allowed for their margin of profit, the remainder of the money is shared out equally as a 'dividend' to the holders of winning tickets.

The Tote's on-course bets include Win, Place, Trio, Dual Forecast and Placepot pools, the last named being a place accumulator on the first six races on the card (although at most meetings there are only six races). The Tote's most exciting on-course wager, holding out the same prospect of great profit for a small stake as an off-course betting-shop Yankee, is the Jackpot. This is a pool-bet operated at all major race meetings and consisting of a straight win accumulator on the first six events. If the Jackpot pool is not won, say on the first day of Cheltenham, then it is carried forward to the next day and if it's not won on the second day, then it's carried forward to the third day and so on. Pot hunters have been known to turn up at Lingfield on the Friday after Cheltenham dreaming of scooping a fabulous un-won pool but, inevitably, if six easy-to-pick favourites triumph, the pay-out will be much smaller than if the winners are all difficult to fancy but big-priced outsiders.

Tote betting shops provide access to the on-course Jackpot and Placepot pools and accept bets at Tote odds Win, Place and Dual Forecast.

The greater portion of the Tote's profits, once its operating costs and expenses have been deducted, is returned directly to racing. Yet given that the Tote still enjoys only a modest overall share of a betting market dominated by private bookmaking companies, and given that the profits of those companies are split mainly between their shareholders and the Treasury, a sincere lobby would like to see a complete or off-course Tote monopoly in Britain, a move it believes would be in the best interests of the Turf.

The idea of gambling with the Tote is anathema to any serious betting and racing enthusiast, be they a cash punter in Tattersalls or a professional on the rails. This is because the Tote does not let you take a price at the time you place your bet which means that although you are not betting entirely blind you have only an imprecise idea what odds you will receive if your selection wins. And the whole point of both serious and recreational gambling on the horses is that you are always trying to beat the market, to get your money on at a price ahead of the likely starting price and at one which you consider is an underestimation of your selection's likely winning chance. This is why punters of all types and classes get so much pleasure and excitement from dashing up and down the pitches at a racecourse and trying to get on at the 4–1 that Fred Binns or John White may be offering about a horse before they fall into line with the odds of 7–2 or 3–1 that William Regan may be quoting further down the line.

A majority of race-goers may bet with the Tote, but these on-course customers are not true or indigenous gamblers but the occasional visitors and small-stakes punters who are either unsure of how to bet with a bookmaker or who, like the rather niggardly old toff in the box at Cheltenham, feel slightly intimidated by the urgency, the patter and the lack of deference of the betting ring. There are occasions, such as when an outsider from an unfashionable stable wins in a big field, when the Tote dividend, due to so few punters having subscribed to the winner, will be quite a bit larger than the odds returned by the bookies. Conversely, when the form horse wins in a small field, the Tote dividend is frequently smaller than the odds that were available in the ring.

The situation is even worse abroad. In France there are no bookmakers and all racetrack betting is pool betting organised under the aegis of the monopoly PMU or Pari Mutuel Urbain. With no bookmakers to compete with and no free betting market it takes only a small amount of money to cause the odds of a fancied horse to fall right through the floor. One of the most infamous recent examples of this lamentable state of affairs came in the 1991 French 2,000 Guineas at Longchamp when the winner, the François-Boutin-trained Hector Protector was returned at the absurdly short price of 1–10 (ten to one on), which means that you would have to have gambled ten pounds or francs on him to win one. Hector had a favourite's chance all right but it was still a classic race with other good horses in the field and not even the meanest English bookie was offering worse than 2–5 (two and a half to one on).

The Tote in Britain deducts 16 per cent from the Win pool and 24 per cent from the Place pool. The PMU deducts 28 per cent. There are betting situations with bookmakers when the over-round or margin in the bookmakers' favour is higher than 24 per cent but also when it is lower than 16 per cent – and that is a statistic of vital importance to the serious gambler. The bookmakers are fully entitled to claim that the great majority of authentic British punters understandably prefer to bet with them when they can. The Tote's daily average on-course turnover at the 1991 National Hunt Festival was £1,588,581. The on-course bookmakers no longer reveal their precise figures but the figures for 1986–87, the last year for which figures are available and the year prior to that in which the Conservative government abolished on-course betting tax, reveal that the Tote's share of on-course turnover at that time was a mere 16 per cent.

There is no minimum stake in most betting offices. The Tote's on-course minimum is £2 Win, Place and Dual Forecast and £1 on the Jackpot. On-course Tattersalls' boards bookmakers mainly insist on a £5 minimum at meetings like Cheltenham either as a straight-win bet or as a bet of £2 or £3 each way. Credit-wagering generally begins around the £20 to £50 mark and rises as high as the bookie, not the punter, wants to go.

If you don't like the Tote and don't want to deal with the

legitimate on- and off-course bookmakers, there is still one other option. You can step into the entertaining if shady world of the unlicensed or illicit bookie. He may be no more of a sinister big shot than Jeffrey Bernard laying a few loose change bets to some drinking companions in the Coach and Horses. He may be someone running a book for the regular habitués of his pub, club or workplace. He may be one of a party of friends laying bets to the others on a visit to Paris on Prix de l'Arc de Triomphe day. He may be a known private trader working on the 'floor' of the betting ring, someone with whom even the most respectable bookies have been known to lay off if they cannot get on at their chosen price with a legitimate layer.

Alternatively he may, like Cheltenham Tony, be an 'entrepreneur' with a wide variety of business interests who is prepared to strike large credit bets with a high stakes punter who, like A.J. Kincaid, may already have substantial debts with other legitimate layers along the rails – which he is not presently able to pay. The illicit bookie will charge no tax on- or off-course and he will pay none himself to either the Customs and Excise or the Inland Revenue. Which is not to say that his services do not come with a price attached: if you never settle any part of your debt with him or if you ever outlive your usefulness either as a conduit of information from owners and trainers you may know or as an agency for getting his own bets on without the straight bookies being aware of the real source of the wager . . . well, how can one put it? In those circumstances there *are* one or two unlicensed practitioners who you'd really rather didn't get their hands on your private address or home telephone number . . .

The trouble with all flat, ironed-out descriptions of betting and bookmaking is that they may explain certain technical aspects of it to the uninitiated but they also tend to make dynamic gambling situations seem static, ordered and unmoving. The truth about real racetrack betting is that most of it takes place not after a span of calm reflection but in a hectic, ten-minute period of trading just before the off. And it's not at all calm and ordered. It is loud, crowded and intensely confusing, punctuated by sudden moments of high drama and frantic, whirling movement. If it's taking place at Cheltenham ten minutes before the fifth race on the third and final afternoon of the National Hunt Festival, it confronts you with a cocktail of colour, noise, energy and adrenalin that is at once exhilarating, intoxicating and impossible to resist.

CHAPTER THREE

Whistling Dixie

Kincaid, Moynahan and I followed the Major down the respectable side of the Members-Tattersalls' partition until we came to the two on-course rails representatives of the Major's firm. Known in the trade as Dick and Harry, they were standing side by side with and breathing the same air as such élite on-course credit bookmakers as Victor Chandler, Stephen Little, John Henwood, Dudley Roberts and Colin Webster, names that may mean nothing to the uninitiated but which describe some of the biggest shrewdies and high-rollers in the game.

There was no shortage of custom, credit and cash for these men today. No shortage of pushy young hustlers with trenchcoats and personal jewellery or of older, suaver men in camel-hair coats and bespoke suits. Across the other side of the rails in the fifteen-pound-a-head Tattersalls' Enclosure (we were paying £30 a day for access to the Members' while entry into the Course Enclosure was £7 a time), the boards bookmakers, too, were under siege. Though unlike the urgent, but at least swiftly moving, queues on our side of the wall, the crush over there was so intense that even the shortest journey from pitch to pitch was a slow and strenuous undertaking. The boards customers included weather-beaten countrymen in once-a-year suits, pale and under-nourished-looking town-dwellers in 'not quite' Barbours and flat caps and little jolly Sam-the-Fisherman types in red polo-neck jerseys, brown leather coats and little Bing Crosby black-and-white check hats. Some of these would-be punters were just standing motionless in the scrum. Grinning, gawping, studying and frowning until every now and again one of them would suddenly break free from the surrounding crowd and rush to join one of the manic, jabbering queues fighting dementedly to place their money in a bookmaker's outstretched hand. And then, the business at the end of the queue swiftly done, they would reel away equally suddenly and dive back once again into the mass.

The boards bookies were going 11–8 and in one or two places even 5–4 the field. You could better those odds by several points on the rails. 'I'll lay 2–1 this favourite. 2–1 if you want it,' yelled Ruislip's John Pegley, the man with the loudest voice on the racecourse. John's sober grey suits and his modest, unassuming manner may make him look like a rather dull and desk-bound manager with the Norwich Union but when he's standing up on the rails and shouting the odds he assumes all the authority and vocal power of a drill sergeant at Aldershot. 'I'll lay 2–1 this favourite. I'll lay 2–1.'

We had all agreed in the bar beforehand that there could be no cop-outs with each-way betting here. No savers without the 'jolly'. Only the favourite could possibly be backed because he was the class horse of the race, because he was fresh after a mid-season rest and because he'd love the ground. In the circumstances that 2–1 with Pegley was surely a generous price? There were also some market moves for the second favourite, another firm-ground specialist and dual Cheltenham course winner and also for a promising young Northern chaser who had 'made the long journey down from Cumbria', so a trade paper said, and, as Kincaid remarked, let's hope he had a window seat and a rousing British Rail breakfast to get him here in decent shape.

It was at this point, just as our money should have been going on, emphatically, on the nose, that we momentarily succumbed to an affliction all too familiar to the regular punter. We started to change our minds. More specifically we began to try to find reasons why the favourite wouldn't win. It was Kincaid who initiated the slide. Had we not been here before? he suggested. And could we really be serious about wanting to back a 2–1 favourite in the penultimate race at Cheltenham? Particularly when it was trained by a grinning, chinless, trilby-hatted idiot (or so at least Kincaid's malign and probably irrational prejudice believed). Would any serious gambler even dream of putting his all on a racehorse prepared by this joker?

Admittedly the Major, who just happens to play cricket with the trainer every summer, had often assured us that this same chinless smiler who had already rattled up more than ten Festival winners to date went to a very good school and that in some quarters he was regarded as absolutely splendid, a first-class off-spinner withal and entirely without faults. But this ringing social endorsement was still not quite enough to satisfy Kincaid.

Then we hesitated again. Had we not made this mistake before too? On the very first day of this gruelling, sybaritic race meeting? We had wanted to back the favourite in the first. Twenty points clear on Timeform and form about two stone superior to the rest but also a short-priced favourite in the first race at Cheltenham and trained, what's more, by a man who even the Major agreed made the off-spinner look like a combination of Vincent O'Brien, Jonathan Miller and Bertrand Russell. This fellow, over six feet tall with glasses and a booming voice, always wore either a regulation flat cap or a brown trilby, sometimes turned up at the front for effect. We had often suspected that he was not an ordinary human being at all but some monstrous bespectacled alien from another planet. A chortling, intergalactic buffoon in a wax jacket and cherry-red shoes. Surely no punter with any frontal lobes left could possibly have backed him to get it right in the first at Cheltenham? Not at 11–8. The horse, naturally ignorant of this uncharitable assessment, turned out to be so good that he won anyway. Albeit only by one-and-a-half lengths proving, claimed Kincaid, that the trainer's ghastly interference had whittled down his form book advantage from twenty. But our money inevitably had gone elsewhere. On some wretched whispered good thing, hopefully soon to be dog food, some joke from the Curragh who had finished very nearly last. That had been the beginning of a hopeless downward spiral, which, in Kincaid's case, had been relieved by just two winners in two-and-three-quarter days. It was unthinkable that we should go and screw it again now in the next to last race.

Our resolve stiffened and, our commitment to the favourite affirmed once again, we turned to address the bookies. Typically and predictably, as other punters will understand, the 2–1 had now all gone although we were able to get on at 13–8 with the Major's firm. Roughly translated that means that we had backed the favourite, the off-spinner's representative, on credit, to win us $1\frac{5}{8}$ times our respective stakes. (Though we guessed that Kincaid's recorded wager was probably but a fraction of the off-the-record bet that he'd already placed with Tony in the bar.)

We stayed to watch the race in the company of the hard, smart boys who had gathered half-way up the rails on the Members' side of the line. Up above us stood the bookmakers – Chandler, Webster, Henwood, Little – their figures silhouetted dramatically against the sky as in the magnificent black-and-white images of the forties' photographer Bill Brandt. Whatever state of excitement the rest of the crowd might have been in on the lawn and on the terraces, the layers were giving nothing away. Most of them had their binoculars up but anonymous and unspecified wagering was still taking place and their cordless blowers and bleepers continued to flicker with nervous, electronic energy, constantly receiving or sending back information to and from their off-course offices or perhaps to other more mysterious off-track connections. Just as the runners went past the winning post for the first time a tic-tac man jumped down from his box in front of Colin Webster and ran off down a line of boards bookmakers' pitches shouting unintelligibly. By the time he returned to his precarious vantage point, his urgent message presumably delivered, the horses had taken the water jump, the second fence out in the country.

Without my own 'bins' which I had left on some bar counter or hotel-bedroom floor, it was difficult to make much sense of the first half of the race. I could tell that the second favourite and course specialist was marginally ahead, that the favourite was disputing second place on the inside rail and that at least two or three other runners were still in with a winning chance. A few feet away from us was the famous Glaswegian bookmaker John Banks who was concentrating on the proceedings through his powerful Zeiss Jena × 40 binocs. As the second favourite kicked on into a two-length lead, starting up the rising ground on the far side of the course, a man from John Henwood's pitch, a minion in a minion's suit, suddenly appeared at Banks's feet. The minion gabbled something into Banks's workman's ear. The workman relayed the information to his boss. The Scotsman calmly put down his binoculars and issued a few brisk instructions to the workman. A phone was picked up. A brief but inaudible conversation ensued. By the time that conversation was over the horses had made another left-handed turn and had begun their descent down the famous Cheltenham hill. The favourite – and object of our fervent hopes – had made up ground on the leader but now an unconsidered outsider from Herefordshire was also closing. And there were still three fences left to jump.

All that stuff about snapping birch, divots of mud and

courageous Corinthian endeavour is strictly for the fruitier commentators and for form book journalists looking back at their videos. Try spotting or noticing one flying divot while packed into a crowd of 40,000 gamblers all crammed together on the lawn or in the ring at the climax of the Cheltenham Festival. The fate of your money and of the various contestants has to be gauged from the noise variations alone. As the three leaders made their final turn into the home straight the second favourite looked beaten, and it was not our horse but the outsider who now held a definite advantage. Jumping the penultimate fence there was still half a length in it but at the last it was the rider of the 'jolly' who went for a 'big one' and who appeared to recapture the initiative in the air. If I had been holding binoculars my arms would have been shaking. I was certainly trembling with nervous excitement but I still had time to notice that John Banks on our right appeared to be completely unmoved.

As the two horses began their climactic battle on the long uphill run towards the line the whips came out. You couldn't hear them in that crowd but you could see them and you could imagine the effect of them too. Those long slim and painfully severe-looking implements scorching through the air and on to those horses quarters while all the expert jockeys in the grandstand roared and roared their selections home. Up the hill they came. The eight-year-old gelding and the seven-year-old gelding. Straining, straining and striving for the wire. The pair of them seemed to reach the winning post simultaneously. Except that they didn't. The angle was deceptive. And so was at least a part of the pain. The favourite's jockey wasn't actually using the whip quite as much as we thought. He was mainly just waving it through the air. Waving, persuading, coaxing and steering, which was clearly still enough to fool the horse. And that's how they got the race. By a short head.

Kincaid wanted to resume the celebrations immediately back in the bar, that reeking outdoor pen beside the hamburger van. But first there was another little drama to observe rather closer to hand.

John Banks had put his binoculars down and turned for one moment to look back up the rails. He seemed to be oblivious to everyone and everything but his indifference to the crowd enabled one to study him more closely.

Twenty years ago John Banks was the biggest thing in racecourse bookmaking: the boldest and most exciting operator on the rails. His was the archetypal sixties' success story of the streetwise boy made good, only in his case it described a tough and pushy Scot rather than a self-made Cockney photographer. His long march from Anderston to a millionaire's mansion overlooking Wentworth golf course was achieved through nerve, enterprise, hard work and quite brilliant self-promotion. 'John Banks. Where will he be tomorrow?' the adverts in the trade papers used to say, often accompanied by an unforgettable photograph of a large, laughing man in a black hat and dark glasses.

His success, though, posed a threat to the cosy hegemony of the big firms. Here was a bookmaker who was prepared to stand up in the tradition of the late great William Hill and pit his judgement and nerve against the punter's. If his knowledge or instincts or inside contacts told him that a particular heavily touted horse was by no means certain to win, then, whether it was the Derby or a selling race at Pontefract, he would lay that horse at several points over the odds being offered by his rival bookies. Not surprisingly, high-rolling racetrack punters all flocked to bet with him rather than with the established figures. And Banks offered them bets about everything. He was laying odds on golf, cricket, tennis and the Eurovision Song Contest long before it became fashionable. He would even accept a wager about the outcome of next week's episodes of *Coronation Street*.

Banks's problem, if problem it was, was that whenever he was interviewed by either the trade or the mainstream press he couldn't resist making witty, irreverent and generally uncomplimentary remarks about the racing and bookmaking establishment. He mocked Ladbrokes for being terrified of high-stakes gamblers and for trying to manipulate the betting market, and he mocked the Jockey Club for their lack of professionalism and their resistance to change. When the news broke in April 1978 that he was to be hauled before the Club on a charge of paying money to John Francome in return for information about the horses that the brilliant jump jockey was riding for the Fred Winter stable there was a distinct feeling that however valid the charges, a decision had been made to put the upstart in his place. Guilty or otherwise, a perfectly legitimate defence might have been that if he was buying information he was only following the practice of nearly every major bookmaking company, who all have their paid-up spies in the leading yards, be they lads, work riders, jockeys or the trainers themselves. And, for all Banks's artful willingness to occasionally act up to the image of the sharp-suited 'businessman' whose offers should probably not be refused, he was never a villain. He was and still is a charming, humorous and intelligent man with an incisive racing brain.

It didn't do him any good, though. The chaps in brown trilbies had built him up as a sort of malignant predator in much the same way that they tried to depict the Irish professional gambler Barney Curley ten years later. In the words of one patronising ex-amateur rider turned racing correspondent, the man who had billed himself as 'the most famous Scotsman since Rabbie Burns' had become 'excessively visible' and needed to be taught a lesson. So off the track and out of sight and sound he went for the next four years. During that time he wasn't even allowed to make a book or set foot on a racecourse. His star waned and his high-rolling clients inevitably went elsewhere. He returned, appropriately, at Cheltenham in 1982 but, although he's still there, still active and still laying after all these years especially in the now lucrative area of American football, he's nothing like the force that he used to be in the days before the ban. You experience less of the wit and banter but also less of the sense of danger, real or simulated, that you used to get just from standing around near his pitch.

The John Banks bookmaker of this National Hunt Festival was visible, yes, but hardly excessively so. Gone was the big black hat of yesteryear. In its place was a sober, grey Homburg with a black hatband worn with a fawn suede coat. The shades were still largely the same, though: brown- to black-coloured, slightly misty, and the eyes still bloodshot and puffy underneath. I tried to imagine how much he might have won or lost on this last race. John Moynahan and I had doubled our money very nicely and we imagined that Kincaid had won a four-figure sum. Not J. P. McManus standards maybe, but at Cheltenham still something to cheer about. But where did Banks stand? I could see Henwood's assistant at the workman's shoulder once again. And other hardly down-at-heel-looking punters were beginning to gather round. Did the once irresistible Glaswegian really still have the appetite and the resources to take on not simply the accountancy-minded Big Three, whose rails representatives were perhaps celebrating another starting price triumph even at this moment, but also the new breed of independent bookies-turned-punters? Before turning back to deal with his customers he uncharacteristically took off his shades for a few short seconds and rubbed his eyes with the thumb and index finger of his right hand. Perhaps he feels tired, I thought

Hardly surprising. Perhaps he's had a bad week. Perhaps time is catching up with him at last. Then again . . . how easy it is to misrepresent a bookmaker, to distort or over-romanticise him simply because he is perceived somehow to operate on the margins of respectable and conventional life. Perhaps John Banks was not lamenting his losses or considering his imminent retirement at all. Perhaps he was simply thinking to himself, Why don't these pathetic apologies for gamblers, these three-day-Festival wankers . . . why don't they bet big money the way that they used to do in the past? That way they'd lose . . . and I'd win . . . a lot more.

The gallery of tiered terracing that surrounds the unsaddling enclosure at the top of the Cheltenham paddock was only half full. Most of the punters with the strength left to stand and the wits left to think were either back up in the ring trying to mount one final assault on the bookies or back in the bars continuing the party. No packed-out gathering, and not even a full complement of reporters, awaited this officially returned 13–8 winner as his impossibly shy jockey steered him through the little white gate and up past the handful of photographers to the number one berth.

Yet the absence of cheering onlookers could in no way deflate or diminish the understandable elation of the winning horse's connections. Foremost among them was the co-owner, Mr Michael Buckley, not a man for whom the bar behind the hamburger van would have had any more meaning than for his friend J. P. McManus. Like J. P. the English city high-roller is a tycoon of the ring. Not on quite the same scale maybe, but a serious bare-headed punter none the less. A serious backgammon player, too – in fact, an all-round gentleman and sportsman be it at Cheltenham, Ascot, or York. 'Well done, team. We've done it at last,' he cried in ecstatic delight, rather generously attributing his success not simply to his trainer, the beaming off-spinner, who had risen triumphantly above Kincaid's malign suspicions but also to the loyalty and support of his considerable band of friends and admirers who included a number of ravishingly well-coiffured and sweet-smelling blondes in suits and coats and expensive-looking burnished brown leather boots.

Racing and betting on racing may enjoy a predominantly male image, in spite of the best efforts of outstanding women trainers like Jenny Pitman and mould-breaking jockeys like Alex Greaves, but, according to a Racecourse Association Survey conducted in

July 1991, up to 44 per cent of race-goers and punters at an average meeting are likely to be women and on the big prestige occasions at venues like Cheltenham and Royal Ascot the proportion will be even higher. And, while all the attention may outwardly and apparently be centred on the serious business on the track and in the ring, there can also be a strong sexual undercurrent at a racecourse, attractive to both men and women alike. There are moments at Cheltenham and Newbury in winter and at Ascot, Newmarket and Goodwood in June and July when the whole atmosphere can suddenly begin to resemble that of a rather lush party or wedding reception. Everyone is wearing their best and most expensive clothes. They seem to be more tactile than usual. They want to enjoy themselves. They want to let go. Alcohol's flowing, glasses are full and opulent designer brands of male and female scent blend with the equally pungent aromas of horseflesh and cigar smoke, crushed grass and champagne. If you add to that mixture the potent ingredient of large sums of ready money you have an erogenous concoction that is enough to make anyone tingle with desire.

The particular and amusing application of all this to the gambling side of racing is that at least one spur, one incentive, to the male gambler is the touching belief that if he is seen to risk and win, or even just to lose large sums of money, this braggadocio display of fearless *élan* might be enough to persuade certain rich and desirable racegoing women to jump into bed with him. Though, given the state of most cock-and-bull punters with their expanding waistlines, receding hairlines and usually empty wallets, it is hard to believe that the objects of their desire are very often won over by their doubtful charms – unless, perhaps, they have the financial resources of a Michael Buckley, a Robert Sangster or a Lord 'Gordon' White.

Buckley's moment in the spotlight didn't last long. The trophy presented, the pictures taken and the winner led away, the co-owner and his party were soon swept out again towards their private box. The runners in the last, the sixth, race of the day and the eighteenth event of the meeting, were already circling impatiently around the parade ring.

It would be difficult to exaggerate the extent to which 'consuming' horseracing, once the betting and racing gets under-way, is not a steady, ordered experience – like watching or even joining in a baccarat game in a smart casino – but entertainment savoured at the gallop. Even at the National Hunt Festival where there is a forty-minute interval between the main races there simply isn't enough time to do everything and certainly not to do anything slowly: you can't see the winners return to the unsaddling enclosure *and* celebrate in the bar *and* look at the runners for the next race in the paddock *and* get a bet on with the bookies *and* still be in time to get a decent vantage point to watch the race. At least two of those activities have to go, and as for most of us the gamble is the *raison d'être*, and as already less than fifteen minutes remained before this final 'heat' would be under-way, there could be no more drinking, for the time being at least, and no further delay in my own return to the betting ring.

CHAPTER FOUR

The Getting Out Stakes

UP IN THE grimy unromantic world of Tatts – not at all the sort of milieu to put you in mind of tactile, wedding-party sexuality – the 'trading floor' was awash with bookmakers' and punters' litter: discarded odds tissues, pieces of chalk, cast-away betting tickets, abandoned racecards and pages of form.

Some of the big rails bookies, while obviously still trying to get the punters' business on this last race, were also beginning to work out their final likely margins of profit and loss on the week. As far as they were concerned, Cheltenham was already nearly yesterday's news and, 'don't let that suave bastard with the Burberry get away without confirming that ten grand he said he wants on the French thing in the Guineas,' etc.

For the boards bookmakers there was no time to consider their balance sheet as they were being inundated with almost as much custom for this concluding event as they had taken on the Cheltenham Gold Cup.

The last race on any card is traditionally known as the 'Getting Out Stakes', the opportunity for punters to back a horse to win them enough money to recover whatever losses they may have sustained earlier. At the three- or four-day festival meetings the Getting Out Stakes assumes much greater significance than usual. It is the final betting opportunity of the week, your last chance to try to rectify the imbalances in your own speculative trading. Of course, professional gamblers wouldn't dream of betting more than their usual stake on a race just because it was the last event on the card. They only ever gamble when they seriously fancy a horse and believe that they can get on at good or value odds. But to the rest of us poor fools – 'mugs, losers and tourists', to quote one layer's brutal description – the Getting Out Stakes at Cheltenham annually and hypnotically demands that we empty our pockets of their last penny and push our credit limits to their highest point to conform with the prevailing dementia.

I caught up with Kincaid and Moynahan back up by the Major's men, though this time the Major had stayed in the bar and the rest of us were all standing on the Tattersalls' side of the divide. This was because Kincaid had wanted to collect the winnings on an each-way bet without the favourite that he had unusually placed with a boards bookie on the Sun Alliance Hurdle at the start of the previous day.

By contracting ourselves to midget-apprentice size we managed to squeeze into a precious little corner of space beside the Major's joint thus affording ourselves the opportunity for two or three minutes' concentrated study of this climactic and concluding heat. We began by fetching out of our coat pockets not Timeform or the Chaseform Notebook but a tipping sheet sent to us by a rather strange and enigmatic character from the south coast. This compendium of selections, which had been produced with the aid of some kind of desk-top publishing kit, gave us the considered views of 'The Professional Investor', as he calls himself (not to be confused with another tipster known as 'The Professional' or the tipping agency entitled 'The Professional Sporting Bureau'), on the Festival programme. His 'inside information service', for which we had paid £30 each, was similar to that provided by a dozen or so other phone and mail-order tipping services, all regularly advertised in the racing press and mostly fronted by characters with intriguing pseudonyms such as 'The Whisperer', 'Computer Kid', 'The Faces', 'Top Dog-Top Horse' and 'Master Spy'.

If betting and horseracing have always been inextricably linked, the once raffish figure of the tipster and tout, still only semi-respectable even today, has been an ever-present and entertaining element in the equation. The most famous tipster of them all was Peter Mackay, better known as Ras Prince Monolulu, the irresistible con-man who, according to the National Horseracing Museum, came to Britain around 1920 from 'an unknown source'. The Prince's magnificent feathered headdress and resounding cry of 'I got a horse' were regular features of all the big race meetings between the wars.

The period between the twenties and the mid-sixties was the

heyday of the sealed letter and the late-wire service usually recommended by small, sly and patently wide gentlemen who always found it necessary to adopt an air of mystery when addressing their clients and to talk in a low voice preferably out of the side of their mouth. These characters recently made a crafty but colourful return to some of the big outer-London tracks. As you got out of your motor in the bottom car park at Sandown on a winter Saturday, you were quite likely to be accosted by a tanned programme seller with tinted shades and a sheepskin coat. His 'programmes' would turn out to cost at least £10 each but as he pressed one into your hand you would find that contained within it was a little white envelope. If you duly parted with the necessary smackers and then opened up this interesting missive the piece of Basildon Bond notepaper inside would say, 'Desert Orchid. 3.00. Win Only.' Now, given that the famous grey had probably been tipped already in about seventeen national newspapers and was certain to start at odds of around 4 – 6 (6 – 4 on) this could hardly be described as inspired advice but by this stage it was too late to get your money back.

Of course, the top-drawer tipping services and trade-paper form experts regard themselves as in a wholly different league from the common tout but they are all engaged in the same commercial enterprise of trying to sell the public their opinion, cash in advance. At the top of anybody's list of tipsters would have to be the incomparable Timeform Organisation which was founded in the 1940s by Phil Bull, a maverick Yorkshire miner's son and former schoolmaster who died in 1985. Bull introduced to British racing the then revolutionary concept of trying at least partly to 'rate' or evaluate horses by comparing their achievements against the clock. He started going to race meetings with a stopwatch in his pocket and if, say, he found a two-year-old winning over six furlongs at Goodwood in an appreciably faster time than it took an experienced four-year-old sprint handicapper to win over the same distance and in the same conditions half an hour later, he would know that he had something worth betting on next time out.

For more than forty years Bull's technical knowledge of racing – and in particular his precise understanding of all betting and gambling issues – which always vastly outstripped the collective capacity of the Jockey Club, was probably equalled by only one man, his close friend and one-time partner William Hill, the greatest course bookmaker in the history of the game. For a while even Hill was reduced to closing the accounts of some of Bull's clients, so effective were his handicapping methods. The same rigorously empirical techniques are still applied today to all of Timeform's publications from their authoritative annual reviews of the abilities and performances of the previous year's horses to their weekly black books and their indispensable daily racecards.

Yet even Timeform are prone to the occasional fault, principally to a rather pious self-assertiveness, a sort of 'fact-is-fact,-boy,-and-nothing-else-will-do'-Mr-Gradgrind approach. Prospective employees used to have to undergo a daunting oral examination to enable Bull to satisfy himself that their heads were not empty or their approach unsound. It's not hard to imagine the junior members of the Timeform staff at their head office up in Halifax still being compelled to sit at high desks like inky Victorian schoolboys, poring over their slates and forbidden to look round at the clock before lunchtime on pain of serious punishment.

A majority of the telephone hot-line tipping services that share Timeform's advertising space in the *Racing Post* and the *Sporting Life* prefer to cloak themselves with the aura of privileged contacts, of mysterious access to stable information that marvellously inflates the ego of the tipster and leaves the ordinary mug punter wishing that they too were somehow a part of this magical inside world. It may often be that the source of this inside advice is no closer to the horse's mouth than the Newmarket postman or Steve Cauthen's chauffeur's brother's newsagent but the really mug punters are still taken in. An important part of the tipsters' approach is always to talk about top trainers and jockeys by their first names as if they are on terms of close personal intimacy with them. Never mind the fact that your 'mole', a half-deaf stable lad from another yard, was simply standing at the back of a group of work watchers when Henry Cecil mumbled a few scarcely audible comments to the owner of the long-range 2,000 Guineas favourite on the Limekilns gallop one Saturday morning. By Saturday night's phone message this incident has been transformed into an illuminating first-hand account. 'Henry is privately confident that this tall, imposing son of Green Desert who he recommended exclusively to our subscribers at the beginning of March is at least two stone superior to the rest of this season's three-year-olds . . .'

These days so many so-called racing correspondents are making at least part of their income from their telephone hot-lines that at some racecourses the press room is barely big enough to cope with them all. (Particularly when you throw in the usual scattering of bookmakers' public-relations representatives, such as Major Tom, who are frequently to be found either very charmingly attempting to lure the more gullible journalists into plugging the firm's sup- posedly generous odds on the big betting races coming up or 'accommodating' the same journalists' latest credit-account wagers.) Anyone who makes a habit of regularly ringing the tele- phone hot-line services should occasionally do so from a public phone box. Watching how swiftly the money speeds out of your pocket and away into theirs offers an instructive way of assessing the quality and value of the information that the various lines provide. The ones to avoid particularly are usually the most florid. 'It was a really quite beautiful morning here at Cheltenham today with a light mist and dew on the track early on. By the time we returned to our hotel for our post-gallops breakfast both my com- panion and I agreed that we had rarely seen the Cotswolds looking quite so quintessentially charming so early in the spring' and so on. With this sort of service the caller is going to be at least £5 out of pocket before they even get to the first of six races. And if they ring back later for the afternoon update message they are unlikely to get far beyond what the tipster had for lunch.

Yet, for all that, eccentric personal preferences are bound to play their part in the selection of a tipster, just as they do in any other consumer transaction. Kincaid and I had always retained a soft spot for the Professional Investor's views partly because his phone messages are entertaining but not over-garrulous and partly be- cause of his improbable working address: 2l b Norman's Bay Road, Hove. Hove is not renowned as a barometer of racing opinion. We suspected him of being an at least mildly eccentric if not barking mad ex-racing correspondent and down-at-heel toff of public- school vintage who probably commutes between his lodgings in a once Palm Court seafront hotel and his dingy basement office in a terraced back-street. We also suspected that this minute office is probably piled high with form books and annuals, copious videos from the TV and endless old editions of the trade press.

The Professional Investor regularly informs his clients that before publication all his deliberations are fed into his 'private handicapper' or pocket computer. Generally these computer rec- ommendations are either for obvious odds-on favourites or for quite ludicrous 50–1 shots with no credible chance at all. But these wildly contrasting tips often have one thing in common: they almost all hail from the ranks of the least fashionable stables and five- and ten-horse trainers, for it is among these fringe characters that the Investor has his premier contacts. And, perversely and incredibly, there are days when these 'little men' (why never women?) as the Channel 4 racing presenter, the terrier-like 'Bruffscott', likes to call them, whose usual stamping ground is Hexham or Carlisle, do indeed do the business. And do it well enough to elevate the Investor into a bit of a character and no doubt one worth keeping on the right side in his local Ladbrokes and Corals offices in Shoreham, Brighton and Hove.

And all credit here to the Investor's enterprise and initiative because some seriously compulsive punters, as well as the habitually thriftless idiots like ourselves, do occasionally send off their cheques or pick up their telephones to gain access to his latest selections. (Partly because we can't often be bothered to do all that form book study and want to have somebody else's opinion ready-made so that we can either disagree vehemently with it or pass it off as our own while still retaining the option to deride the Professional Investor for it afterwards.)

For this final race at Cheltenham, this cathartic end to the meeting, this twenty-six-runner two-mile handicap hurdle with more tips flying around than in the World Darts Championship, the Investor had surprisingly opted neither for the favourite nor for a 66 –1 shot and was recommending a five-year-old gelding from a small yard in north Yorkshire. The name of the gelding's trainer must remain anonymous. Let us just say that he was based somewhere near Outer Malton and that he had a squeaky-voiced head lad called Foggy who was the principal source of the Investor's information.

Foggy's 'guv'nor' was, according to the Investor, a 'shrewd handler who gets on with the job in a quiet way but is quite up to the task when the horse is good enough'. What this really meant was that he was a complete nonentity who had rarely managed to train the winner of anything except as the result of some improbable equine fluke. His representative in the County Hurdle, who was to be ridden by a wily old northern 'job' jockey, equally adept at 'pulling' his mount or thrashing it within an inch of its life according to the circumstances, had pissed up in a couple of egg-and-spoon races at, yes, Hexham and Carlisle and seemed to be 'thrown in at the weights'. (The County Hurdle being a handicap, all the runners had been allotted weights by the official handicapper, the object being to take a race between runners of mixed ability and make it as competitive and interesting a betting medium as possible. A horse 'thrown in at the weights' seems to have got into the handicap with a remarkably light or generous weight assessment given its recent performances and possible or estimated potential.)

The Investor's tipping sheet went on to observe that, 'the right men are on' and urged all his subscribers to bet to their maximum stake. Anything better than 4–1, he said, would be value all the way. Well, well, well. All very exciting. And the maximum stake, eh?

Just then Moynahan dashed across briefly to the pitch of the experienced boards bookmaker Pat Whelan, who had chalked the gelding up at eights. We heard the Major's representative calling 17–2. We didn't like this at all. These men wouldn't get it that wrong. If the gelding was the good thing that the Investor insisted and if the right men really were on he ought to have been half these odds at least. Feeling a sudden rush of bullish self-confidence we decided that we would reject the Investor's advice and pour scorn on his reading of the race. Why was this dour northern trainer, this Terry, this Brian, this dark horse from Lesser Habton-on-the-Moor, not holed up in Newmarket with a 150-box yard, two cupboards full of Gucci shoes and a glamorously bejewelled wife to entertain the owners and ride work first lot? Why, for that matter, was the Professional Investor always hunched over his books in his Hove basement office instead of being out on the track with swanky fellows like us where he could watch the action, listen to all the rumours and get informatively drunk? Why was he not here right now at Cheltenham, spooning caviare down his throat with McManus and Buckley in a private box? And if he really was any good, why was he not wiring us his selections from his poolside cabana in the Caribbean rather than mailing them off dutifully from some wretched little postbox on the Sussex coast?

'I'm going to oppose him,' John Moynahan muttered to himself uncharitably, using a phrase much beloved by all punters rash enough to believe that for one brief moment they may just have got ahead of the game. And, disloyal though it may well have been to our original tipster, both Kincaid and myself decided to follow suit. Our selection was to be a horse who had won a big handicap only five days before, a horse turning out again very quickly but with only a modest penalty. A horse on a winning streak. And how much were we going to put on him? How much of our remaining

43

capital were we prepared to put at risk? We were going to do the lot. No hedging and trimming. No weak, pathetic and usually over-cautious attempts to save ourselves here. We were going to go out on a limb and go for it with one grand slam bet on the nose.

Our minds made up, we got on as quickly as we could with the Major's representatives and then realised that, having made the unwise decision to step into the ring, we now had about as much chance of being able to get out again and watch the race from the Members' as we had of being invited up into the Royal Box afterwards for tea and crumpets with the Queen Mother. Only the tallest bookies, high up on their crates by the rails, could see anything over the heads of the crowd on the lawn next door. We wanted to get in there. We had badges which entitled us to be in there but the Cheltenham management's arrangements for funnelling punters out of one enclosure and back into the other are unbelievably prehistoric and incapable of any justification at all unless, presumably, you are the spiffingly busy and smooth-shaven racecourse manager, who has clearly never had to fight his way out of the ring just before a race on the last afternoon of the Festival and thus risk having his kneecaps, wallet and balls hideously and agonisingly squashed on the stout iron railings that border the insanely narrow exit paths, as the morons behind push, elbow and pile up into the desperate frantic souls already trapped in the bottleneck up front, resulting in an inevitable churning collision with much wailing and exhaling of air. It's too much. We were ready to leave our shirts behind with the bookmakers as a reasonable price to pay for an unforgettable week but we were not prepared to be castrated too.

In the end we managed to battle our way out of the back of the ring and up to where we hoped to catch at least a glimpse of the action on a giant close-circuit television screen hoisted up high on the brickwork between the Turf Newspapers' kiosk and the caterers underpass. Dozens of anxious, greedy and expectant faces craned their necks close to ours, their breath reeking of alcohol and their bodies of stale cigarette and cigar smoke, aftershave and sweat. They, too, longed to be rich. To win as big a pot as imagination could conceive in as short a time as possible and with as little oppressive work or labour as could tolerably be allowed. If you think that all punters are basically platonic sportsmen and women engrossed simply by the spin of the wheel, the romantic hand of fate and the turn of the cards, then you are wrong. They want to win. Money. Lots of it. They want to win and to explode with elation or to lose and complain and commiserate and to re-run the race again and again the way it should have gone. And then, if it's the Cheltenham Festival, they want to rush off to order more Bell's and Gordon's, Bollinger and Krug and plastic pints of Guinness and Fosters and lukewarm beer, before the whey-faced youths retire, the security men slam down the hatches and the hail-fellow racecourse manager and his staff declare that enough is enough, that all good things must come to an end and that the Festival is over for another year.

They were under starter's orders. They were off. You could hear more of the course commentator's voice than you could of the SIS voice-over behind the television pictures. We tried hard to concentrate on the unfolding drama. Twenty-six horses already reduced to twenty-three by the time they passed the winning post on the first circuit. With one fallen and one brought down and one pulled up before the second hurdle and maybe broken down too, with an off-fore hanging pathetically smashed and wrong, and the jockey now dismounted and standing on the ground apparently waiting for the green screens and the bullet. We wanted to get away from this melancholy scene, this imminent death that the cameraman kept lingering over uncharacteristically, so we walked down the steps and through the underpass, free of crowds now that the race was on and down along the Members' side of the rails.

The bookmakers all had their 'bins' up on the leaders, who were already way out on the far side of the track at the foot of the majestic backdrop of hills and fields and dry-stone walls, the sky grey now with dark rain clouds and maybe even snow coming up from the South West. How many other ordinary, mundane, rich or poor, grand or banal but non-racing, non-gambling citizens, I thought, could possibly understand the beauty, the poetry, the pain and emotion of this scene moving relentlessly towards its climax? The last race of the last day at the Cheltenham Festival. Save it. Store it. Hold on to it. Hang on to these images, these sensations for the next twelve months because very few other racing and gambling moments – maybe one, two or three, the Arc, the Derby, the Breeders' Cup, if you're lucky – are ever as intense, as pure, as undiluted a combination of adrenalin, sport, fate, tragedy and elation as these.

Forget all that romantic toss, the bookmakers (and the dry, mainline punters) would say. This is still only horse racing and that all comes down to winners and losers, profit and loss. And suddenly, as the half-dozen leaders swept towards the second last hurdle, a very real possibility of imminent profit was speeding in our direction.

For as they raced towards the elbow it was our stand-out, on-the-nose, hat-trick-seeking-selection that was challenging, strongly, for the lead. And as they landed over the last, an indistinct blur of shapes and colours, mud and whips, the rails bookies on our right were already confidently calling him the winner. Starting up the run-in, their voices, ours, the crowd's and the commentator's all embarked on a rising arc of volume, passion and hysteria. A great baying, yelling tumult of noise that rose and reached and strained and then finally at the climax peaked, broke and shattered around the winning post. Signalling the end. The closing titles of another March meeting and the triumphant salvation of another charmed life. John Moynahan, in a rare outburst of emotion, grabbed me triumphantly by the shoulders. A. J. Kincaid had already flung his Basque beret up high into the air.

Back in the Kerstin bar, the 'convenience outdoor drinking outlet' behind the hamburger van, we squeezed, pushed and elbowed our way up to the counter. Two bottles of vintage Bollinger were soon ours with which we then hacked an equally murderous path back to rejoin the company of Cheltenham Tony and the Major.

Tony was grinning happily while totting up A. J. Kincaid's liabilities on the bets that he had struck with him (and these days Kincaid struck almost all his big bets with Tony) in the inside margin of his Timeform racecard.

'Now then, A. J. I've got you down for two grand on that Irish thing in the Triumph.'

'Terrific.'

'Followed by the grand on the favourite in the Foxhunters and likewise plus a £200 forecast in the Gold Cup.'

'If you say so, maestro,' said the Bold Punter, taking another puff on his cigarette.

'And then you had your nice piece of luck in the fourth and fifth . . .'

'And sixth.'

'Which almost put you even on the week.'

'Almost.'

'If we hadn't had that unfortunate horlicks in yesterday's last.'

'We?'

'I'd have been in there with you, A. J. I tried to get Corals to accept my monkeys at the off and they said nothing doing. Can you believe it?'

'Diabolical.'

'But never mind, eh, my son? It's been an almost winning day.'

'Except for the odd twelve and a half thousand that he's left lying around the place,' added Moynahan sourly.

'Well, you can always look on the negative side,' said Cheltenham Tony, accepting a proffered glass of champagne.

'Tony offers very good prices,' confirmed Kincaid. 'Much better than Hills or Ladbrokes.'

'Better than the "Old Firm"?' asked the Major, doubtfully.

'Better than most.'

'And all strictly illegal,' said Moynahan. 'Not that I object, you understand.'

'Prompter settlement, though,' reasoned Tony.

'And longer to pay up, too,' added Kincaid. Moynahan simply shook his head: he was confidently expecting to be well up on the week once all the calculations had been done.

'"An almost winning day . . ."' repeated Kincaid, as if it were a toast.

'"An almost winning day,"' we echoed loyally.

Whatever the truth of A. J.'s position – and whatever the profit and loss figures that the big bookmakers and professional gamblers were now looking at – in the course of the last three days I had spent and gambled enough money, in cash and on credit, to sustain a full-scale family holiday and Christmas and New Year celebration combined. I had begun the week in the manner of most mug punters by 'borrowing' funds from my bank account that it could ill afford to lend. By the end of day two, I had been hopelessly down, in urgent need of extended credit on the rails and cash loans from generous friends simply to keep me afloat. The tide had been stemmed by a lucky decision to lay the losing Gold Cup favourite to a fellow punter and those two provident victories in the last two races, particularly the handicap hurdler's thrilling 9–1 triumph in the finale, had brought me back to a position where, like Kincaid, I was *almost* even on the book. And at Cheltenham in March that is a situation of which you can feel entitled to be, well, almost proud.

Later, in the gathering dusk, as the Kerstin bar slammed down its hatches, the hamburger van doused its stinking flames for the final time and long after the leading bookmakers had packed up their satchels and headed for their Jags and Mercs, we all walked slowly away. Bottles rolled, paper drifted in the wind and the long, white running rails glowed with phosphorescent brightness against the enveloping dark.

Down in the bottom car park – where a heavy tractor was attempting to pull somebody's Roly Poly out of the mud – we paused for a necessary pee on the grass. The tall, thin wireless masts on the top of Cleeve Hill were already lost in the blackness and the heavy escarpment was itself about to blend indistinguishably into the shape and colour of the night sky. Behind me I could hear the normally bold and intrepid A. J. Kincaid muttering some strange and morbid incantation beneath his breath. I turned round to upbraid him for his maudlin sentimentality, taking care not to piss on my shoe in the process, only to discover that he had at that moment passed out – or at least fallen down – and was now lying flat on his back on the ground beside his car. And, while I cannot say for certain, it seems reasonable to believe – I should like to believe it and I think it would have been an even-money shot at best – that he had his eyes on the stars.

This is how it sometimes is at the National Hunt Festival. Yet Cheltenham in March is not, more's the pity, typical of the average contemporary British race meeting. That is not simply a reference to the infectious profligacy and indulgence: Cheltenham is the best of what we have left, some would say that it is all we have left, of a style and tradition of betting and bookmaking that once flourished right across the land.

If you talk to any veteran bookie, punter or racing journalist, they will tell you that for all the manic betting at the Festival and at Royal Ascot the gamblers of today risk only a small proportion of the stakes that used to be common currency on British racecourses during the last century and until the period of William Hill's retirement in 1955. They will also tell you that the bookmakers, so often and so easily cast as the villains, were not always timid, suspicious characters preoccupied with their balance sheets. Even a great monolithic institution like Ladbrokes was originally built up by enterprising individuals possessed of every bit as much flair and daring as the high-rolling punters with whom they did business. There were other layers too, fabulously bold, gaudy characters, who might never have bequeathed similar betting-shop dynasties

to the modern high street but who, in their heyday, richly epi-
tomised the truth of J. P. McManus's observation that good bookmakers make good punters and vice versa.

Which is why to appreciate the character and complexity of
contemporary betting and bookmaking you have to begin by celebrating the high life and fast times of some of those earlier buccaneering figures on both sides of the rails – bookies and punters
who demonstrated that to gamble – in the sense of being prepared
to put at risk what you cannot really afford to lose – was not simply
to indicate a preferred investment policy . . . but to express a
fundamentally rebellious as well as acquisitive approach to life.

CHAPTER FIVE

The Old Enemy

ANYONE WANTING to know about the great bookmaking characters of the thirties, forties and early fifties, a golden age of racecourse gambling, has to begin by talking to Geoffrey Hamlyn, the charming and dapper old gentleman who at the sprightly age of eighty-one is still actively employed as the public relations spokesman for the Victor Chandler firm. Hamlyn's connection with Chandlers is an entirely appropriate one as the Chandler business is not only one of the oldest but also one of the best – in the sense of being one of the most daring – credit and independent rails bookmaking companies in the country.

Geoffrey, who bears a remarkable resemblance to that much-loved actor Richard Goolden, who used to play Mole in traditional productions of *The Wind in the Willows* in London each Christmas, is well qualified to understand the gambling psychology. His father was a semi-professional card player and Geoffrey's youthful family holidays were invariably spent in the major casino towns of Europe. Not surprisingly the scale and duration of these vacations depended in large part on Hamlyn senior's successes or otherwise at the bridge, poker and gin rummy tables. Geoffrey's passion has always been horseracing rather than cards and dice and for over forty-five years he was the official starting-price reporter for the *Sporting Life*. During that time bookies and punters were his daily working companions and he has retained a wealth of memories and anecdotes about the truly colourful personalities of the 'better days'.

And, in Geoffrey's opinion, there was never anyone more colourful than the pre- and post-war layer Percy Thompson, known to his peers as the greatest board bookmaker of all time.

Percy used to tap his board at meetings like Royal Ascot and declare loudly to the punters: 'Any horse to win five thousand.' It would be unthinkable for a Tattersalls' cash bookmaker to offer to lose that kind of money (£100,000 at today's prices) on a single race today. And as soon as one contest was over Percy would have his odds up for the next event, no matter the size of the field. The only time he omitted a name was if it was one of his own horses and he was hoping to get a price about it.

The Percy Thompson years lasted from the late thirties to the early fifties and, if he was fearless about taking the public's money, he was equally fearless about staking his own. At one time he had upwards of thirty horses in training and he went for some colossal and, as it turned out, losing touches on the likes of Coubrador in the 1948 Cesarewitch, and Querneville in the Lincoln of 1949. He also owned an almost all-white steeplechaser by the name of Solo III. 'What's Solo? What's Solo?' cried Percy's workman, Jack Stein, uncle of the current Ladbrokes chairman, Cyril Stein, while dashing up and down the rails and trying to 'get on' for the firm at Liverpool one day. 'Ace, King, Queen, Jack, Ten,' retorted the rails layer, Willie Preston.

Percy brought a touch of panache to everything he did and Hamlyn says that, if you hadn't known he was a bookmaker, you might have taken him for a big band leader or a particularly stylish impresario in the West End. When he went up to the north west for Grand National week, which back in the forties was still a much bigger occasion than the Cheltenham Festival, he used to hire a whole floor at Manchester's Midland Hotel and then arrive with his entourage, which would include numerous delectable shantoosies, in a fleet of six Daimlers. Not surprisingly he had friends everywhere, including among the London underworld, and, according to Geoffrey Hamlyn, was much liked by all of them. Perhaps he was too well liked. Perhaps he was an imprudent gambler because in 1951 his firm, Percy and Warwick Thompson Ltd, went suddenly and spectacularly bust with unpaid debts – money owed to them by defaulting punters – totalling several hundred thousand pounds. Countless other boards and rails layers, then and now, have been plagued by similar 'knockers' or slow and non-payers. Gambling debts are not, and never have been, legally enforceable and Percy's fate should give the lie to the idea that the bookmaker always goes home rich. If he's a genuine bookie and not a corporate accountant trading under a false name, if he takes risks and stands proper bets, he can sometimes lose. Heavily.

Jack Butchers, a one-time night porter at Brighton's old Metropole Hotel, tells a story of a suave, cigar-smoking ghost that was supposed to haunt the hotel's third-floor landing during the sixties and seventies. One night Butchers saw the phantom for himself. It was wearing a chalk-stripe suit and correspondent shoes and it had a white gardenia in its buttonhole. The ghost appeared by the lift shaft, strolled slowly down the carpeted corridor and then disappeared. The aroma of cigar smoke lingered on. When Butchers enquired about this strange haunting among the other Metropole staff he received a cheery response from the hotel's senior barman. 'Oh yes,' he said. 'That's the bookmaker, Percy Thompson. He always drops by during August. He used to stay here then during the races. And did you see the ghost of Jack Spot walking a few feet behind him?'

The Lincolnshire born Laurie Wallis, who used to make a book on the rails in the thirties and forties, was another intrepid operator who would regularly lay horses to lose him five- and six-figure sums in a single bet. Laurie's contemporaries originally thought that he was something of a Stan Laurel character with his pale face and naïve, disarming manner. His prosperous longevity in the trade proved that he was no idiot, though by today's standards one of his bookie–customer relationships would have been classified as completely barmy.

Wallis used to permit his neighbour, the wealthy Lincolnshire landowner Frank Dennis, who worked all day on his farm and never went to the racecourse, to bet with him in the evening after racing was over. Why? Because he trusted him, naturally. The bookmaker would talk to the punter over the phone and relay to him his odds on the afternoon's cards. The farmer would place his bets and then Laurie Wallis would tell him the results. The arrangement apparently suited both men very happily. Mr Dennis won sometimes, especially on his own horses, but if he did ever know the results in advance he never made use of that knowledge to embarrass his bookie. Any Ladbrokes, Hills or Coral employee suggesting such a relationship with a punter today would probably face instant dismissal followed by psychiatric testing and a suit for damages.

Nobody ever mistook Willie Preston for a sucker. One of

Wallis's principal rails competitors he was born into a bookmaking family and began working on the tracks as a bookie's clerk in the 1920s when he was in his early teens. In the classic manner of the close-knit and interrelated on-course bookmaking fraternity he then progressed to betting in his own right on the boards in the ring from the pitches established by his father Alf Preston. Throughout his career Willie always knew all the right people and when Harry 'Snouty' Parker, the then foremost rails layer and the father of Cyril Stein, was forced out of action in 1941, Willie teamed up with Snouty's clerk Issy Isaacs, another Stein brother and another one of Cyril's uncles, and started operating on the rails with great success.

A short, stocky man with well-groomed wavy hair, Preston is remembered as another strong, self-confident personality who, like his contemporaries, was never afraid to accommodate a punter or to take a view about the likely outcome of a race. Yet the period when Preston made his biggest impact on the betting ring was not when he was trading in his own right but later, in the early sixties, after he'd sold his off-track and racecourse business to his partner Issy and joined the William Hill Organisation as their number one rails representative in the south of England. Looked at objectively Preston's belief that his own firm would never be able to overtake or outstrip the level of business being taken by the company that still trades today in the name of 'The Big Man' was surely a realistic one. That may have been an era when there were numerous high-rolling bookies, all of them worthy of respect, but there has certainly never been any doubt in Geoffrey Hamlyn's mind or in those of senior and respected racing writers like Peter O'Sullevan and Richard Baerlein that William Hill was the greatest racecourse bookmaker of all time.

What made Hill so popular with his punters, and initially with his shareholders, was his comprehensive knowledge of racing and the formbook coupled with his absolute willingness to take a bet, to embrace a risk, to strike a wager. If somebody wanted to back a horse with Hill to win themselves £100,000 in forties money, he would accept that bet – and then proceed to frame his odds on the other runners in a way that would quickly enable him to find enough punters to back them in sufficient proportions to guarantee himself a profit whatever won. This may seem like stating the obvious when you're talking about the bookmaking practice of brave contemporary independents like Victor Chandler and the

Uppingham-educated Stephen Little, but it is not the automatic approach of the Big Three. Yet Hill would not have been able to operate like this were it not for the much larger numbers of serious gamblers and customers patronising racetracks forty years ago. The one breeds the other as both Chandler and J.P. McManus would be the first to agree.

Hill, who was the son of a West Midlands farmer, started making a book while he was still a teenager at the BSA works in Birmingham during the First World War. He began to go racing in the 1920s but, except for a brief period betting on the rails at the old Northolt Park racetrack between 1933 and 1939, he didn't stand up and bet in Tattersalls until 1940. From then until 1955, when he retired theatrically at the age of fifty-seven in the middle of Royal Ascot, he was the king. But despite his exalted reputation as a layer, it would be a great mistake to perceive him as some sort of benign pussycat surrounded by cowards, con-men and thieves. Hill may have been a devout Christian and a socialist, too, but he was also an enthusiastic womaniser and on the racecourse he was every bit as tough if not tougher than the other hard men of his era from Willy Preston to the Parker-Stein family. It is said that he had a fierce temper and would tolerate nobody standing in his way. Neither did he conform to the conventional pre- and post-war image of the bookmaker as a spry little type in a check waistcoat and spotted bow tie: he was nearly six feet tall and weighed seventeen stone. In his prime, he looked like a cross between the West German Chancellor, Helmut Kohl, and the sort of burly and bespectacled northern police superintendent who might have ridden shotgun for T. Dan Smith.

After the First World War, Hill escaped from the dreariness of factory life by enlisting in the Black and Tans and saw active service in their ugly campaign in Southern Ireland. Ironically, thirty years later he is supposed to have told Vincent O'Brien, after the great Irish trainer and astute gambler had landed a major betting coup at York races one day, that he should have had him shot back in 1919 when he had the opportunity. Vincent, a native of County Cork whose population suffered acutely from the Tans' sickening brutality, didn't see the funny side. When Hill's one-time employee Ron Pollard, who later became Ladbrokes' euphemistically entitled 'director of public affairs', published his autobiography *Odds and Sods* in 1991 he couldn't get beyond page three without describing how he once acted as a bag man for Hill and carried money to a jockey's agent to reward the jockey for throwing a race at 'Glorious Goodwood' at the bookmaker's behest. Of course, Ladbrokes' management and field men have never had anything to do with that kind of disreputable activity.

In the 1930s Hill had concentrated on building up his starting-price business and, after several years in a couple of rooms in Jermyn Street, expanded into much larger premises in Park Lane, only yards away from the Dorchester. (There are two William Hill betting offices near that site today.) In view of his increasing financial commitments he decided that his only way forward was to increase his number of high-rolling off-course clients. He left the off-track business to his minions and began to go racing in person six days a week. Four- and five-figure bets were nothing to him in that period and he was in his element when it came to the big gambling handicaps like the Lincoln and the Grand National in March and April and the Cambridgeshire and the Cesarewitch in October, races that are still called the Spring and Autumn Double. For every shrewdie who might try to jump him in the ante-post betting market, Hill reckoned that he could smoke out a dozen or more mugs who would plunge on a losing horse. Sometimes even he lost, as over Airborne's victory in what became known as the 'Servicemen's Derby' in 1946. For most layers the 50–1 result was a skinner but Hill laid £1,000 to £15 ten times at the off to another rails bookie and later laid the same man £30,000 to £9,000 about Airborne winning the St Leger. (The grey horse followed up comfortably in a sub-standard field.) Hill was a bookmaker, though, who was always willing to accept a bet at the punter's preferred odds and stake and not at some reduced safety-first price of his own.

One of the best William Hill stories is told by Geoffrey Hamlyn and concerns the last race of St Leger Day at Doncaster in 1952. Hill's workmen were happy to pass on the contest, the two-and-a-quarter-mile Rufford Abbey Handicap, to make sure of catching the 4.30 p.m. train back to London, as to miss that would have meant a two-hour wait for the next service. Just as they had persuaded Hill to leave, the secretary to the famous and quite manic woman gambler Mrs J. V. 'Pat' Rank came up and asked for a £10,000 bet for her on her husband's runner in the last. Hill accepted the bet instantly, turned his staff round and marched them back to the rails. He climbed back on to his stool and within a matter of minutes had laid four other horses to take out a similar sum as the

Rank runner. The race was won by a 20–1 outsider and Hill's enterprise had cleared him a £50,000 profit. When he and his men got back to the station they found that the 4.30 p.m. train had been delayed due to signal failure and was still waiting at the platform. They settled down for dinner in the dining car and Hill travelled back south a happy and wealthier man.

In 1954 the William Hill Organisation went public. It was the first ever bookmaking concern to receive a stock exchange quotation and was ploughed into a shell company known as Holders Investment Trust. The deal was masterminded by Hill's close friend and associate, the accountant Lionel Barber. He was the Abbadabba Berman (the American financial genius who advised the gangster Dutch Schultz) of the Hill business and his finesse with numbers was helping to turn the rails layer into a man of substance. Hill ploughed much of the profit from his racecourse business back into racing, considerably more than any of his leading rivals at the time: he was an early sponsor of big gambling events like the Ebor Handicap at York, the Manchester November Handicap (at a time when Manchester racecourse was on the verge of closure) and Redcar's William Hill Gold Cup. He also invested large sums, with remarkable success, in the breeding industry. In 1942 he purchased Sezincote Stud in Gloucestershire and Whitsbury Stud in Wiltshire (yards away from what is now David Elsworth's training stable) from the executors of the former owner-breeder Sir Charles Hyde. Within seven years he had bred the 1949 2,000 Guineas and Derby winner Nimbus, by Nearco, the grand sire of Northern Dancer, out of a mare called Kong bought for him by Phil Bull for 750 guineas. A subsequent mating between Kong and Nasrullah produced the champion sprinter and leading sire Grey Sovereign and other homebred triumphs came with Cantelo, in the 1959 St Leger, and Be Careful, in the 1958 Gimcrack Stakes.

Hill's removal to Wiltshire, as a lately arrived bookmaker cum country squire, perhaps predictably offended the sensibilities of one or two of his two new county neighbours. Invited to dine near Whitsbury by a former Lord Mayor of London, his host was somewhat put out by Hill's robust approach to a whole Stilton which he spooned directly into his mouth as if it were melon or ice cream. 'We don't do it that way here,' he was informed, whereupon he gave his host a quick lecture about the basic diet and eating habits of undernourished Brummies pre-1914. The ex-

Mayor was told that he could either like or leave Hill's table manners. He decided to like them.

Hill always maintained that it was easy to make his breeding ventures pay and frequently castigated those who wanted some kind of public subsidy for breeding or owning racehorses. Both of these activities, he insisted, were strictly rich men's hobbies and entirely undeserving of financial support from the pockets of working-class punters.

Yet Hill was not universally wise, inspired or successful: at the time of his retirement in 1955 he was supposed to have been owed more than £750,000 by credit-account clients who had failed to honour their commitments, a loss his company could ill afford to bear.

In the early 1950s he started a fixed-odds football betting business and soon became involved in a costly price war with a rival firm which resulted in heavy losses for both companies. One of them went 33–1 for three draws so the other went 35–1. Then 40–1 and 45–1 and eventually 50–1. The odds for four score draws went up at one point from 100–1 to 250–1 and impulsiveness and ignorance of the form, which would never have been tolerated in their racecourse bookmaking, was rapidly leading the rivals into ever deeper water. In 1964 the new Labour government introduced a 25 per cent tax on fixed-odds football betting to bring it into line with Tote betting on the sport but instead of abandoning it as a losing streak Hills continued to deal in this area for another eighteen months, simply compounding their losses.

Hill's biggest mistake, however, was his failure as a would-be businessman to appreciate the commercial possibilities of legalised off-course betting shops. Geoffrey Hamlyn believes that it was his social conscience that allowed him to convince himself that only a third of the new offices, which he described as 'a cancer on society', would still be in business at the end of their first year of trading. When the William Hill Organisation belatedly realised that they would have to open shops to compete they found that all the value-for-money sites had gone and that they would have to buy in at the top end of the market.

Initially Ladbrokes, who had taken on Hills over fixed-odds football betting, were equally reluctant to identify themselves with the new breed of off-course punter, but the determination and enterprise of their top management enabled them to take the initiative in this rapidly developing field. Their founders, not to mention their most celebrated on-course representative, would have found it all distastefully vulgar and commercial.

In the twenties and thirties it used to be said, only half jokingly, that you had at least to have an entry in *Debretts* to open an account with Ladbrokes. The firm was established in 1886 in the Warwickshire village of the same name, moving to London at the turn of the century where it was bought by a smooth-wheeler dealer, Arthur Bendir. Bendir shrewdly calculated that his best hope for expansion lay in concentrating on the patronage of the aristocracy, many of whom still had the kind of private wealth that could support a major gambling habit. Cultivating the gentry, which the firm proceeded to do with impressive finesse, depended on a discreet approach to the business of actually laying bets. In keeping with this strategy the Ladbrokes' credit office in Burlington Street contained little curtained-off desks like polling booths from which their clerks could accept bets from clients, including royal clients, in complete anonymity. People may have thought this off-course office was bizarre but never was there a more discreet or indeed bizarre rails representative for a major bookmaking company than the petite Mrs Helen Vernet who executed that role for Ladbrokes for over thirty years. This remarkable lady, whose real name was Helen Monica Mabel Cunningham, was born into a good upper middle class Scottish family in 1877. She acquired a taste for gambling as a teenager after being left a not-inconsiderable legacy on the death of her father. She enjoyed a brief career on the stage, married twice in quick succession and then, rather like Barney Curley in his early twenties, developed a potentially serious tuber-cular illness. Her doctors advised that the best remedy would be to spend as much time as possible in the healthy, restorative, fresh, open air. So she started going racing.

One of the more comical aspects of the British Turf is the habit of old toffs, especially the female ones of the sadly impoverished or downright-mean school, betting in nothing but the smallest deno-minations. 'I say, darling, would you be a darling and see if you can get me a pound each way' – it used to be a shilling – 'on that frightfully nice little bay horse that Charlie Brooks trains.' These parsimonious gamblers wouldn't dream of setting foot in the bet-ting ring in person, unless it is a point-to-point and they have no alternative. They usually confine their custom to the bland respec-tability of the Tote, but back in 1918 there was still ten years to go before its introduction. That's where Mrs Vernet came in. She let it be known among her own social circle that the patrician loose-change punters, particularly the women, could henceforth place their bets with her if they wished, simply by slipping her a piece of paper inscribed with the name of their selection, underwritten by either credit or cash, while she was circulating among them on the Members' Lawn. This foray into illicit bookmaking proved an instant success but, not surprisingly, it quickly earned Mrs Vernet the opprobrium of the professionals, some of whom regarded her poaching activities, even if they were only in the shallows of the betting stream, to be every bit as 'diabolical' as others view the behaviour of Cheltenham Tony and his like today. Had it not been for the intervention of Arthur Bendir, that might have been the end of the career of Helen Vernet, bookmaker, but Bendir had observed her activities and decided that it would be another shrewd commercial move to bring her operation within the Ladbrokes fold. If more rich and well-connected women could be persuaded to bet on racing, especially in larger sums, then before long their husbands, fathers, brothers, sons and lovers might be persuaded to follow suit.

At first the introduction of a woman into the hitherto exclusively, not to say aggressively, male world of rails bookmaking was regarded by Ladbrokes' rivals with a mixture of sarcasm and incredulity. Due to her respiratory problems Mrs Vernet's limited vocal range would have made it difficult for her to dominate a polite drawing room let alone compete with the Jazz Age equivalents of John Pegley. Her way of dealing with this potentially disastrous liability was simply not to try to compete. She stood at her position at the major meetings, dwarfed by her umbrella on wet days, and let her ever-widening circle of punters and acquaintances come to her. She called no odds – in fact, she barely spoke but she had other attractions: she was minute; she was a novelty; she was utterly charming; and as her knowledge of both bookmaking and human character grew so did her ability to persuade the dippy ladies and their Wodehousian boyfriends that the prices she was giving them were somehow preferable to the more generous odds available elsewhere in the ring. The Drones Club members simply loved it. They thought it was no end of a caper to strike a wager with this feminine, elegantly dressed woman rather than with the somewhat threateningly masculine gentlemen close by.

In 1928 Bendir made Mrs Vernet a partner in the firm. Her salary was generous. She lived in the Albany and then in Eaton Place. It was said that her houses were always furnished in impeccable taste. Aside from gambling, her other great passion was ballroom dancing and whenever she went away from London for one of the big provincial three- or four-day race meetings at places like Aintree, Doncaster and York she would insist on staying at the best hotel in town. After dinner, Mrs Vernet and her workman, provided that he was a good-looking boy well up to a fox-trot, would dance the night away to the sounds of Roy Fox, Lew Stone and the Savoy Orpheans.

For nearly thirty years the names of Ladbrokes and Helen Vernet were virtually synonymous and it was only the painful onset of arthritis and Parkinson's disease that terminated her career. Even when she was a crippled and grey-haired old lady, Mrs Vernet still insisted on 'turning up for work', as she put it, although by then she had to be pushed down the rails in a wheelchair by her clerks. She died in 1956 aged seventy-nine. One of the great mysteries, as well as one of the sadnesses, of modern racecourse bookmaking is why, in a supposedly much more sexually egalitarian age, there are still next to no women bookies, let alone any Helen Vernet characters, working on the racecourse rails.

The year of Mrs Vernet's death was also the year that Cyril Stein joined Ladbrokes as an administration manager. He was already steeped in the traditions of bookmaking albeit not in such refined areas as Mrs Vernet. Today's regular punters may know something about the life and history of William Hill. Cyril Stein's father, Harry or 'Snouty' Parker, né Stein, is a less familiar handle. Yet Snouty's and his family's influence on bookmaking in Britain in the twentieth century has been as far-reaching as that of those other famous incomers Louis B. Mayer and Harry Cohn to the development of the American film industry.

There were four brothers in all. Harry, the eldest, who was born in 1895, Max, Jack and Isaac. Their parents were Russian émigrés who had settled in the East End of London and their family name was Stein. Harry who was also sometimes referred to as Dick acquired the youthful name of Snouty due to what W. C. Fields would have described as his distinctive proboscis. Parker came with Snouty as in Nosey and pretty soon Harry or Snouty Parker had taken the place of Harry Stein.

As a young man in the 1920s Snouty was an illicit starting-price bookmaker in Whitechapel and Bethnal Green. In the 1930s he branched out on to the rails at the leading southern and Midlands race courses, quickly acquiring a reputation for laying and staking large bets. It appears that Snouty's rise to a position of pre-eminence on the track owed not a little to the polished dexterity with which he executed the 'knock-out', a technique still notorious in bookmaking and racecourse gambling circles today. This practice, which was supposed to have been invented by one Charlie Gardner, father-in-law of the Reading bookie, Alf Turner, was a way of trying to beat the market by means of a little delicate manipulation. Snouty would invest heavily on fancied horses at SP, meaning that he stipulated that his bets were to be settled at the officially returned starting price. He didn't reveal himself by trying to get his money on in person. He organised teams of kids on bicycles, junior bookies runners in knee-length grey shorts, who would be sent out to hit all the illegal street-betting pitches in the East End. Then Snouty, operating from his pitch on the course, would offer – though not necessarily lay or accept bets for – the horses he'd backed at several points over the going odds and in stentorian tones hope to convince the SP reporters, who would be circulating in the ring, to return his selections at his own extended odds.

If the horse that Snouty had backed was being offered by the other rails layers at 3–1 then he would offer it at 7–2. If he could persuade the market to follow him out to that price, then he would try to knock out the odds again to 4–1, 9–2, 5–1 and as far out as he could go before the off. Anyone trying to get a decent bet on with Snouty at those prices would be tactfully ignored or steered in the direction of another layer who might well have been in on the scam. The whole sting depended on the SP reporters being taken in or convinced that the knock-out odds were those prevailing at the off.

A knock out is an inspired way for a rails bookie to try to enhance his profit margins, but he's got to be clever to get away with it. There was a celebrated instance of J. P. McManus pulling off a knock-out coup with his Cheltenham hero, Mister Donovan, at Punchestown races in Ireland in 1984, and some English rails layers still occasionally make a play with it today.

By 1939 Snouty Parker was *the* man on the rails. William Hill had yet to move out on to the racecourse and until he did Snouty was the undisputed Lord of the Ring in spite of the rivalry of other formidable personalities, such as Willie Preston and Laurie Wallis.

Manipulating the odds on his own bets was winning Snouty considerable sums of money and furnishing him with a sizeable betting bank for other legitimate wagers. He was extremely popular with the racing press of that era which contained many stylish and colourful individuals, almost all of them regular and heavy gamblers. One such man was Jimmy Park, *bon viveur*, proficient tipster and principal Turf correspondent for the *Evening Standard*. Park was convinced that Royal Mail, twelve lengths second to the incomparable Golden Miller in the 1936 Cheltenham Gold Cup, was a stand-out certainty for the 1937 Grand National, and he shared his thoughts with Snouty at the outset of the 1936–7 steeplechasing season. The bookie began quietly backing the horse, incognito, at the start of 1937 and continued with his investments throughout the early spring. By the day of the race his selection's odds had dropped from 33–1 to 100–6 and Snouty had further commissioning agents in place at Liverpool to get even more money on before the white flag went up. As every student of racing history knows, the eight-year-old Royal Mail, ridden by that fearless pre-war jump jockey Evan Williams, came home by three lengths from Cooleen and Pucka Belle. The winning prize money was £1,307. Snouty was reckoned to have profited by about £100,000, which at today's rates would translate into a sum in excess of two million.

Snouty celebrated his success by throwing a spectacular Grand National night party in the Prince of Wales hotel in Southport, where he and Jimmy Park always stayed for the Aintree meetings. The successful punter, the game's big winner, told the *maître d'* that he wanted to commandeer every bottle of champagne in the house, and if any guests asked for one they should have it at his expense. All the hotel staff were awarded lavish tips and Park's present was to be fitted for a new suit, price no object, at a tailor of his choice in Savile Row. Happy days all right – but they didn't last. Eighteen months later Royal Mail's owner Mr Lloyd Thomas was killed in a fall sustained while riding Royal Mail at Lingfield Park. Then, in the summer of 1941, Snouty Parker was 'warnedoff' by the Jockey Club for (shades of the Banks-Francome affair thirty years later) allegedly bribing jockeys and attempting to buy information. Four years later he died.

It would not be hard to believe that the circumstances of his father's premature exit from the track, followed by his equally untimely demise, were a source of considerable grievance to his son Cyril who was only seventeen years old in 1945. If Cyril Stein, no Parker for him, did feel any pain or resentment he has never expressed those feelings in public. What he has done is carve out a career for himself that has insured that the name of Stein can never again be taken lightly, either by the racing establishment or the most establishment financiers in the City of London or indeed worldwide.

When Cyril joined Ladbrokes in 1956 he brought with him a qualification in accountancy, an abundance of energy and an unusually sharp mind. Even at that early stage of his business career he is remembered for his consuming fascination with how 'prospects' might develop, not simply the following week, month or year but in five and ten years' time. In 1957 his own prospects were given a considerable boost when his uncle Max Parker – an exceptionally shrewd character who had taken over Snouty's position on the rails – bought Ladbrokes for £100,000 by . . . instalments. When Max died in 1966 it was his nephew who assumed the chairmanship.

The early years of Cyril's and Max's tenure of Ladbrokes were rough and controversial ones. Their aggressive policy of trying to take on Hills in the area of fixed-odds football-betting was as big a financial disaster for them as it had been for their rivals. Hills accused Ladbrokes of plagiarising their coupons, took them to court and won the first round. Ladbrokes won an appeal, and then the House of Lords came down in favour of Hills. Ladbrokes backed out of the football-pools business and didn't return until their purchase of Vernons in 1990.

Cyril was still determined to try to expand the Ladbrokes business into a wider market. He doubted that the firm could depend for ever on an inexhaustible supply of high-rolling untaxed aristocrats with sufficient plantations to sell and mews houses to develop to pay off their gambling bills. He was contemptuous, anyway, of society's snobbish and antiquated attitudes to bookmakers – the notion that it was all right for nice people to bet with a bookie by phone, but quite another for them to be seen talking and mixing together socially. All of Cyril's early battles with his inherited board involved convincing them that if Ladbrokes wanted not simply to survive but to prosper and thrive, they would have to expand their market base. They could continue to exploit their exclusivity if they wished, but they would also have to go out and actively recruit new customers. Crucially, Stein had already and accurately assessed the commercial potential of an event that was to have far-reaching consequences for both the future of British bookmaking and for the British Turf: the legalisation of off-track cash betting.

CHAPTER SIX

Out of the Shadows

THE ACT of parliament legalising off-course betting offices in Britain from 1 May 1961 was, in one sense, merely restoring a privilege that had existed over a hundred years before. In 1850 some 400 betting shops were operating quite legally in London. They had grown up in response to the greatly increased popular interest in horseracing in the early nineteenth century. On-course and credit-betting has always been legal but in Victorian England it was perceived as mainly the preserve of the toffs. The new off-course shops or 'listers' were designed to cater for the smaller bets of the riff-raff and hoi polloi who had neither the money, the chance nor the initiative to go racing.

One of the best-known shops was Dwyer's, located in a former tobacconist's in St Martin's Lane, with a reputation for fair trading and full and prompt settlement. It also claimed to offer better prices than many of its competitors. Yet hedging was not so sophisticated in the nineteenth century as it is now, and one spring day in 1851 the shop was cleaned out to the tune of £25,000 after a fancied horse that it had laid at several points over the odds won the Chester Cup. The proprietors' response was a moonlight flit and when their punters turned up the following morning to collect, they discovered that every stick of furniture in the place had been removed and that only the empty shell of the old cigar store remained.

It was supposedly to protect the innocent public from these welshers, and to try to curb the activities of those spicy Victorian underworld figures who had taken over proxy ownership of many of the gambling premises, that all of the nation's List Shops were officially closed down in 1853. This piece of legislation instantly brought into being a thriving, illicit, off-course cash-betting industry with much attendant comedy, hypocrisy and semi-visible crime. Villains continued to own or extract protection money from many of the illicit pitches and their biggest partners in graft were frequently the local police who, at the very least, accepted back-handers or a percentage of the take not only to look the other way but to tip off the bookies when a token raid was to take place. In some instances, they actually supplied uniformed constables to direct and drum up custom on the beat.

Generation after generation of working-class punters, the descendants of those cash gamblers who had been fleeced by the likes of Dwyer's in 1851, now had to break the law to indulge in the harmless past-time of putting a few shillings on the horses, usually while they were either unemployed or toiling though long hours of manual labour. Illegal pitches flourished outside factory gates, dockyards and pitheads. Others were to be found up alleyways, in rooms over chip shops and in gents lavatories at the back of pubs. Some legitimate credit layers, like William Hill, ran an illicit cash business from the same offices that they used to take telephone wagers from 'the quality'.

A vital component of any illicit bookmaker's enterprise were his runners who were responsible for fetching and carrying the bets. To be a runner for a street bookie in the 1930s and 40s was an attractive cash-in-hand occupation greatly preferable to a lifetime of drudgery, working in a cotton mill or down the mine. The runners were equipped with special brass-topped betting bags which they locked into betting clocks – machines which validated that all bets had been placed before the 'off' and that none had been tampered with afterwards.

Peter Smith, one of the most intelligent and hard-nosed council members of BOLA, the Betting Office Licensees Association Ltd, today owns forty independent betting shops in Yorkshire, and is regarded as a champion of the smaller off-course bookmaker. In the late fifties he was working in an illegal cash-betting office in Leeds and vividly remembers the daft music-hall-routine of the once-yearly prosecution. 'There was always a mysterious "warning" beforehand. The drill was to put a stooge behind the counter and leave two punters in the shop. We'd pay their fines when they came up in court and then everything would carry on regardless.'

It was the unenforceable nature of the old law in the face of widespread disobedience, and the time-consuming absurdity of carrying on with these annual ritual prosecutions, that played a major part in convincing senior politicians, like the liberal-minded Conservative Home Secretary R. A. Butler, that something had to change. And, while no formal betting tax was introduced until 1966, some shrewd Treasury civil servants had already begun to calculate the potential benefits that would accrue to the Exchequer from legalising the activities of a prosperous section of the black economy that was currently paying no income tax at all.

In April 1960 a Home Office committee, chaired by Sir Leslie Peppiatt, reported that in its august opinion the nation was ready to experiment once again with legalised off-course cash-betting shops. The Betting and Gaming Act named May Day 1961 as the date from which the new order could begin. William Hill may not have approved of the way that things were going but other established bookmaking firms, who had assiduously lobbied both parliament and the committee, counted Peppiatt's decision as a major triumph in their long battle to gain the imprimatur of respectability.

There were, inevitably, religious objections to the government's encouraging the 'vice' of gambling. There was also some pressure, though by no means overwhelming pressure, from horse-racing interests – some owners, breeders and racing correspondents – for the new betting shops to be run as a purely Tote Monopoly rather than passed into the hands of private entrepreneurs. To the advocates of such a monopoly, and to those sections of today's racing industry, most sorely affected by the recession of the early nineties, the 1961 act was the moment when British racing was sold down the river. They point to countries like France, where there are no bookmakers, America, where they are outlawed in all except two of the fifty states, and Australia, where they may make a book on-course but where off-course betting is operated by a Tote-based system. They see racing interests in those countries enjoying a much higher proportion of the revenue generated by off-track betting than British racing receives from its private bookmaker-run system. They look at the disparity between average prize money on the British Turf and the much higher levels in France; the prohibitive rates of admission to British racecourses compared with the much lower French rates. They compare the deteriorating value of the Derby with the Prix de l'Arc de Triomphe, the Breeders Cup series in America and a whole host of fabulously endowed races that take place in Australia, New Zealand and Japan. They cite the numbers of trainers in Newmarket, Lambourn and elsewhere who can no longer attract enough owners or racehorses to stay in business, whose yards are mortgaged to the hilt and who cannot find a buyer even though they are desperate to sell. And they blame it all on off-course bookmaking companies and that infamous licence to print money – John Banks is supposed to have coined the phrase – handed to them thirty-one years ago. It's a debate that goes on . . . and on . . . and on.

The Jockey Club of Great Britain, the self-elected and self-perpetuating body with near life-and-death power over the nation's 1,300 or more professional trainers and jockeys, has lately put itself at the head of a campaign to wrest more money from the off-track betting industry, money that it proposes should be spent on racing's behalf. Yet, in 1961, the same Jockey Club showed absolutely no interest in taking a direct stake in the new betting-shop businesses, and clearly had no intention of sullying their hands with common trade. Jakie Astor, then a Tory MP and subsequently a Jockey Club member himself, tried to organise a parliamentary lobby in favour of a Tote monopoly, but to little effect. It was an open secret that the leading Jockey Club Stewards at the time, such as Lord Willoughby de Broke, Lord Rosebery and Major General Sir Randle Fielden, who were used to their word being law in racing circles, all quite liked betting with bookmakers themselves and, when the Home Office civil servants came round to canvass their views, did nothing to discourage the government from opting for a free market system. They still didn't regard bookies as gentlemen – perish the thought – and they certainly wouldn't have dreamed of allowing them in their Club but they got on, no doubt, at a few points over the market odds in return for their accommodating attitude.

Yet, however preposterous the likes of Fielden and Rosebery may have seemed as conductors of democratic opinion, they were quite right to imply that British punters were accustomed to betting with a bookmaker, that they enjoyed betting with a bookmaker and that to attempt to channel their custom through a European-style off-course Tote system would be unlikely to succeed and would probably simply result in a continued proliferation of illegal betting.

In the end the majority view accorded with the sentiments of Sir

Winston Churchill (that great example of the British politician-as-bookie-figure, as opposed to clergyman – to invoke Malcolm Muggeridge's famous line) who some years previously had gruffly intoned that he saw 'no reason why the bookmaker shouldn't be allowed to make a profit just like the next man' and, 'as a staunch upholder of democracy', he would 'never be party to any sugges-tion that bookmakers should only be allowed to bet on the racecourse'.

As legislation drew near the *Daily Mirror* reported a 'gold dig-gers' rush' to acquire sites to take advantage of the anticipated gambling boom. One or two enterprising speculators bought in-itially mediocre or unpromising sites which they sold on at a profit to the bigger chains, particularly to late entrants like William Hill. Peter Smith, whose own first legal betting office was in what he only half jokingly describes as a 'chicken hut' outside Fryston Colliery near Castleford, recalls that to begin with Yorkshire became a bookmaking jungle: 'Illegal shops had been common and everyone knew their potential. At the first licencing session at York magistrates court there were over fifty betting-office applications. That was in just one day and they were all granted.' Yet anyone who thinks that off-track betting has only ever been a licence to print money for small traders and big combines alike should con-sider the situation in York today where there are just twenty-two shops left in the entire city.

Not the least ironic aspect of the new regime was that, whereas the illicit shops had frequently been open in the evenings, had offered televised races, provided comfortable furniture and a sym-pathetic ambience for their customers to bet in, the law now insisted that there could be no television and that the shop owners could offer only the most basic and Spartan amenities. John Morgan commented on this punitive and puritanical attitude when reviewing betting-office culture for the *New Statesman* in 1964. 'With a delicate hypocrisy the government has encouraged gam-bling by making the shops easily available but has salved its conscience by insisting that they are graceless utilitarian places without coffee or soft drinks and even without a television to watch the horses.' What Morgan probably didn't realise is that some punters grew up in the era of fag-ash on the floor and nasal voice-only commentaries of the Exchange Telegraph coming over the Tannoy in the corner, and the sleazy conditions are as cher-ished and essential a part of their gambling fix as champagne and closely cut green grass are to the svelte high-roller at Goodwood.

Not everything about those early betting offices was stark and depressing: some had a homely and sympathetic atmosphere not always evident in the bright-red plastic wonderland of today. Vera Smith (no relation to Peter), the former owner of a small chain of four in West London, fondly remembers how her and her husband's first office was a quick conversion of her mother's old grocery shop. When trading began she found herself as sole cashier and settler sitting up between the former cheese and bacon counters, telephone in one hand and calculator in the other. She remembers the look of utter joy that would cross a regular punter's face if you ever offered them 15 – 8 instead of an officially quoted price of 7 – 4. One day one fortunate customer struck gold and won £250 on a single five-bob-forecast bet. His hitherto undreamed-of triumph was the inspiration for countless other friends, relations and clients to come into the shop for the first time to see if they could emulate his success.

In 1961, as now, the genuinely friendly local betting office was a companionable social refuge with no rules about minimum stakes and no compulsion to bet or get out in a hurry. Vera's husband Ken was often asked to lend money by hard-pressed regulars and would generally try to oblige though only to half the requested sum. But while the punters may have liked their new neighbourhood bookies and enjoyed spending time in their shops, there was still widespread resistance to them in the community at large. It may no longer have been a criminal offence to own a betting office but the new Turf Accountants, as they called themselves in an effort to sound more respectable, still had to cope with the stigma of spivvery and villainy that had traditionally clung to their vocation.

In the spring of 1961, even as betting offices were in the very process of being legalised, a horse called Pinturischio, who was ante-post favourite for the Derby at the time, was sensationally doped. Not once but twice, and so badly that he was never even able to make the line-up at Epsom. Pinturischio was supposed to have been the best colt that his illustrious trainer, Noel Murless, had ever had through his stable and thousands of pounds had been gambled on him at the beginning of the 1961 flat-racing season. As a result of his non-participation, all that money stayed in the bookmakers' satchels.

Only one man, patently not the ringleader, was ever charged

with the Pinturischio dopings but racecourse rumour (and no one should forget that race tracks are always awash with rumour and gossip, all of it enjoyable but most of it unfounded) has persistently whispered that two leading bookmaking figures, whose firm had laid Pinturischio heavily and who therefore had much to gain from his untimely exit, were the real instigators of the crime. The Pinturischio Affair is undoubtedly a story that's just waiting to be written by some kamikaze investigative journalist, providing that they are backed by a publisher with a large wallet and an optimistic approach to libel actions.

If Pinturischio was got at by a bookmaker-recruited gang then he was by no means the first or the last racehorse to suffer in such a manner – which is not the same as saying that all bookmakers are characters you would automatically suspect of horse nobbling and doping. Yet, for all the efforts their industry is continually putting into improving their image, they have to live with the paradox that, for many punters, the faint whiff of corruption that has always been associated with gambling on horses and greyhounds is an essential part of the attraction. Respectable society's disapproval of betting shops in the early sixties (as in the 1850s) put what went on inside them on a par with other deliciously forbidden activities such as sex, drinking and cigarettes – not always a welcome association for a hard-working small bookmaker trying to get ahead.

Vera Smith recalls that because of this aura of insalubrity her husband was always slightly reluctant to reveal the precise nature of his occupation to strangers. This inevitably led to some comical misunderstandings, as the more Ken muttered enigmatically about being something 'in the retail line' the more intrigued and persistent his questioners would become. On one occasion a fellow guest in a holiday hotel leant across to Vera at the dinner table and confided that he and his wife realised she was embarrassed but that it didn't matter one bit about her husband being an undertaker.

The first few relatively uncomplicated years after legalisation were good times for the small betting-shop owner but things became much harder later on. In 1966 the then Labour Chancellor of the Exchequer, James Callaghan, introduced the first betting tax, which was to be payable on both on- and off-course betting and was set at a rate of $2\frac{1}{2}$ per cent or sixpence in the pound. It went up to 5 per cent eighteen months later and, although Anthony

Barber for the Tories shaved it by one point in 1972, continued to climb until it reached the present level of 8 per cent. (The 10 per cent deduction currently imposed on off-course punters includes an extra 2 per cent of which roughly 0.89 per cent goes back to horse-racing and is called the Betting Levy. The remaining 1.1 per cent is counted as bookmakers' handling charges and is partly used to make up their non-recoverable VAT payments.)

As well as attracting the Treasury's attention the Turf Accountants discovered that they were particularly vulnerable to a prolonged spell of severe midwinter weather. There were no all-weather race meetings in Britain in the sixties and seventies and, if a sudden freeze-up curtailed all horse racing for more than three or four days in succession, then the small shop-owners' turnover and profit margins were badly squeezed. Similarly, if one or two punters got lucky with a couple of big-priced outsiders, or if a clutch of favourites went in on a Saturday afternoon, then the two- or three-shop business, lacking the resources to lay-off above a certain level, could be faced with a distressingly large pay-out.

Vera Smith remembers that as the pressures and responsibilities on her husband grew, so did the number of keys that he always seemed to carry around in his jacket pockets. There were the main keys to each betting shop, the keys to the back door, the manager's office, the cash registers, the safe – a key for everything. The ritual of unloading them onto the bedside table each night became a standing joke between the couple, and Ken liked to remind his wife that if she thought that his hardware collection was excessive then just imagine what Cyril Stein's bedroom must look like.

Cyril, along with the managements of Mecca, Coral and Hills, was busily maintaining the pressures on small betting-shop owners. If Ladbrokes owned a betting office in a neighbourhood in which the competition consisted of one Coral shop, one Hills shop and one independent, Ladbrokes would begin by offering punters tax-free betting as an inducement. They would then offer the owner of the small independent office, which would soon be struggling to compete, generous cash terms to sell out. The independent shop owner would be taken on as on-site manager and Ladbrokes would now own 50 per cent of the outlets in the area. In 1966 there were 16,000 betting-shop licences in Britain. In 1973 there were 14,750. By 1987 that figure had shrunk to 10,400 and by the autumn of 1991 it has shrunk again to just over 9,000. And, with Mecca having dropped out of the picture, some 45 per cent of those licences are held by the triumvirate of Ladbrokes, Coral and Hills.

Jim Callaghan's joyless betting tax turned out to be a charge on punters rather than bookmakers as both the betting-shop owners and the on-course layers simply passed the cost on to their customers. To serious professional gamblers, who all bet to percentages, the new tax was a disaster. Further high-taxation policies of the Wilson governments (in areas ranging from income and super-tax to death duties and inheritance charges) combined with the betting duty to cut a swathe through the ranks of high-rolling on-course punters. It wasn't until Nigel Lawson mercifully abolished the tax on-course in 1987 that the racetrack betting and bookmaking business was given some respite. That decision came much too late for an old-style racecourse bookmaker like Willie Preston who, depressed by the developing trends, had retired from his job with William Hills as long ago as 1965.

The now increasingly powerful off-course firms took to employing smoothly effective professional spokesmen to lobby for them in Parliament and in the media on matters effecting their interests. One such spokesman in the early 1970s was Brian Walden, at the time still a backbench Labour MP but later to make a much bigger name for himself as a slick and articulate television interviewer. Another lobbyist was the late Richard Holt who, from 1966 to 1972, was personnel director for William Hills before entering the House as Conservative member for Langbaurgh. Walden, Holt, and other MPs like them, were all behaving quite legally. Their interest was openly declared and their activities considered no more reprehensible than the lobbying of numerous (other Labour and Conservative members who stood up to plead for the trade unions and the City.

Unionisation of their workforce was not on the big betting-shop owners' agenda but big business was definitely taking an interest in the performance of their chains and especially in their cash-flow patterns: takeovers, mergers and amalgamations were the predictable outcome. By the end of the seventies, the William Hill Organisation (its founder and namesake having died back in 1971) had become an adjunct of the Sears Group, Mecca had been swallowed up by Grand Metropolitan and Corals by Bass.

Ladbrokes were taking over other people. On first going public in 1966 it had a market capitalisation of £2 million. Its value today is 1,000 times greater: in the course of this relentless evolution the canny descendants of the Parker Boys have expanded into both the American and the European betting markets. They have controlling interests in racecourses and off-course betting franchises in six different states in the USA, have opened betting shops in Belgium and, until the end of 1991, in Holland and successfully challenged the PMUs off-course French betting monopoly (its café, bar and betting-shop outlets) in the European court. The cash flow generated by gambling has been partly used to fund inter-group and company debt but it has also been diverted into a variety of other activities, not all of them successful.

During the 1970s, Stein moved into a sprawling mélange of leisure businesses from hotels, bingo and holiday camps to electrical retailers, snooker halls and television investments. At one point he owned 20 per cent of Central TV and made an abortive bid to merge with the Granada group. His biggest setback came in 1979 when the company lost its much-vaunted casino licences in London's West End – a bitter blow to the group's image, made worse because the casinos accounted for nearly half of their total profits at the time. The chairman's response was to restructure the group into its present four divisions and to attempt to move into new businesses with international appeal. In 1986 he paid £200 million for the DIY superstore chain Texas Home Care, doubling its estimated market value by 1990. The greatest moment, though – perhaps the greatest in the whole history of 'The Magic Sign' (the racecourse tic-tac codename for the Ladbrokes company) – came in 1987 when Cyril successfully purchased Hilton Hotels outside the US for only £645 million. 'Is that the best deal you've ever done?' somebody asked him afterwards. 'It's the best deal anybody's ever done,' he replied.

Incredibly, in spite of the Big Three's relentless climb up the corporate ladder, no changes were made to the law relating to betting shops until 10 March 1986 when, as a result of a bill ushered in by another Conservative Home Secretary, Douglas Hurd, the rules were relaxed slightly to permit punters to watch live and recorded sports on national television. Shop-owners could now sell soft drinks and light refreshments, provide more comfortable stools and chairs and even, to everyone's relief, install gents and ladies lavatories.

Of even greater import was the launching of Satellite Information Services (SIS), which on 1 May 1987 provided the UKs first-ever live satellite coverage of non-televised race meetings, beaming horse and greyhound racing into a handful of selected betting shops. By the end of 1989 the SIS service was available nationwide. Its initials disguise a company that was primarily set up *by* the big bookmakers: 45 per cent of the shares are owned by Ladbrokes, Coral and Hills. The service begins shortly after betting offices open each morning and continues until after the last race of the day. It comprises a minimum of two horse-race meetings, and one BAGS (Bookmakers Afternoon Greyhound Service) fixture each day plus a full results service and shows of betting from any other meetings. SIS provide their own studio commentators but the race commentaries come directly from the racecourses themselves and simply involve the usual course commentator speaking into an additional microphone. The pictures are supplied by Racecourse Technical Services who currently record every race for possible steward's enquiries. The pictures and commentaries are relayed to the SIS studio headquarters in Corsham Street, north London, using a combination of landlines and microwave signals, edited and mixed in fractions of a second and transmitted to the betting shops who pay for the service. (From 1 May 1992, the pictures will be supplied by Chrysalis Television Mobiles.)

The SIS consortium won the right to supply live racing from the Racecourse Association (RCA), which collectively represents Britain's fifty-nine different racetracks and SIS had to beat off a challenge from Extel, who had supplied betting shops with their old audio-information service, to win the contract. It was a notably bruising competition and dark mutterings came from the Extel corner about some of the canvassing methods and other techniques employed by the winners.

Racing has benefited to the tune of £10 million from the first three years of the SIS service's existence but some people have wondered if it couldn't have been more. The Jockey Club showed no more interest in getting actively and personally involved with high-tech satellite racing than they did with legalised off-course betting shops in 1961 and the RCA's negotiations with the bookmaker-sponsored enterprise were headed by a retired general, Sir Peter Leng.

SIS has indisputably been one of racing's biggest success stories of the past decade. It has revolutionised the lives of betting-shop owners and managers every bit as much as it has transformed the options and entertainment of their customers. Yet, for all that, you feel that those same off-course punters, if not the providers of their entertainment, are still held in much the same contempt and derision that they were subjected to in 1853 and 1961 by the non-gambling sections of the population.

Some people – mainly middle-aged, middle-class professionals, teachers, solicitors, GPs, accountants and such like – have probably never spent more than fifteen minutes in a betting shop but remain convinced that most Ladbrokes, Hills and Corals customers comprise the deadbeats, loafers and shirkers of life. Betting-shop owners, mindful of this impression, have made strenuous efforts in recent years if not exactly to move upmarket then certainly to brighten up their act. The idea that your local betting office will inevitably be located down a side street behind the railway station is history, but as well as moving into the high street the bookies have invested large sums of money in refurbishing their old shops to accompany the bright, cheerful and punter-friendly image of SIS. They say that they want more young and female clients and that they're prepared to open up special non-smoking salons for their use. (Hills opened an entirely non-smoking shop in Doncaster in September 1991 and Ladbrokes have had around a dozen non-smoking shops since 1988.) They have been pressing for evening opening and Sunday opening and while the law restricts them to catering for unstimulated demand – which means that they may not display any material or any advertising that does not primarily show the runners, form or results of racing or another sporting event – it is no secret that their new target punters are interested in sports other than horse racing, which is often perceived as a closed and incomprehensible world by the non-racing public. They feel that if they can suck in the young, upwardly mobile sports fan with golf, tennis, soccer, cricket and American football they can gradually pass them on to the more traditional addictions. Which was partly why Ladbrokes paid out for an expensive Saatchi and Saatchi devised advertising campaign for their 1990 World Cup promotions – to which they were also attempting to direct their twice-a-year punters on the Derby, which in 1990 occurred three days before the first World Cup match was played. Off-course turnover on the World Cup competition was estimated to be in excess of £20 million.

Football and golf are growing, prosperous markets well worth cultivating, but crafty advertising rather than any serious desire to make a book is the main impetus behind the much-touted novelty prices on everything from the date of the next general election to

the name and gender of the next royal baby and the likely discovery date of the Loch Ness monster. Ron Pollard modestly takes
the entire credit for introducing political and novelty betting to the
British punter as long ago as 1963 but this is a form of odds-making
where the attention created usually vastly outweighs the amounts
of money staked. Every time some wily representative of the Big
Three, like the ever-so-amenable Graham Sharpe of Hills, manages
to persuade another newspaper or news bulletin editor to include
yet another item about the sensational million-pound pay-out that
the bookies are meant to be facing over the Booker Prize winner or
the identity of the next Archbishop of Canterbury, his grateful
management can be imagined rubbing their hands with glee at yet
more marvellous free publicity. It's a brilliant way of getting the
company's name off the back and on to the front pages. A few, as it
turned out erroneous, enquiries from Lambeth Palace about the
odds against the Bishop of St Albans for the 1990 archbishopric
race did wonders for the Hills image. 'William Hill . . . God's own
bookie!' Yet any really informed clerical 'insider' who had wanted
to place £20,000 at 5s on Dr Carey would have been instantly
advised to seek closer acquaintance with the Almighty. Similarly if
a publisher, operating on the principle of backing well-bred but
unraced two-year-olds for the next year's Derby, rang up any of
the Big Three companies now and asked for a couple of grand on
William Boyd, say, to win the 1993 Booker Prize, then the best
they'd probably be offered would be £500 at 5–1.

Persistent critics of the multiples contend that this dishonest
advertising, coupled with the cynical hedging of money on-course
to manipulate the market and depress starting prices, proves that
for all the talk of the new-age, new-look betting climate the main
off-course operators are still only interested in mugs and morons
and that, as long as they are allowed to get away with it, they will
continue trying to pare down any real wagers and to force
informed and discriminating punters out of the system. The Big
Three sometimes add to this impression with their own promotional material such as the TV campaign for the William Hill Race Line
service featuring a pair of spectacularly gimpish race-goers, both of
whom spend the entire duration of the commercials with their
mouths open and their heads practically lolling from their
shoulders.

'Why do you think they want to install slot machines on their
premises?' the critics of the cartel go on to ask. 'Do you seriously

think that they're for J. P. McManus? And if they could would they not take up even more of our gambling diet with morning and afternoon greyhound fixtures, horseracing from Hong Kong and practically any activity about which the punters are likely to know as little as possible about the precise form of the various contestants?'

And what about these much-vaunted new 'betting theatres' like Ladbrokes' £5,000 square feet of 'punter space' in their showpiece Arena shop in Birmingham (currently under fire from the Home Office for supposedly trying to be more of a leisure centre than a betting office)? If you hang around long enough and lose enough money these high-tech wonderlands soon begin to feel every bit as squalid and tacky as those old smoke-filled rooms back in 1961. Sometimes they don't feel as fundamentally sympathetic or as tolerant of failure and human weakness: the bright lights and gratingly vivid décor are too uncomfortably reminiscent of the hard sell and unrelenting cheerfulness of a modern homogenised fast-food outlet and, other than the differing colour schemes, there is sometimes as little to distinguish the latest Ladbrokes' from the most recent William Hills shop as there is to mark out a McDonald's from a Burger King.

Which is perhaps exactly the kind of image that the Big Three are after. For, in the age of junk betting, in which high turnover is all, what could be more appropriate than that placing a bet should become as swift, as easy and, some would say, as flavourless a transaction as consuming a flame-grilled Whopper or a Big Mac?

CHAPTER SEVEN

And into the City

IT'S HALF-PAST two in the afternoon on the second day of Royal
Ascot and a crowd of some thirty-two punters, only one of them a
woman, are sitting, standing and walking around in the main
betting parlour of the Ladbrokes' Dover Street office in the West
End of London. The interior feels like a cross between a small-scale
Wimpy and a Kentucky Fried hairdressing salon. There are lots of
bright red-and-orange plastic surfaces and a notice on one wall
encouraging punters to complain if the lavatories are dirty or if the
paper tissues need re-stocking. Sadly, these admirable incentives
to good housekeeping don't seem to have made much impression
on the habits of the customers themselves.

The floor beneath their feet is awash with losing betting slips
and fag packets, dead matches and cigarette butts. 'Frankie drops a
right Bolkonski', proclaims the headline of the *Sun* racing page
which is pinned up prominently next to the *Sporting Life* affording
the more discriminating punters the opportunity to read Claude
Duval's thoughtful observations on one of the previous day's
Ascot events. Next door to the thoughts of Claude are the top
recommendations of the day by Tony Lewis in the *Star*, whose own
column has to contend for your attention with a list of phoneline-
lust box numbers and 'dial my naughty knickers' ads which Tony's
editor clearly feels belong most appropriately on the racing page.
Either side of the newspaper cuttings are the proprietors' own
adverts for their live-line and results-line telephone services.

A dusty-looking green plastic plant sits in one corner of the
room underneath a display of ante-post prices on cricket, tennis
and golf. Four bored-looking female cashiers perch up at the front

behind the counter waiting unemotionally to take the punters' business. And a youthful and crisply shirt-sleeved shop manager paces up and down in the rear.

'And the rain's stopped now at Ascot,' announces the SIS studio commentator. 'So . . . that's good.'

'Do you think this rainpour, this down . . . will affect, will affect the ground . . . Colin?'

'It'll take more than that, Carol.' My goodness me. This is illuminating stuff. Is this what they mean by the incisive, extra-inside information that shop punters now have at their disposal with which to try to fox the bookies?

'It's a tough track actually, Ascot,' continues Colin. You don't say, squire. But according to Carol, the great French trainer, 'France was Bootan,' knows exactly what's wanted. Thank goodness for that then.

It comes as a merciful relief when the SIS Corsham Street team hand over to Peter O'Sullevan's live BBC commentary on the £100,000 Coronation Stakes but within three seconds of the Ascot winner galloping past the winning post SIS cut in again to take us over to some coruscating dogs' action from Canterbury. Their studio director even flashes up the number of the leading dog at each bend as if we are too moronic to make any sense of the race with our own eyes.

The William Hill office further up the street has the sort of fake wooden panelling and phoney library-foyer feel of those second- and third-rate London hotels that cater specifically for the more gullible Americans. The colour scheme is somewhat more res-trained than Ladbrokes, favouring brown wooden rather than red plastic stools with fake blue velveteen upholstery and a blue-patterned carpet on the floor. Unfortunately for the carpet, large squares of it are hidden beneath the same wash of rubbish and litter as bedeck the floor of the Ladbrokes' shop nearby. On this evidence betting-shop punters are contributors to the European litter mountain on a truly epic and heroic scale.

The punters present are a slightly more upmarket-looking bunch than the Ladbrokes' customers although, worryingly for Hills, there are only nine of them and not one is a woman. The two female cashiers are an altogether friendlier and more pleasing pair than any of the Ladbrokes' counterparts while the walls are adorned with a selection of surprisingly tasteful old racing prints as against Ladbrokes' gallery of colour action photos. There is, however, exactly the same tired-looking plastic pot plant sitting in one corner of the room.

If you walk half a mile away to the Hills' Park Lane office you find a much bigger crowd of exclusively male punters packed into its larger but identically decorated dark-brown vinyl library interior. A group of tanned and fit-looking construction workers in navy-blue boiler suits have popped in from a nearby building site. These stocky and intimidating lads, most of them with Geordie accents, swagger around a brilliantly lit room that is otherwise dominated by well-dressed middle-aged Arabs and animated parties of Italian and Chinese waiters. Everyone's attention is glued to the Royal Hunt Cup, the big betting handicap of the day. 'Look at all them Sammy Davises walking up the middle of the park,' remarks one of the Geordies tastefully, as Sheikh Hamdan al Maktoum and his entourage walk across the Ascot paddock. Muttered oaths and resentful expletives issue from both the Geordies and the 'Sammy Davises' standing next to them as three outsiders dominate the Hunt Cup finish. 'Fucking Eddery. Fucking Cauthen. Fucking bastards,' etc, etc, come the unpleasant and aggressive cries.

By the time the last race is over, and the last from Ripon and the concluding dogs' heat from Canterbury, the block of twelve satellite television screens, six over six right along one wall and all endlessly spewing out information, has begun to seem like some sinister and hypnotic prop from *A Clockwork Orange*. Your head, eyes and brain are exhausted and your soul feels grimy and bedraggled from the incessant gambling.

Now, of course, it would be unfair to judge all Hills' and Ladbrokes' offices by the standards of these three inner-London emporiums. There are other Big Two and Big Three shops and numerous small independently owned offices around the country that have a much friendlier and less aggressive atmosphere in which to sit, watch and gamble. Even so, prolonged exposure to that distinctive Big Three ambience and to that feeling that they treat you as a mug from the moment that you walk in through the door (and sometimes who can blame them?) should once again encourage anyone who has the time, the money and the opportunity to 'Go racing, go racing' if they really want to bet.

If it's by no means an undiluted pleasure to be a punter in some big modern shops then neither is it an uninterrupted picnic for some of the staff who have to work in them. Some betting-shop employees (some of them employed by the Big Three) will talk with real bitterness of their long hours and poor pay. There are instances of shop managers working through their lunch hours at flat rate maybe three times a week if there's satellite racing from Hong Kong or Friday-and-Saturday-morning dogs. Many staff are concerned that if there are to be evening opening hours (and maybe one day Sunday opening too), their interests and their well-being are the last things that their bosses will think about. An attempt at unionisation by some Coral employees was brusquely dealt with by the parent company, Bass, a few years ago but even those workers who wouldn't wish to join a union complain feelingly of the stigma that continues to pertain to working in a betting office or for a bookie. Banks and insurance companies, they claim, treat them as on a par with being in the scrap-metal business or employed by a second-hand car dealer.

Ladbrokes, as mindful of the need to raise the profile of a career in the betting industry as they are of the need to improve the public image of their shops, are proud that twenty-four of their junior staff have recently completed a twelve-month course in retail management at the North London Polytechnic, qualifying for the Business Technicians Education Council Certificate. This ranks somewhere between an A Level and a degree and Ladbrokes staged a kind of passing-out ceremony to mark their graduation. To demonstrate the importance they attached to it both Peter George, chairman of Ladbroke Racing and Berjis Daver, managing director, were on hand to pose for the cameras. The young graduates lined up alongside them had the same bright, clipped, neat and respectable look that you see on the young faces in the cosy television adverts for the Big Four high-street clearing banks. They may all have first-class managerial potential but what, you wonder, do they know or care about horse-racing? About jockeys and trainers, horses and courses, stories and characters going back years? With only 5 per cent of betting taking place on the race-course, is this what the legacy of Percy Thompson and William Hill has finally dwindled down to? Are these spruce young executives really the bookmakers of the future?

The truth is that for many years off-track bookmaking (as the leading representatives of the Big Three never tire of telling you) has been not a back-alley game for barrow boys but a big business that must regularly feed and placate its shareholders. Ladbrokes dominate this market, deservedly from a mercantile point of view, because they run their affairs more thoroughly and with a greater degree of professionalism than anybody else. The key management personnel in their racing division always seem to be that little bit sharper, harder and better informed than the opposition. You imagine that they must get up earlier, work harder and stay longer hours.

Behind a friendly, soft-spoken exterior, the forty-eight-year-old Peter George, who also shares the joint managing directorship of the whole Ladbroke group with Cyril Stein, conceals a brain made of razor-wire. George's father and grandfather were bookmakers in south-east London and Surrey and George joined Ladbrokes as an office boy in 1963. In the late sixties and early seventies he worked as one of the company's field men, representing the firm on-course. He will still talk about horse racing with apparently genuine enthusiasm although, as with the rest of his boardroom colleagues, you are always aware that it comprises just one part of his overall corporate strategy. What is also noticeable is that he appears to have a much shrewder understanding of how horse-racing is perceived by the outside world (and therefore of how to exploit that perception to the bookies' advantage) than can ever be detected in the statements and postures of the Jockey Club.

The man who is currently Ladbrokes' most visible and famous on-course representative is the moustachioed and bespectacled 'Marshal' Mike Dillon, their chief press officer and public relations spokesman. The Marshal, a sharply groomed and sober-suited forty-year-old Mancunian, doesn't hedge money or lay bets. He handles the promotional side of any racing event with which Ladbrokes are associated and zealously nurtures the Ladbrokes' name and interests in racing events around the world.

Dillon wasn't born into the bookmaking business like Peter George and Cyril Stein. His father owned a small pub-cum-boarding-house hotel and Mike left Manchester's Cardinal Langley grammar school at the age of sixteen with but two O levels. After a short spell working in the advertising department of Cable and Wireless he joined Ladbrokes as a trainee settler (a back-room cashier who settles up punters' bets) in one of their Manchester offices. Within three years he had been promoted to manage what was then Ladbrokes' Manchester flagship shop in Moseley Street off Piccadilly. What had instantly commended him to his employers was not simply his remarkable capacity for hard work but also his self-evident flair and drive. He had the dedication and imagination of a born salesman, coupled with an almost missionary-like belief that the product was worth selling. All of these qualities were vividly demonstrated when he was charged with promoting the Grand National during the seven-year period from 1976 to 1983 when Ladbrokes stepped in to manage the Aintree race.

These days his responsibilities also include pricing up the leading aspirants for the classic races, after their trials each spring and summer, and the main candidates for the big races at Cheltenham as they compete throughout the winter months. Bookmakers rely on accurate inside intelligence to help them perform this task and it's an accepted racing truth – like saying that the Derby is run at Epsom each June – that Mike Dillon's information is the best in the business – better than any other bookmaker's representative's and better than any owner's, trainer's or jockey's. He often seems to know more than they do about the problems and challenges they're going to face in a particular contest. The source of this prescient knowledge is a subject of much gentle teasing.

Each January Ladbrokes sponsor a valuable handicap hurdle race at Leopardstown in Ireland. Some of the top Irish gambling trainers, such as the inimitable Mick O'Toole from Maddenstown in County Kildare, like to joke about Dillon ringing them up or dropping by some weeks in advance in an attempt, they suspect, to nose out the identity of any likely aces that they might be holding up their sleeves and then offering them surprisingly generous odds about those horses. Before, presumably, making use of that information to ensure that the 'Magic Sign' won't be caught out in any other ante-post gambling on the race.

Dillon disclaims all knowledge of any such Richelieu-style intelligence gathering techniques and insists that for all the overtones of intrigue and guile his fund of information comes not from soliciting tips or eavesdropping on private conversations but simply from being there if trainers and owners choose to talk to him. It's undeniably true that if you stand around chatting with him at a racetrack you are constantly interrupted by a procession of trainers, jockeys, owners, racing managers, journalists and 'faces' coming up to offer him some story or snippet of news. Not that he is by any means wholly dependent on the quality of this information to enable him to make up his mind: he has an intense and all-consuming passion for horseracing and will talk about it, airing his own private views and opinions, for hours on end. Yet, however enjoyable these sessions are and however modestly he makes his points, you are always brought back to his awesome talent for being able to predict spot on what will happen on the racecourse.

Talk to Dillon about the Derby, the Arc or the Cheltenham Gold Cup a few days or even weeks in advance and he can instantly bring the race down to the two or three horses who will really count. He is rarely wrong. Information may play an important part in this process but so too does his own native intelligence and a top professional bookmaker's canny ability to read the form book with even less prejudice and sentimentality than the best professional gamblers. This is why serious punters always scrutinise Dillon's lists of ante-post odds and if they see the Marshal offering a horse at significantly shorter odds than his rivals they invariably take a serious interest in it, if not immediately attempting to get on at the bigger price. Naturally the converse also applies, as John Banks understood way back in 1969 when he advised that 'professionals should not be disheartened when Ladbrokes do not lay them. Instead they should be perturbed when they do.'

There's a story in bookmaking circles that the Ladbrokes' determination to win even extends to employing a sort of house punter to back horses for them, not those whose starting prices they might want to contract in their betting shops but slightly longer priced selections that this form expert believes have a serious winning chance. In spite of all this evidence of impressive endeavour to improve the balance sheet, however, the real or precise profitability of the off-course betting industry is by no means easy to assess.

Tom Kelly, director-general of the Betting Offices Licensees Association, whose job seems to involve endless confrontations with race-horse owners and their interests, insists that off-course bookies are not made of money and that their profit margins are modest. 'About three per cent of turnover for the bigger chains, two per cent for the small bookmaker. Roughly ninety per cent of the six billion wagered is bet in shops but it's really the same pot of money going round and round.'

However misleading this six-billion figure may be, it was still real enough to allow Ladbrokes' racing division to show a profit of £91.1 million in 1989, part of total group profits of £302.2 million. In the light of this achievement, the advice given to City investors that year by Ron Littleboy, an economic analyst with Nomura Securities, was that 'rather than put a bet on the horses you should invest in Ladbrokes shares. If you look at the profits of Ladbrokes betting division they go up in a straight line over twenty years. No punter can say that. And now is the ideal time to buy.' Well, as it turned out Littleboy's upbeat prediction was over-optimistic, hardly surprising given that when he made it, no one had foreseen the outbreak of the Gulf War and its devastating impact on tourism worldwide and on Ladbrokes' hotel business, or the scale and intensity of the impending recession.

One corporate tycoon who may have read Littleboy's analysis and believed that high-rolling times for off-course bookmaking firms were here to stay was George Walker. It was in the summer of 1989 that 'Gorgeous George', who seems to have fancied and gravely over-estimated his chances of taking on Cyril in open combat, paid £685 million to enable his Brent Walker property and leisure combine to purchase Grand Metropolitan's 1,600 betting shops which had been trading under the names of Mecca and William Hill.

By the standards of the old days, George Walker seemed made to measure for the role of a bookmaking baron. Here was the original rough diamond, a former Billingsgate fish-market porter and light-heavyweight boxing champion with East End roots as indigenous as those of the Stein family. You might have thought that George's new competitors would have admired him for the enterprise and skill that he'd shown in getting himself accepted as a dealmaker and businessman by even the most snobbish City boardrooms. His achievement surely mirrored their own success in moving out of the shadows and into respectable daytime society. The trouble was that, as well as colour and individuality, George brought with him other, shadier, associations that his rivals were anxious to forget. Their youthful 'indiscretions' were never mentioned and, in any case, mostly impossible to trace. Some of George's were fashionable dinner-table gossip.

Had not 'Square Georgie' once been employed by Billy Hill, London's leading post-war racketeer and, along with Jack Spot, a man who had taken protection money from numerous illicit bookmaking pitches and controlled some of the most lucrative on-course pitches at tracks like Epsom and Brighton? Had not George done two years in the mid-fifties for being caught in possession of that most evocative of the spivs black-market items, a lorryload of stolen nylons? It all happened an awfully long time ago but it still wasn't the sort of commercial track record that long-since-respectable bookmaking companies wanted to be associated with.

Their concern was ridiculously exaggerated and in some cases deliberately manufactured. There were no more battles with knuckle-dusters and shooters, and George's business associates soon found that they were in much greater peril as a result of Brent Walker's massively vulnerable indebtedness than they were from any contamination from George's iffy past.

In Brent Walker's 1989 company report and accounts George wrote: 'We now have a well-balanced group and have enjoyed another record year during a period of major expansion . . .' Three months later it was clear that he was in deep trouble. Within six months, loan covenants were being breached and Brent Walker needed a refinancing package to survive. With horrifying rapidity the recession closed in, the leisure industry went into reverse and it was suddenly clear that the assets against which the banks had fallen over themselves to lend George money were hugely overvalued.

At the end of May 1991 George was forced to stand down as Brent Walker's chief executive. He felt, with some justification, that his bankers, who he believed had never really liked him and had always despised his Stepney origins, were simply using the recession and its vicissitudes as a weapon with which to get him out. At the time of writing the future of the William Hill betting-shop chain, which was never under direct Brent Walker management and which is regarded as a model concern within the off-course bookmaking industry, is still unclear.

It is long odds against that George Walker's fate will ever overtake Cyril Stein, not that he can go on for ever and not that Ladbrokes are unscathed by the depressed trading conditions and mounting interest payments of the slump. In 1990 the group's total profits rose by just a modest £3.4 million to £305.6 million with the racing division advancing by a mere £600,000 to £91.7 million. The low level of profit growth was attributed to the bad last three months of the year when both profit margins and turnover in the company's 2,000 British and Irish shops came under pressure. The Ladbrokes' credit-betting division was particularly hard hit. Results elsewhere in the multi-billion-pound group were equally undramatic. The Hilton Hotel chain recorded just a £6.5 million profit increase to £174.3 million which was none the less regarded as a good performance, given the marked downturn in world travel and hotel bookings during the last five months of 1990 due to the Gulf crisis. Profits from the Texas DIY stores were down

£400,000 on the year before at £39.7 million, further underlining the effect on the group of the drop in consumer spending and the impact of high-interest rates.

Against this gloomy background, the City was expecting less than good news when the group declared its 1991 half-yearly figures at the end of August, and was not disappointed. In the context of a general 6 per cent drop in betting turnover Ladbroke Racing could take some comfort that it suffered only a 2.8 per cent drop in turnover in its own shops but profits from its racing division were down by 23.21 per cent from £58.6 million to £45 million. This profit represented some 3.6 per cent of turnover approximating pretty closely to Tom Kelly's official claim. The Ladbroke group as a whole announced a 3.5 per cent drop in half-yearly turnover from £2.03 billion to £1.96 billion. Its profits had fallen by 17 per cent from £188.4 million to £156.5 million with a reduction of earnings per share from 13.07 pence to 8.18 pence. The company management announced that as a consequence of these figures they would be asking shareholders to fund a rights issue of £464 million through the issue of 216 million new shares which would be offered at 220 pence each on the basis of one new ordinary share for every four ordinary shares already held. The rights-issue move was fully expected by the City who showed continued faith in the Ladbrokes' management by pushing the company's share price up by the end of that day's trading.

Yet when all the tributes and reassuring noises had been made the betting industry was still left to reflect on the unpalatable fact that it was in the middle of the worst recession in its history. And, according to a report on the profitability of the whole spectrum of British gambling compiled in 1990 by ICC Business Ratios, even Ladbroke Racing's £91 million 1989 profits were an exaggeration of bookmaking's actual position. The ICC survey argued that there had been a diminishing return on capital employed in the late eighties with the figure dropping from 20.6 per cent in 1987 to 11.8 per cent in 1989. The ICC view was that the domestic off-course betting industry was now 'mature' and that further expansion would increasingly have to be sought abroad with the major companies attempting to benefit from introducing their advanced technology into countries previously served by only a monopoly pool-betting system.

The ICC assessment may have been an overly pessimistic one but the Ladbrokes' performance of the past few years demonstrates that however low-risk each individual Ladbroke betting shop may seem (and however heavily the odds are in Ladbrokes' favour, as they do everything within the law to make sure that the punter shall not win), a large off-course betting shop business *is* vulnerable to outside economic factors and in that sense is a riskier undertaking than the critics of the Big Three care to admit. At the same time, if any hard-pressed racehorse trainer had heard Paul Heath of City stockbrokers, USB Phillips and Drew, discussing the Ladbrokes' rights issue many of their worst fears would have been confirmed. 'On the basis of Ladbrokes making £220 million in 1991 its interest cover starts to look pretty thin,' said Heath. 'It has about £1.7 billion of debt which, including betting-shop licences as tangible assets, means its gearing is getting near to 75 per cent.' The part about 'betting-shop licences as tangible assets' simply underlines what many have suspected and others have always known. Namely, that multi-billion pound conglomerates like Ladbrokes have always used their betting-shop chains (with their, until very recently, buoyant cash-flow status) as assets against which to borrow money. And have therefore been using betting on horse-racing quite cynically, but perfectly legitimately, as a means to enable them to move into other even more profitable markets.

You still have to say that Ladbrokes' skill in accomplishing this feat, however contentious their methods, and the proficiency with which they have transformed a spivvish racket into a respectable nationwide habit, breaking the public's automatic connection between bookmakers and racehorses in the process, demonstrates once again just how triumphantly and comprehensively they have made a business out of betting. They carry that professionalism with them wherever they go, including whenever they come up against the representatives of horse-racing. It's rarely an even contest. You would be hard pressed to find many observers of racing and bookmaking, gamblers or non-gamblers, on- or off-course, who even in their most bitter and disillusioned moments would back the Jockey Club Senior Steward, the Marquis of Hartington, or the Tote Board Chairman, Lord Woodrow Wyatt, to run their businesses or even one solitary betting shop anywhere near as effectively as Cyril Stein.

Which is not to say that Cyril is a popular figure. Some people like him. Some fear him. Everyone respects him. He is, as they say, a very private man who, these days, is rarely seen in public. He is a generous contributor to a wide range of charitable causes including several pro-Jewish and Israeli organisations. He is devoted to his children and grandchildren. His senior management are all accorded the status of 'family' and have been with him for at least fifteen years. Together they have twice recovered from the brink of commercial disaster: once over the fixed-odds football business in 1964 and again over the Ladbrokes casino licences in 1979. When he does decide to stand down, perhaps not before the turn of the century, it's already odds-on that Peter George will succeed him. The Russian emigrés' grandson has come a long way from Whitechapel.

CHAPTER EIGHT

Pitch Battles

THE BIGGEST single difference between contemporary on-course bookmaking and the betting ring of the 1940s and 1950s is the aforementioned paucity of punters and custom. In the words of the experienced southern boards bookmaker, Dave Saphir, there are 'too many books chasing too little money in often contracted rings'. The most disturbing consequence of this weakness, at least from the punters' point of view, is the opportunity it gives the most powerful off-course firms to manipulate the market to their own, though not necessarily to their customers', advantage.

The situation is every bit as bad along the rails at it is on the boards. The imposition of the betting tax inevitably restricted high-stakes racecourse gambling in the sixties and seventies. Throughout the last decade, and in particular since the on-course tax was lifted in 1987, there has been a heroic resurgence in the numbers of daring, independent rails bookmakers like Victor Chandler and Stephen Little who will in no way flinch from accepting a large credit wager from a high-rolling client and who continue to embody both the enterprise and the gambling spirit of William Hill and his peers. The problem that bedevils these layers, one sharply exacerbated by the recession, is the same that confronts their colleagues elsewhere in the ring. All too often there simply isn't enough money around to enable them to make a decent book.

Yet in spite of this fundamentally weak market there are other respects in which the character, parlance and organisation of on-course bookmaking has remained remarkably similar to the styles and methods that prevailed thirty years ago. Compared with wagering in a betting shop, gambling on the racetrack still has a distinctly old-fashioned and unreconstructed feel about it. You sense that the language and sounds, the hoarse-throated and bloodshot-eyed ambience of it all is still pretty much as it must have been in Percy Thompson's time. The patter, the front, the chalk on the boards and the swift-thinking manual dexterity of the tic-tacs and clerks have hardly altered. The layers are still predominantly male, too. You'd be lucky to find one woman standing up in five racecourse rings.

It would not be unfair to say that some boards bookies share certain distinctive facial characteristics. They look hard, sharp and quick-witted, qualities traditionally associated with their trade. Then there are other boards bookmakers who look middle-aged and cosy or elderly and bronchial or just tired and resigned. They may all still be bracketed under the punters' traditional title of 'The Old Enemy' but at first sight they don't exactly come across as villains. Some may refuse to pay a quarter the odds a place or turn down three-figure wagers and sometimes they refuse to accept bets under a fiver and even under a tenner. At the same time the bookmakers themselves can occasionally lose, by standing a bet on their own judgement and failing to lay it off, by taking a view, like the men on the rails, laying one horse and getting it wrong, or just through nothing more dramatic than a simple lack of custom.

Stand in front of a classic boards bookmaker like the permanently worried looking Lewis 'Lulu' Mendoza with his curly hair and his Charlie Drake features and you seem to be looking at a man in a direct line of descent from those archetypal bookmaking figures who traded under names like 'Honest Joe' and 'The Firm You Can Trust' and who always seemed to figure prominently in the black-and-white newsreel footage of Derby Day before the war. Lulu favours the conservative brown trilby hat and collar and tie but he wouldn't look at all out of place in a sepia-coloured curly-brimmed bowler with a well-sucked cheroot in his mouth. Not that he emanates any great sense of bravado or risk. He always seems to be fussing about something or other. Fussing about his take, fussing about his liabilities, fussing about what his competitors might be up to or just fussing about his junior assistant workman who keeps leaving the top off the Thermos flask and spilling sausage-roll flakes down the front of Lulu's made-to-measure suit.

It may not be Damon Runyon but it's fun to observe for all that.

A timeless and unchanging scene. Warm, cosy and companionable
. . . except that someone disagrees.

There may be no Jack Spot or Billy Hill edging through the
crowd with a chib in their hand but there is none the less a
malcontent lurking along the rails. A shark in the harbour. A
troublemaker who likes to pose contemptuously by the exit out of
Tatts. And his name? Mickey 'The Asparagus Kid' Fletcher. A
forty-year-old bookie and punter with a fondness for large aro-
matic cigars. You'll never see Mickey Fletcher in a brown trilby hat
or a tie. He prefers white, well-laundered, open-neck shirts or
black polo-neck jerseys worn with expensive black suit trousers.
He has been known to turn up at some evening meetings in
summer in a rather snappy-looking dark-blue blazer but don't let
that country-club image fool you. Fletcher's got a face like the Black
Panther wanted poster. It's partly to do with his short black hair,
black eyebrows and look of lowering intensity. It's also to do with
the thick covering of designer stubble that he strokes all the time.
Of course he's no more of a villain than John Banks ever was but
this somewhat threatening appearance suits his purpose to perfection. Mickey Fletcher is a hustler. A lean and hungry West
Midlander but clever and articulate with it. A Walmley boy made
good, made up, in fact, into a high-stakes independent rails bookmaker – or, at least, one who would like to bet high stakes when he
can do the business and who would also like to bet on the boards in
the ring if only he could get a pitch.

Mickey has never gone on record with any specific comments
about Lulu Mendoza or Lulu's late brother Charlie and son Paul,
but he has specific general views about the old bookmaking
families and about the grip that they and their descendants still
hold on the ring. And his views don't flatter them. Mickey believes
that most of them are not bookmakers in the true sense of the word
at all. As he sees it, up to 75 per cent of them 'refuse any reasonable
wager'. So how do they get away with this apparently flagrant
disregard for the principles of their trade? Because of the out-
moded and restrictive procedures whereby these Tattersalls boards
pitches are allocated.

Most on-course bookmakers belong to the NAB or National
Association of Bookmakers and it is the area branches of their
related body the BPA, or Bookmaker's Protection Association, that
literally hold the ring as to who will bet where on the track. The
NAB and the system that it operates was set up nearly forty years

ago by the bookies, with the Jockey Club's blessing, to try to end the often bloody and internecine conflicts between different individuals and owners or 'protectors' of pitches that had been the less savoury characteristic of racecourse bookmaking immediately before and after the Second World War. These battles and the infamous razor gangs who invariably conducted them were another consequence of bookmaking's villainous and disreputable image in the days long before off-course legalisation. The gang bosses taking protection money from illicit back-street betting pitches realised as early as the turn of the century that rich pickings were to be made from moving in on the on-course boards bookmakers' pitches too and installing their own nominees in the most favoured spots. Without gangland muscle to back them up, many would-be on-course layers were either relegated to the back row, forced into the Silver Ring or kept off the racetrack altogether.

The police, for their own frankly cynical reasons, rarely disturbed the serious villains like Spot and Hill but they did eventually smash the most conspicuous of the razor gangs (as early as 1936 sixteen members of the so-called Hoxton Mob were sent down for a total of 432 years for offences relating to the 'Battle of Lewes Racecourse' that summer) and the NAB's code of restrictive practices was the bookmakers' own attempt to legislate against any similar Wild West scenarios recurring in the future. The main criticism of the NAB today is not just that its controls are completely out of date but that they are stifling competition, excluding new blood and giving both the punters and the racetracks a raw deal.

At present, seniority and longevity determine where individual firms can bet. You have to put down a deposit and join a waiting list to apply for both a boards and a rails pitch. The deposit is still considerably higher on the rails as, in spite of the depressed market, the expectation remains that you will be taking much larger bets in that area of the ring. The waiting list on the rails is shorter: up to three or four years for a pitch on a premier track and considerably less than that for an opening at the gaffs. (Where very few independent rails bookmakers ever seriously make much of a profit.)

Your period on the list before obtaining a boards pitch can seem like the wait of a lifetime but cannot be circumvented and you don't move into the ring and you don't move up from the back row to the potentially more lucrative front-row pitches adjoining the Members' unless somebody dies who is not, as usually happens, handing his pitch on to his son or his brother or to somebody else in the family. As the Asparagus Kid sees it, this system (mockingly labelled 'Dead Men's Shoes' by its critics), with its emphasis on age, seniority and family connections, simply ensures that it's always the same interrelated nepotists who make their way up the list, consistently denying access to a new breed of dynamic, upwardly mobile layers like himself. Which is why he has to stick to dealing mostly in credit on the rails. 'They inherit the best pitches. It's impossible for young blood to come in. Anyone wanting to be a racecourse bookie would be better advised selling his recipe for how to live for two hundred years to the British Medical Authority.' Furthermore the Kid damns this nepotistic cosy gang as not even being prepared to live up to their trade description and make a proper book, not, he believes, because they can't attract the custom but because they're terrified of running real risks. He wants the NAB and the Racecourse Association to administer the pitches as they do in Australia. There, if a bookie doesn't lay a horse at least up to an agreed amount stated in print in advance in the racecard (and accepted as reasonable business levels by layers and track management alike), he forfeits his pitch. In other words, he has a minimum target like a salesman and if he can't reach his quota he's out. But to do that level of business, which at the bottom line means taking money off the punters, he must in theory offer competitive or attractive odds and have the knowledge and the nerve to stand big bets when the customers want them – the best incentive being that if he doesn't he won't be back next meeting. Thus pitches can be freely obtained and proof of ability will earn a better one. So adopt this buccaneering Southern Hemisphere method and get the old farts out and the young blood in . . . says Mickey.

Now someone who enthusiastically supports these propositions and who has been around too long to be described as new blood, but who would hotly object to being classified as an old fart, is the man who has done more to bring the world of betting and bookmaking alive for the average armchair viewer and punter than any other contemporary broadcaster or journalist. He is, of course, that inimitable half-ton of hickory roast ham, the bewhiskered pundit and former course bookie and board bookmaker's clerk, Mr John McCririck.

You rarely get a restrained or carefully modulated response to John McCririck. His very appearance on a television screen is guaranteed to induce as much apoplectic rage in some quarters as it does cheering delight in others. One of the main criticisms directed at him, particularly by some of his fellow hacks, is that his TV persona is nothing but a buffoonish charade and that the more he is allowed to play it up the more it simply trivialises the sport that he purports to represent. 'This is no tribune of the people,' these other people say. 'He's just a bloated self-publicist, a bombastic old-Harrovian right-winger who uses his screen time to promote himself and to act as a shameless mouthpiece for the bookies.'

Well, perhaps the first thing to say about this accusatory tack is that in the minds of some people racing *is* a pretty trivial matter – at least, when compared to such daunting subjects as economic ruin, global warming, third-world famine and drought. But if we believe that Prince Monolulu with his bogus title and chieftain's headdress was basically a sympathetic and entertaining character then where is the real harm in McCririck's pith helmet and fly whisk? And would racing's image and position in the TV ratings be obviously improved by trotting out a series of worthy trade-paper industry spokesmen to bang on about such fascinating subjects as the new travel allowances available in EC countries or the state of the fillies premium scheme in Ireland? It is also a mistaken assumption to deduce from McCririck's outward garb and his apparent willingness to play the fool that he is lacking in either intelligence or depth. He has a quicker mind than most racing correspondents and a coherent if uncompromising view of racing and betting, which is not something that can be said about all of his critics in either the press room or the Jockey Club. In one of his earlier journalistic incarnations with the *Sporting Life* he was named as Campaigning Journalist of the year in the 1979 British Press Awards, and when he bothers to exert himself he can still turn out a style of bold argumentative prose that makes one or two other regular columnists seem tame by comparison.

He is also a partly genuine rather than a wholly contrived eccentric. He does prefer capes, deerstalkers and salmon-pink suits to tweeds and brown trilbies, and while he may look a twerp in that white woolly hat that he resorts to in midwinter, his black silk topper and brocade waistcoat at Epsom and the resplendent Napoleonic field marshal's overcoat that he seems to have dug up for Cheltenham in March are not without style. He does ride a tricycle and he is almost wholly insulated from the routine aspects of domestic and everyday life by his long-suffering wife Jenny, without whom, it is said, he can scarcely get out of the front door each morning. If McCririck's television guise is an artful extension of these traits, a contrivance, a pose, then the same can be said of almost every regular TV personality from chat-show presenter to politician and serious actor. Any professional performer is a different character in front of the cameras from the person they revert to when the lights are switched off. It is precisely this ability to turn it on that makes people hire them in the first place and what matters on a televised racing programme, as with any other live show, is not whether you are acting but whether you do it badly or well and, on the whole, in his field, McCririck does it very well indeed.

Yet the reason why he succeeds as a racing broadcaster is only partly to do with his act and a lot more to do with the substance of what he has to say. His contributions are in an area of direct and vital interest to most ordinary spectators: the movements in the betting ring.

Until the old ham was let loose along the rails in 1981 neither the BBC nor ITV expended much coverage on betting matters. Horse-racing has been disgracefully let down and cut back by the BBC's *Grandstand* programme over the last decade but when they are given the chance the pick of its racing team, like the extra-dry Raceform analyst and paddock commentator John Hanmer, and their matchless race-reader Peter O'Sullevan, can still muster superbly professional and informed transmissions, particularly of the big mid-week Festival meetings like Cheltenham, Aintree, Royal Ascot and Goodwood. Yet even today the BBC format still devotes comparatively little time to the punters' transactions with the bookmakers, although in Hanmer, O'Sullevan and Julian Wilson the Corporation has on its books as shrewd and intelligent a trio of gamblers as you could wish to find. When you remember again that it is the punters who, outside of the biggest meetings, provide up to 95 per cent of the day's betting turnover, from which the betting levy payments are deducted that help to finance the sport, this seems an incredible omission.

It may be true that the hardened betting-shop regulars can get all their up-to-the-minute betting data from SIS but not everyone who patronises a betting office stays there for the entire afternoon. When there's a big televised Saturday or mid-week racing fixture they are more likely to go down to a shop to place their bets and then to pop back home again to watch the action on their own TV.

And they don't have to be J. P. McManus or Barney Curley to want to know what the market's doing.

What John McCririck has done on Channel 4 is to bring the betting and bookmaking side of the sport right into the nation's sitting rooms. And if you think that this achievement is an easy one to pull off, you should go down into the scrum at York or Sandown on a big Saturday or crowded sponsored afternoon and watch him in action. He may change over suddenly and unpredictably from being Mr Jolly to Mr Nasty when some moron tries waving his arms around behind his head but he still manages to put across rapidly, succinctly and with no lack of flair a considerable amount of usually accurate and always pertinent information. This material, drawn from racing's most brutally unsentimental crucible of opinion, the bookmakers, lets the viewers know which horses are being backed, what the 'shrewdies' are on, what the layers feel about crucial fifty-fifty questions such as whether a horse is 'right', whether the connections fancy it and whether it's been working well at home and generally makes it clear whether the market is saying that an animal has a leading chance or whether it's about to take a walk into the wide blue yonder. And through his vivid renditions of the language of tic-tac McCririck has created a popular new cult out of assorted bookmaking expressions from Bottle (2–1) and Burlington Bertie (100–30) to Double Carpet (33–1), Up the Arm (11–8) and The Magic Sign (Ladbrokes).

Of course, he can have his less congenial moments on screen. It's not only ardent feminists who bridle at his endless designation of his poor wife (willing accomplice though she may well be) as the 'Booby', or who cringe when he starts groaning on about the many fantastic women standing next to him around the paddock at Longchamp or wherever. Neither is he ever quite as much fun when you take him away from his natural gambling setting. Standing in front of a piece of bland and anonymous seating and recounting the betting patterns on the Breeders Cup races at bookmaker-free Belmont Park or Churchill Downs in America he seems a strangely lost and superfluous figure. The flamboyant costumes and tic-tac gestures don't really work when there are no shouting bookies or crowds of teeming punters visible in the background. By complete contrast get him on an ordinary chat show and his ego seems so overblown that at any moment you expect him to come crashing and hurtling out of the screen like some deranged water buffalo on speed.

But, for all these low points and questionable asides, there is no doubt in the mind of the Channel 4 racing producer Andrew Franklin that most of his viewers switch on first to watch the horses and secondly to watch John McCririck. And with new talk of possible cutbacks and staff reductions once the company is forced to compete for its own advertising after 1992 it's not hard to imagine a day when McCririck will be the only Channel 4 racing presenter left, rather like the Tony Hancock character who, in his unforgettable send up of early sixties radio soap operas, became so powerful that he was able to write all the other characters out of the script. 'And here come the Channel 4 racing team walking up the straight at Doncaster. And, oh dear, the controversial drainage works have given way yet again and they have all fallen down that dark and terrible hole just before the two-furlong marker. And yes, there goes the terrier-like Bruffscott, the grinning Thompson, the geriatric Oaksey, the smirking Goode, the crafty Francome and the dour McGrath. All fallen into the bowels of the earth and all wiped out at a stroke. And that leaves just me, your ever popular Big Mac, to guide you through this afternoon's card and indeed through all the remaining cards unto perpetuity,' etc.

Next to the allegation that he trivialises the sport, the principal objection to McCririck is that he acts as a sort of one-man propagandist for the betting industry. Yet, almost alone of the contemporary racing press corps, he has had some direct practical experience of bookmaking from when he worked as a boards bookie, a floorman and a board bookmaker's clerk. Neither is it axiomatic that looking at racing issues from the perspective of the betting ring will automatically result in the expression of views that will be inimical to the interests of the ordinary race-goer. Like the gamekeeper who will yield to no one in his love for the pheasants in his care it is often the past or present bookie who professes the keenest understanding and advocacy of the punters' rights. Which is not quite such an outrageous cheek as it may at first seem. Of course, it doesn't mean that everything the bookies say about their financial position should be accepted at face value. Neither does it follow that there are not some disingenuous bookmakers who are giving both racing and their punters an extremely raw deal, both on- and off-course. But at least the more intelligent of the layers all realise that they have an obviously self-interested reason not just to ensure the survival of their existing clients but to encourage more people to bet. The interests of the wider racing community lie in the same direction but the supposed leaders of that community, the Jockey Club, have traditionally displayed not only complete ignorance of the bookmaking business but also an indifference bordering on contempt for the interests of the punters – even though they are partly dependent on the same betting-shop population for their own financial well-being.

There used to be a handful of serious and experienced racing writers like Peter O'Sullevan and Clive Graham at the *Daily Express* and Richard Baerlein at the *Observer* and *Guardian*, who as intelligent gamblers always put their money where their tips were and well understood that it is not fatuous to claim that the genuine bookie *is* the genuine punter's best friend. Baerlein, now over seventy but with undiminished enthusiasm for the ring, has always framed his copy primarily in the context of what the discriminating punter will want to know about and, over the years, has provided considerable entertainment by sharing with us, his readers, the details of his own ante-post betting manoeuvres and his attempts to make a profit on the big events. But some of Baerlein's and O'Sullevan's contemporary fellow pundits, one or two of them inveterate and hopeless punters who will plug the bookies one day, slag them off the next and then be back seeking more credit the day after that, tend to fall into the same trap as the Jockey Club and indiscriminately to lump together all the layers. Big Three, small betting-shop chains, rails independents and boards men, they characterise them all as money-grubbing parasites with deep pockets and short hands. McCririck challenges these assumptions often bluntly and abrasively (Paul Hayward once wittily compared him to Oliver Reed stomping up one of those open-ended late-night discussion forums) but by stirring things up he forces others to think through the logic, or lack of it, in their own positions. In particular he punctures the rather complacent notion that because racing is perceived to be in the midst of a financial crisis and bookies to have lots of money, why, if the Jockey Club could just get its hands on the bookies' money then everything would be all right. And to hell with the consequences for the punter.

And there seems to be no doubt that most punters, or at least most betting-shop punters, genuinely like him as anyone who has seen him stopping the traffic when opening a new town centre Ladbrokes, Hills or Coral office can testify. The fact that, like

Gazza or Frank Bruno, he can command a sizeable fee for perform-
ing these services is again often used to adduce that his bellicose
free-betting-market advocacy is motivated by nothing but hypocritical self-interest and should not be tolerated. But whether they are
being duped by the show or whether they are truly exercising their
free and independent choice, he certainly packs in the customers
and in a way that some struggling racecourses can only envy.

The most conspicuous and self-confessed propagandist for the
off-course betting industry is Tom Kelly of BOLA, a former racing
journalist with the now defunct *Sporting Chronicle*. Kelly is
regarded with particular venom by those current racing writers
who most passionately believe that off-course bookmakers are
going to be the death of the British Turf. Kelly defends himself
against these criticisms by claiming that it is part of his job to state
unpalatable truths that the rest of the racing community would
prefer not to acknowledge. They retort that his job is simply to
recite the party line for money and that because he does this in
such a generally narrow and unbending way it is impossible for
them to take anything he says very seriously.

John McCririck is a lot less predictable than Tom Kelly and by no
means always says what the bookmakers want to hear. You can
find some on- and off-course layers who positively loathe him,
especially when he cracks one of his jokes on TV about the revolt-
ing sight of the horrible bookies counting all their horrible money
after the defeat of another well-backed favourite at Epsom or
Newmarket or wherever. And if his celebrated belief in the free
market leads him to scorn any notion of a Tote Monopoly then it
also leads him to be every bit as hard as the Asparagus Kid on what
he, too, thinks are the restrictive practices of the NAB and their
clients in Tatts. As well as castigating the system whereby longevity ensures a comfortable life – he has described it as a 'total
anomaly' – this controversial populist has also criticised the terms
of the 1963 Betting Act, which drew together all the elements of the
'61 act and which restricts the Badge Money that individual courses
are allowed to charge bookmakers for their pitches to only five
times the cost of admission to the relevant enclosure. All very well
and good at Sedgefield on a midweek midwinter afternoon, but
does it really make sense to charge a layer just £40 for himself and
£40 each for his two workmen (five times the Tattersalls' entry
price) to bet in the front row at Sandown Park on such a profitable
and well-attended occasion as Whitbread Gold Cup day?

McCririck is not alone in maintaining that the racecourses should remember that it is they and not the bookmakers who own the pitches and has urged them to find out what they are really worth by stipulating that the six prime slots at, say, Royal Ascot will only be available for £500 a day, the next ten for £400 and only the back row at the far end at the current legal rate of admission. The racecourse could then adjust its prices depending on the quality of the racing and the time of the year. What's more, the successful bidders for pitches one to six at Royal Ascot and at the Cheltenham Festival would have to conform to the Australian practice, recommended by bold independents like Mickey Fletcher and Barney Curley, and lay bets of anything up to £2,000 a time while in the back row the limit could be just £50. McCririck, the orotund disciple of Margret Thatcher and Adam Smith, is emphatic that such a liberated system would compel healthy competition between the senior bookies and benefit both the racecourses and the punters because a bookie would need a good rate of turnover to justify his investment.

At the beginning of 1991 one bookmaker, the then fifty-year-old Barry Dennis from Romford who bets in Tatts at seven of the southern racecourses, got fed up with waiting for things to change and tried to buy his way into the front line. Dennis, who at the time had been waiting for nearly twenty years to be allowed to bet in the ring at Sandown and who had only just been told that he would be allotted a pitch on the July course at Newmarket after another wait of similar duration, organised a consortium with five other layers and offered Lingfield racecourse, where he bets in the back row, £18,000 to bet in the front line on the then thirty remaining days of the 1991 all-weather racing season. On 5 January that year the twelve Tatts bookmakers present at Lingfield paid £15 each, five times the all-weather Tattersalls entry fee, to stand up and make a book. The Dennis proposals would have meant the course receiving £100 a day for each of his six pitches and if the Racecourse Association, who at the time were earning just £2 million a year from Betting Badge money, had adopted this scheme at all of their fifty-nine tracks their income from this source would have increased three fold to £6 million per annum. You might have expected them to fall upon this with glee when you consider the racing industry's constant refrain that it is desperately short of money in general and receiving an inadequate return for its product from the bookmakers in particular. Celebration however proved premature.

On 8 January 1991, Ian Pithers, a spokesman for the RCA, declared, 'It would be chaotic at Lingfield if Mr Dennis's proposals were implemented tomorrow. The Bookmakers Practice Committee will look into the whole situation when it reviews the matter. We have invited bookmakers to write to us with any thoughts on Pitch Administration and we look forward to receiving their views but as for making any changes, that will take time.' Pithers was unable to say when the initial meeting of the RCA and the National Association of Bookmakers review bodies would take place. Paul Massey, secretary of the NAB, was equally unforthcoming. 'There will be no changes to the rules until such time as they emerge from the joint review. As far as changing pitch fees is concerned, we can do nothing because they are enshrined in legislation and can be changed only by Parliament. There is no way that the NAB could fly in the face of the law.' Heaven forbid. Except that at greyhound tracks up and down the country, bookmakers eager to get a pitch are known to make light of the five-times-admission-fee rule by making 'voluntary contributions' to the individual greyhound stadiums said to run into hundreds of thousands of pounds a year. Massey was adamant, though, that a scrupulously honest organisation like the NAB would have no part in such practices on the racecourse. 'We'll have nothing to do with voluntary contributions; it is breaking the law.' So there.

Barry Dennis's reaction was that the NAB were simply and typically trying to delay things. 'They don't want changes. They have a vested interest in everything staying as it is.' Yet there were comparatively few other bookmaking voices raised in support of the Dennis-McCririck-Asparagus Kid line. Alex Farquhar, managing director of the Edinburgh based on-course firm Macbet, pointed out that the legislation concerning pitch fees had been introduced to protect the bookmakers and maintained that it was still a good law. Farquhar, who bets in the back-line pitches at nine racecourses in Scotland and the north of England, was prepared to concede that the pricing arrangements now mitigate against the racetracks but would have nothing to do with *ad hoc* proposals to change the rules. 'I have been on the waiting list to bet at fourteen tracks for fourteen years and I agree with the system. It's tried and proven. I realise we should pay more to bet but I'm not unhappy with my on-course pitches at the back. Punters will move about for value. Anyone trying to buy front-line pitches is trying to buck the system.'

The Leeds-based Graham Lyles who bets on every flat race-course north of the Trent conceded that there was some merit in buying and selling pitches as long as it was done in an organised manner. 'But just letting the pitches go to the highest bidder would cause utter chaos,' he said. Concern was expressed for the fate of the small-time layers who might not be able to afford the new prices for a pitch and who might be forced out of the game altogether. And Bob Jacobs, president of the Birmingham/Midlands Bookmakers Association and a director of the NAB, insisted that nothing could be done unless it was discussed through his organisation first. 'If people want change, let's talk, but you can't just let these rebels come in, take up arms and move into the best pitches.' Now how many times must that refrain have been heard in the bad old days of Square Georgie, Jack Spot and Billy Hill? The veteran layer Leslie Steele tried forcefully to remind his colleagues of just what things were actually like in the cowboy era before regulation. 'They're talking about improving the public image of racing. Well, I can tell you, the image *has* improved. I remember going to Ascot forty years ago and being turned away from the heath at ten o'clock in the morning. In those days they'd be fighting for pitches with choppers and hammers and the line of bookmakers would be half a mile long. It's people in poor pitches who are doing the screaming but we all started out in poor pitches.'

As to the Asparagus Kid's contemptuous disdain for most of his on-course colleagues one or two of the layers had some caustic things to say about him too. 'Mickey Fletcher?' jeered one rails layer. 'Don't talk to me about Mickey Fletcher. He did buy a drink once. I think it was at Ascot the day Park Top won' (which for the uninitiated is a reference to the Saturday afternoon in 1969 when the famous mare, Park Top, won Ascot's King George VI and Queen Elizabeth Stakes).

The most reasonable defence of the traditional practice of keep-ing bookmaking pitches within individual families came not from some elderly stooge or self-interested racketeer but from Graham Greene, not the supreme now sadly deceased novelist but the likeable and intelligent on-course bookmaker of the same name.

Large and courteous with well-cut collar-length grey hair, Graham wears tailored suits and monogrammed Pierre Cardin shirts beneath his trench coats and waterproof jackets but in other respects he couldn't be less like the malign and stereotypical image of the bookmaker that you find in an archetypal Dick Francis novel like *Whip Hand*. A proud father and family man, he lives in the Warwickshire town of Alcester, not so far from Asparagus Kid country, is not obviously senile or corrupt or cowardly about taking a risk but can see little logic or justice in being expected suddenly to hand over the pitches of his firm, Walters and Williams, to disaffected critics of the system just because they've got a wallet full of notes. Particularly given his suspicion (widely shared by his colleagues) that some of these new boys and revolutionaries already have other money-making enterprises ranging from antiques to florists shops and would not be the only or even the main financial investors in their pitches. In fact, their racecourse ambitions could be nothing but a front for other undisclosed, conceivably underworld, figures, who have always regarded the betting ring as an ideal environment in which to launder their dirty money. 'I've been in the game for thirty-five years and I would like to think that I could hand over my pitches to my son, just like the owner of any high-street business. The trouble is that these people who are trying to buy pitches at Lingfield have other businesses. Unlike me they don't have to rely on the racecourse to make a living. What I would like to know is what their other businesses are and then perhaps I could get into them.' He also echoed the words of the rails independent, Stephen Little, in pouring scorn on the notion that there is an infinite amount of cash that can be taken at most racetracks or a limitless customer potential not being fully tapped by the present layers. 'At tracks like Warwick and Wolverhampton on a Monday or Tuesday I'd be lucky to take maybe £100 on each of the last two races, so you could hardly say that business is booming.'

The argument flared up again in September 1991 when Rodger Farrant, clerk of the course at Chepstow, announced his intention to charge bookmakers in advance for their pitches for the calendar year 1992. He wanted to ensure that all the available pitches were paid for whether they were used or not and aimed at putting an end to the situation whereby a boards bookie can have pitches at several different racecourses but if he chooses not to turn up to bet at one of them on a particular day's racing (whether because he doesn't fancy his chances of making a profit or just because he's gone elsewhere) the racetrack is unable to collect any Badge Money for that pitch on that day. Under the current rules they cannot go ahead and allocate the pitch to any other bookie who turns up and is prepared to pay for it, but only to those bookies who are already at the top of the Tattersalls' reserve list and who may not all turn up to bet either.

The Cardiff-based bookmaker John Lovell, who has pitches at several courses including Chepstow, was wholly in favour of Farrant's initiative. 'This thing needs stirring up. The NAB is quite happy with the status quo, but under the present conditions bookmakers wanting a pitch will never get one. There's no movement whatsoever. That's the truth of it.' Other bookies predictably saw things differently. Many of them questioned the legality of such a move while warning that if Farrant's ideas were to be implemented nationwide a lot of boards bookmakers would soon be forced out of business. 'This is the thin end of the wedge,' lamented Gus Oppenheim from Wilmslow in Cheshire. 'If I have pitches at Chepstow and Haydock on the same day and I cannot get to Chepstow, I shall be paying for a badge I haven't taken out for that particular day.'

Gus needn't have worried. On 17 September, one week after the Bookmakers Association of Wales had indicated that they were happy to co-operate with the Chepstow plan, the NAB, acting in apparent conjunction with the RCA, scuttled it. It had no basis in legality, they declared. Farrant was furious. So was John Lovell. 'The NAB are running a kind of closed inner sanctum,' he said. 'When they say, "it's not legal," what they really mean is, "We don't like it." It's impossible to become a course bookmaker at the moment. You don't have to wait until you're a hundred. You have to wait until you are a hundred and sixty.' More passionate support for Mr Mickey Fletcher.

Discussions between the NAB and the RCA were continuing at the time of writing and it is always possible that some modifications to this antiquated system may have been announced by publication. It should be remembered, though, that there are as many shades of grey and as many different truths about the betting and bookmaking industries as there are bookies and punters themselves, and what you believe and what common factors you try to deduce will depend very much on your position, experience and vested interest. Yet for all that the Asparagus Kid and those like him may appear to be directing a kind of metaphorical razor gang menace, if not at any one bookie personally then at the NAB and its code of restrictive practices, even Mickey would accept that in the minds of most impartial observers the difficult customers of race-course bookmaking, if difficult customers there be, are located not on the boards but along the rails. And they are not the indepen-dent credit bookmakers but the on-course representatives of the Big Three or, as they usually manifest themselves, the Big Two – Ladbrokes and Hills. These scrubbed, clipped and beady-eyed gentlemen need have no fears about where they are going to bet or whether they will be able to drum up enough custom to make a book. But their intercessions in the on-course market, quite legal though they may well be, are the source of as much bitterness and controversy as the Badge Money row and the nepotistic pitch allocations of the NAB and the RCA.

CHAPTER NINE

A Nasty Little Business

In the early days of his Ladbrokes chairmanship Cyril Stein, who quite liked to place as well as take a bet, used to go to all the major race meetings and, although he was never mistaken for William Hill, would often stand up on the rails in person at the head of the Ladbrokes on-course team. Among the Ladbrokes and Hills race-course representatives in the sixties, seventies and early eighties were genuine characters like Ladbrokes' fast talking Dickie Gaskell and the courteous, silver-haired Leslie Spencer of William Hills. These men were old-school bookmaking figures in the best and least derogatory sense of the word. The contemporary on-course representatives of the Big Three firms may be as neatly turned out as Leslie but theirs is an altogether more uniform and less indivi-dualistic style.

Mike 'Pretty Boy' Burton of Hills, he of the smooth, baby-faced good looks and the immaculately coiffured hair, exudes the kind of slick but impersonal managerial competence of some aggressive chief executive of a high-street store. His colleagues Mark Fogarty and John Bates of Ladbrokes, both of whom stand on the rails at the southern tracks, have a similarly hard-edged book-keeping air about them, while also conveying a faint but discernible im-pression of the sort of men's outfitters' who can never be entirely trusted not to kit you out with a pair of trousers one or two inches too tight in the crotch, or too huggingly close-fitting across the thigh, or an inelegant wave too far above the ankle.

At the smallest midweek race meetings there are rarely more than half-a-dozen rails bookmakers present but two of that number will always be on-course representatives of Ladbrokes and Hills.

They are not merely there to make themselves available to any high-rolling credit-account clients who might suddenly decide to turn up at Salisbury or Huntingdon and want to strike a decent wager. Their primary responsibility is to influence the starting-price market on their employers' behalf or, as they see it, to correct the imbalance between the 5 per cent of on-course betting at most racetracks and the 95 per cent of off-course wagering in betting offices nationwide, which is what their shareholders expect them to do and which, in a free-betting market, they are fully entitled to do. Without these interventions there would be days, as Stephen Little has frequently pointed out, when the on-course layers, rails and board, would barely be able to drum up enough business to make a book.

In December 1990 a Channel 4 documentary in the *Despatches* series essayed a look at the more controversial aspects of these hedging activities. According to the figures it came up with, the Big Three annually bet in the region of £25 million on-course in their efforts to contract starting prices and reduce liabilities, and this investment or 'manipulation' deprives punters of a total of £150 million a year. In fairness to Ladbrokes' who totally rejected the £150 million figure the programme hardly bothered with even the flimsiest presentation of the bookmakers' case and in the course of its research employed hidden cameras and microphones during an afternoon's filming at Southwell races. These underhand methods brilliantly captured the secretive, almost Masonic, nudge-nudge, wink-wink relationship between the on-course layers and a Ladbrokes' agent rejoicing under the evocative name of Harry 'Boy' White. Harry was seen wagering £3,400 on one contest at the all-weather track but when confronted by a reporter at the end of the day he denied placing a single bet. Ladbrokes denied that there was anything illegal or reprehensible about Harry's activities and issued both Channel 4 and the programme's producer and director, Charles Thompson, with a writ for libel. (The case was settled and involved Channel 4 paying Ladbrokes a sum in excess of £50,000.)

One of the contributors to the documentary was the genial starting-price reporter David Smalley, whose principal occupation is as a lecturer in Mathematics at Brunel University in Middlesex. Smalley felt that the selective editing of his interview, whereby a twenty-minute exposition of the whole spectrum of betting in the ring was compressed down into one and a half minutes of actual coverage, may have suggested to some people that racing 'was quite a nasty little business' at heart and that people might have been deterred from betting because of it. 'In the interview I had pointed out that the racecourse market was a free and open one and that there was nothing illegal in the office agents hedging money at the racecourse.' Even so Smalley was emphatic that late money from the offices, usually for the favourite, can distort returns, because if it happens at the last minute no time is left to compensate by pushing out the prices of market rivals. 'At poorly attended meetings it is relatively easy to influence the market when money is placed in the period around thirty seconds before the off. All activity is centred around the horse that is the object of the agents' bets which then shortens up rapidly as in the case of Haky at Southwell, for example, which dropped from evens to 2–5 in no time at all. Without the other horses being shortened accordingly due to the lack of time left before the off, at which instant the starting price applies, the markets are distorted. Nothing annoys me more when returning starting prices than to see this late flurry of activity.'

The incident that Smalley was referring to, involving the horse called Haky, so enraged the Southwell course manager Richard Muddle that he went as far as to suggest that he might ban Ladbrokes from betting at the track in future. Stephen Little preferred to see the Haky race as a perfectly normal illustration of the laws of supply and demand exactly as you would expect from a free betting market. 'When Ladbrokes' punters backed Haky to the extent which suggested 2–5 was a fair reflection of his chances (a view borne out by the ease of his win), how could it be right to seek to prevent the operation of those laws? The second favourite in Haky's race drifted from 7–2 to 11–2 in face of the support for the favourite; would Mr Muddle be complaining that this was detrimental to bookmakers if he had won?'

For all Little's eloquent exposition of the basic logic of the market place it would be difficult to exaggerate the effect that the Magic Sign can have on the rest of the ring at a provincial racetrack with a seriously weak market. At some of the gaffs the Ladbrokes' representative only has to move ten yards from his pitch and the boards bookmakers run scared. The leading southern rails bookie Robin Grossmith sees it happening all the time. 'Once they [Ladbrokes] start asking for a price about a horse, without even laying a bet, the price is rubbed off and a new price appears. They know that they only have to ask and the price is shortened up.'

This policy is widely used when the 'first show', which means the first set of odds about a race, is about to be transmitted by SIS to the betting shops. Ladbrokes and the other big firms may have had enquiries from informed punters about, perhaps, a particular two-year-old running first time out. To ensure that the first show for the horse to the nationwide network of betting offices will be short they merely have to spread rumours that they intend to back that horse and as sure as the Oaks follows the Derby the opening price will be decidedly skinny. The consequence of this operation is that in reality the price of the animal will drift as the on-course market, which means the punters at the racetrack, will have little desire to back the horse at such short odds. In turn the off-course punters will see this apparent weakness, assume a lack of confidence in the horse and, as a result, may no longer be interested in backing it. Either way, the effect will have been to attract a minimal amount of money for a genuinely well-fancied runner.

The one indisputable point, underlined equally by the *Despatches* programme, the views of the free marketeers and the testimony of other working bookies like Grossmith (who is quite realistic about Ladbrokes looking after the best interests of their business) is that you must go racing if you seriously want to bet. It's not simply that you don't have to pay any tax on-course: even the briefest scrutiny of starting-price returns in racing's two trade papers will show you that at some time most prices will have been bigger during on-course exchanges than the eventual SP. The likes of Southwell and the other midweek gaff fixtures suffer from a shortage of players and a dearth of ready money, which is why it is possible to see the interventions of the Big Three as actively strengthening the market in those instances rather than simply manipulating it. But it is only at the big festival meetings like Cheltenham and Royal Ascot, with their much bigger attendances and full complement of high-rolling gamblers, that the big book-making firms cannot dominate, thus demonstrating the inestimable advantage of having so much more money around.

David Smalley's advice to those punters who, whether through necessity, laziness or preference, insist on staying in their betting office is that if they want to avoid being turned over as a result of late interventions by the offices they should take the board prices (that is, stipulate they want the price being currently quoted in the shop when they place their bets) at around a minute or so before the off if they are backing strongly fancied animals at the head of the market. The only trouble, as Smalley would be the first to concede, is that understanding in theory the importance of choosing the right moment to get on and actually being able to put that theory successfully into practice are two very different things.

High-stakes punters who wouldn't dream of doing their gambling in a betting office must also be always on the look-out for value if they nourish any serious hopes of making a profit at their bookmaker's expense. A value bet is quite simply one where you believe, suspect or – if it's a set up betting coup where the trainer and connections have been deliberately misleading the market – definitely know that the price you are being offered greatly underestimates the horse's winning chance. But once again understanding the notion is one thing: recognising value when it's in front of you is another.

The market on a horse race (assuming it's not a classic or a big handicap for which ante-post odds will be on offer for several weeks, or even months, in advance) begins to emerge when the on-course boards bookies chalk up their 'first show'. This is based on the bookmakers' 'tissue', a set of odds worked out before the meeting by a form expert. These odds reflect, to a degree, the realistic chances of the runners, but the bookies are also trying to guess the proportions in which the public will want to bet. If a stable is on a roll with its two year-olds, the bookie can expect a big demand for almost any juvenile from that yard. Similarly, if there's been a lot of overnight rain and they've got a fit, attractively weighted, soft-ground specialist in a big handicap, they're bound to get a lot of enquiries for it.

Regular gamblers rarely go in on the first show, knowing that the course bookies will generally have to loosen their first set of odds to encourage betting. The layers must also allow room to extend or contract the odds sometimes drastically to cover their liabilities. All the racetrack bookies, be they on the rails or on the boards, will react to public demand as in any other market place, but from time to time a horse's odds will be artificially extended by a clever rails bookmaker trying to engineer a Snouty-Parker-style knock-out manoeuvre.

Sometimes the ordinary and least well-informed punters will act like sheep, and pile on to a horse whose form book-chance, to a shrewd and experienced player able to read the signs correctly, doesn't merit a really low price. That's one time when value may be available elsewhere because, as all the professional betting gurus, from the famous Lancastrian punter the late Alex Bird to the former racing writer Mark Coton have consistently pointed out, value betting is partly created by the stupidity and delusions of others – as when the tide of rumour, media hype and sentiment forces a horse's odds down far too low. Such was the weight of popular emotion surrounding Desert Orchid before the 1990 Cheltenham Gold Cup that he was sent off a ridiculous 10-11 favourite although his 1989 Gold Cup triumph had been his only previous Cheltenham win and only the second of his thirty-one victories to be recorded around a left-handed track. After the race everyone was asking how the winner Norton's Coin, not an obvious selection but an improving horse for all that, could have been allowed to start at 100–1.

Twelve months earlier, the massive Irish gelding Carvill's Hill was backed down to 9–2 for the same race, partly because the exceptionally testing conditions were thought ideal for him but partly because of the intense longing of thousands of success-starved Irish steeplechasing fans to celebrate another champion. Yet Carvill's Hill was an inexperienced and unreliable jumper who had been treated for back problems, whose training preparation had been interrupted due to a bout of lameness and who was competing in only his fifth steeplechase. He fell at the fifth fence. A much more attractive each-way betting prospect would have been the 1988 Gold Cup winner, Charter Party. He started at 14–1 in 1989 and finished third.

One popular misconception about value betting is that it is in some way the same thing as backing longshots or outsiders. Not true. Desert Orchid was fantastic value at 9–4 favourite for the 1990 King George VI Chase at Kempton because at the time he still had few peers around the sharp Middlesex track and although he was greatly helped by the fall of a leading rival he proved the point with a decisive twelve-length success. Even money or 'levels, you devils' can be a value bet if your knowledge or form book study tells you that a true or fair price should be five to two on (2–5).

The average margin of profit for the bookmakers is much greater over longer-priced runners than it is with those horses who start at shorter odds. 10–1 may seem to represent an attractive price in a wide-open race like the Stewards Cup at Goodwood but it constitutes only a 9 per cent chance of victory, which is why the top bookmaking firms like Ladbrokes and Hills are understandably delighted to sponsor these big betting handicaps. There are always plenty of runners with little to separate the majority of them on form, and the over-round and profit margin in the bookies' favour will be considerably higher than in a seven-runner two-year-old Group race at Newmarket. Mug punters look at the odds for events like the Stewards Cup, the Lincoln Handicap and the Cambridgeshire sponsored by Hills, the Ayr Gold Cup sponsored by Ladbrokes and the Cesarewitch sponsored by the Tote and think, 'Oh, great. A five-to-one favourite in a field of thirty-two.' But the bookmakers know that the market on these contests will always be balanced heavily in their direction.

Hills and Ladbrokes aren't the only bookmaking companies to sponsor important horseraces. Victor Chandler, the independent credit bookmaker whose own pitch is just down the rails from the Big Two and Three at all the leading racetracks, sponsors a valuable and prestigious prize at Ascot each winter. It is not, however, a baffling cavalry charge with umpteen runners and near negligible prospects of picking out the winner. The Victor Chandler Chase is a two-mile limited handicap, which invariably attracts a small but select field and has twice been won by Desert Orchid. Chandler's Ascot sponsorship is rightly praised as an example of a bookmaker supporting racing and putting something back into the sport which creates the gambling opportunities that provide both the rails bookies and their boards counterparts with the major portion of their income.

The race, which is covered by BBC Television, is also good publicity for the firm. It does a bookmaker no harm to be associated with a top-drawer racecourse and that is particularly true for Chandlers. They have a wide-ranging clientele drawn from right across the social and financial spectrum and they will as readily accept a bet from a skint Jeffrey Bernard as they will from a comfortably well-heeled racehorse owner or trainer. At the same time they probably have more titled and upmarket clients on their books than most of their rivals: Ascot is their kind of course.

What makes Chandlers very nearly the ideal credit bookmakers for the discerning punter is partly that they have some personality and style but also because you know that they won't refuse a genuine wager or instantly try to beat down the stake or halve the odds. Neither do they immediately close a winning account. It all adds up to the kind of personal one-to-one service of an old-fashioned gentlemen's tailor but with a full range of modern technological services also supplied. Men like Chandler are the heroes of the betting and racing game, just as much as the top horses, jockeys and trainers, because they are keeping the authentic book-making ethos alive. Without them, the historic character and atmosphere of the British racetrack would be diminished still further. The market would be even more at the mercy of the big off-course firms than it is today and the already dwindling number of high–rolling players would have little alternative other than to emigrate to Australia.

Of course, these independent rails bookies are businessmen too in their fashion. They can be hard and sharp and are not at all sentimental. They will draw on all their knowledge, cunning and skill to try to come out ahead of their clients. But they have not yet all sold out to the accountants. There is still some spirit flickering within them that is made up of the same elements of enterprise, risk and adventure that motivate the gambler. And, as a result of this triumph of individualism over the corporate ethic, they comprise a far more interesting and diverse cast of types and personalities than the on-course reps for the Big Three.

Victor Chandler, curly-haired and boyish-looking, is a fourth-generation bookmaker. His grandfather, Billy, was an absolutely fearless rails layer in the thirties and forties, right up there with Snouty Parker and William Hill. He was also an indomitable gambler and cleared over £200,000 when Ocean Swell won the Derby in 1944. 'Old' Victor Chandler, who was actually only fifty when he died, owned Brighton and Walthamstow dog stadiums and was another high-stakes bookie-punter. Legend has it that he had nearly £50,000 on the 1948 Cambridgeshire winner Sterope. At odds of 40–1.

Victor senior sent his son to Millfield where he encountered numerous dedicated adolescent punters and racing enthusiasts. From there he went on to study catering in Switzerland, not generally renowned as a finishing school for the betting industry, and worked for a year in the hotel and restaurant business in Spain and Paris. Inherited genes proved stronger, though, than the attractions of a career in a 'respectable' trade. In 1974 he took over the family firm which was based in a house in Great Portland Street and still runs it today though not from the same elegant and capacious offices. The atmosphere inside those rooms was masculine and slightly old-fashioned with lots of brown leather upholstery and panelled bookcases containing all the volumes of Timeform's Racehorses of the Year along with classic racing books by authors such as George Lambton and Jack Leach. There were

numerous framed prints and portraits of famous horses and greyhounds as well as a photograph of Sterope hanging proudly on one
wall. It was the sort of place where you expected everyone to be
smoking smart cigars and drinking whisky and soda even at half-
past ten in the morning.

Victor now has a small chain of betting shops in London and the
suburbs but he's only a minor player in the off-course business.
His credit clients number around 5,000 of whom about 800 are
'active'. He makes a book on all the big sporting events as well as
on horse-racing and roughly 70 per cent of his business is conducted by telephone. Only the remaining 30 per cent still takes
place at the racecourse. Chandler has a maximum pay-out of
£500,000 on a single bet but his biggest racetrack loser of recent
years was a 'mere' £90,000 to £20,000 (resulting in a £110,000
cheque for the punter) that he laid about Vagador, winner of the
opening race at the 1988 Cheltenham Festival.

When Victor goes off to work at places like Cheltenham and
Newbury he might don a countryman's well-cut brown tweed suit.
When he and 'the boys' fly over to Deauville for the day in the
middle of English flat racing's traditional quiet period in early
August they sport a rather different image. Gold cigarette lighters,
glinting signet rings and designer shades. All very appropriate for
Deauville in season but also a charismatic reminder of both the
colour and the frisson of danger that has always attended the
bookmaking game. It's the same kind of deliberately flash homage
to those earlier days that John Banks used to exploit so entertain-
ingly in the sixties and seventies and it still sends out an erogenous
message to the more imaginative punters. A bit like having a
retired gangster or former train robber on the guest list at your
first-night party or midsummer ball.

Stephen Little, who says that he never bets on anything that
talks, is cast in a very different mould. In many ways it would be
hard to find a rails bookmaker less like the traditional John Banks
big shot. Little, short-haired and clerical-looking, may have become synonymous with the ankle-length Bud-Flanagan-style fur
coat in which he regularly appears on the rails, but he wears this
resplendent garment not to draw attention to himself but simply to
keep warm and comfortable. He reckons that he spends an average
of 230 days a year standing out beneath the elements on the
racecourse and he feels the cold keenly. Underneath 'the bear' he
wears conservative grey or green tweed suits in winter and respec-

table cream linen jackets in summer. He seems a shy and self-effacing character but, like the quietest and least conspicuous player at the poker table, his outer image is entirely deceptive. Stephen Little stands the biggest bets on the racetrack.

His father was an Anglican clergyman and Stephen was educated at Uppingham. His decision to aim for a career in bookmaking came about as much due to his talent for mathematics as to any fledgling interest in horseracing. In fact he was considered to have had sufficient mathematical ability to have won a scholarship to Oxford or Cambridge had he been interested. Little wasn't interested. He left school at sixteen and started cycling around the country going to race meetings and finding out about the betting business from the bottom up. He worked for a while for a variety of other bookies, including Ladbrokes, until one day they suddenly and without explanation sacked him. He thinks that it was probably because he was asking too many questions and sounding a shade too clever for the company's liking but when he asked them for a reason they told him to go away and mind his own business. So he did.

Today he runs the telephone and credit side of that business from his home in a Georgian terrace overlooking the comfortably liberal city of Bath. He also has a rails pitch at nearly all the Group One British racecourses, although his local beat and acknowledged territory is the beautiful weathered West Country circuit from Hardy-esque Wincanton to Taunton, Chepstow, Cheltenham, Newbury, Salisbury and Bath itself. He has about 500 clients on his books, many of them from the prosperous and educated middle class. They range from middle-aged millionaires in the financial sector, to self–made West Country businessmen, accountants, restaurateurs, record-industry executives and Oxford-educated antique dealers. They also include a small number of serious professional gamblers. Some of them wager between £300 and £500 a week, others £10,000 a fortnight. The professional punters have a yearly turnover amounting to hundreds of thousands of pounds, though for most of them their profit will be only a small percentage of that sum.

Little feeds each day's betting data into his private computer when he gets home in the evening and keeps a tape recording of all his transactions at the big meetings like Cheltenham. But the real key to his success, like that of Victor Chandler and like John Banks before him, is the personal one-to-one bookie and punter service that he provides, coupled with the fact that he doesn't quake at the suggestion of a hefty wager.

Some of the old-time giants of the betting ring like Thompson, Hill and Billy Chandler were themselves inveterate punters who would often argue passionately about the merits of different horses and expose their own and their firm's reputation accordingly. Not Stephen Little. He is renowned for rarely taking a personal view. To make his book he relies predominantly on his skill with numbers and percentages and theories of statistical probability, all strictly related to the basic free-market laws of supply and demand. He's rarely caught out but that doesn't mean that it's easy. 'Racecourse bookmaking,' he says, 'is now one of the most competitive businesses in the world. Nowhere else do you get so many trying to sell the same thing in one place.' Little's skill at selling can be partly measured by the size of the bets that he continues to strike, bets much larger than anything accepted by the Big Three. He laid a punt of £100,000 to £50,000 about Magic Ring, winner of the 1991 Norfolk Stakes at Royal Ascot and one of £90,000 to £40,000 about the 1988 champion hurdler, Kribensis. At the same year's Cheltenham Festival he got £90,000 back from a punter who wagered all of that sum to win £40,000 at odds of 4–9 (nine to four on) on the losing Cathcart Challenge Chase favourite, Rusch de Farges.

But, in spite of these winning races and winning days, all credit bookmakers can be bedevilled by bad debts and slow payers. If you owe a lot of money to Ladbrokes or Hills they may not wait for very long before reporting you to Tattersalls' Committee, the bookmaker-constituted panel that still officially arbitrates all betting disputes. If the Tatts' committee passes your name on to the Jockey Club as a persistent debtor or non-payer you are likely to find yourself 'warned off' or summarily banned from all racing premises until your debts are cleared. The independent layers very rarely take a punter to Tattersalls, which is another reason why serious gamblers prefer to bet with them if they can. But bad debts can ruin a bookie who has probably had to lay off his liability and pay his tax and VAT demands in the meantime. In 1989 the southern rails independent Duggie Goldstein, already a millionaire from another business, suddenly and dramatically defaulted with unpaid accounts in excess of £600,000. The 'knockers' or debtors notwithstanding though, the rails contingent's biggest worry continues to be that there just aren't enough serious or seriously loaded punters coming racing any more.

In the face of this pervasive insecurity, made worse by their dependence on the honour and solvency of others, one or two credit bookmakers have, with increasing frequency, reverted to Percy Thompson's and Bill Chandler's example and become gamblers themselves – except that they don't back horses they expect to win. They lay horses, often just one horse, that they believe will lose.

Every gambler understands that it's usually far easier to work out those runners that you think won't win a race than it is to find the winner. The business of laying horses, of standing up on your pitch and loudly and repeatedly encouraging the punters to back one animal ('I'll lay 11–8 Jeune. I'll lay 11–8 this favourite,') can be extremely profitable, particularly if you are in possession of valuable inside information. This kind of insider trading which goes on all the time at the racetrack and involves the Big Three just as much as the rails independents is not the sort of subject that the bookies want to talk about because of the inevitably sensitive nature of how they got their information and who from. One incident, taken from the safe distance of a few summers back, is enough to establish the general picture. The individual involved was Dudley Roberts, one of the biggest and most colourful rails bookmakers in the south of England. Dudley, along with his colleague John Henwood, can often be seen standing up to the might of all-comers in the ring, including Ladbrokes. Other bookmakers may automatically lay off their liabilities. These two prefer to use their own judgement and field against a market leader if their instinct or information is strong enough.

The race in question, a mile-and-a-quarter maiden event, which means a race for horses that have yet to win, took place at Lingfield Park and the betting patterns on it were closely observed by Richard Thomas, former ante-post odds maker for Corals but at the time employed by Alan Kinghorn, another leading on- and off-course credit bookmaker. Thomas describes what happened:

'The Guy Harwood-trained Bushido was, on form, one of the most promising maidens in the stable and duly opened at 1–2 [2–1 on] in the ring. Ladbrokes were keen to shorten him up as the race was the first of the afternoon and there would have been thousands of combination bets, doubles, trebles and Yankees, starting off with the apparent "good thing". However, Dudley Roberts stood up and constantly called against the favourite, in the process taking a large measure of the Ladbrokes' money. He layed one horse in the race and would have lost thousands had the favourite obliged but Dudley was prepared to take the risk. At one point the horse touched 4–5 [5–4 on] but interestingly, as soon as the race was under way, Roberts was calling odds *against* the favourite. So why didn't he do this earlier if he believed it couldn't win? Well, there was no need as Ladbrokes were prepared to take odds on about the horse. In the event Bushido trailed in fourth, beaten a total of eighteen lengths, having at no stage looked likely to threaten the leaders.'

Dudley's willingness to back his own judgement over Bushido was one kind of gambling triumph but the rails layers and their clients will all tell you that landing the other kind of gamble, the one where your money is on the first past the post, is getting harder all the time. One of the main ingredients necessary for a successful betting coup is secrecy, but obtaining it is far from easy. Never mind the covert intelligence gathering. There is so much open information around as well via form books, trade papers, videos, television and SIS. All of these organs of communication specialise in highlighting promising or suspicious runs by both fancied and dark horses. The gamblers of earlier generations were rather luckier. They didn't have to worry about the Timeform Organisation or the intrusion of high technology. There were no TV pictures or even on-course commentaries until the early fifties and not the detailed declarations of runners and riders in the daily papers that we have today. Money was more plentiful then, too, along with layers prepared to take it and to risk their own. Coups, strokes and touches flourished in that kind of climate but although there were some punters who made their fortunes on the racetrack many others blew them away . . . or simply made the fortunes of their bookmakers instead.

CHAPTER TEN

Heroes and Villains

THE MASSIVE and incorrigible plungers who frequented the race-tracks in the late nineteenth and early twentieth centuries were often as reckless one day as they had been astute the day before but no one was ever more wholeheartedly reckless and self-destructive than the 4th Marquis of Hastings who did 'his pieces' on the horses unto ruin and even unto death.

The Marquis, handsome, charming and dangerous to know, was a notorious Big Loser who lost £120,000 in a single bet when a horse he had backed called Marksman was touched off by a neck by the colt Hermit in the 1867 Derby. The loss was made all the more poignant for Hastings as his lover, the celebrated beauty Lady Florence Paget, had been engaged to Hermit's owner Henry Chaplin until she had jilted him on the eve of their wedding to run off with the twenty-five-year-old gambler instead. Hastings dropped a further £89,000 at the two big Newmarket meetings that autumn by which time he'd been forced to sell his Scottish proper-ties for £300,000 and to give up all titles to his securities and to his Donnington Castle estate in Berkshire.

To try to keep himself in the game, he raced his brilliant two-year-old filly Lady Elizabeth no fewer than thirteen times in the 1867 season and her only defeat, in the Middle Park Stakes, was said to have been caused by her jockey's over-confidence rather than any lack of gameness on her part. Two days after the Middle Park the Marquis subjected the filly to a match race for a purse of £1,000. Her opponent, Julius, who had finished third in the St Leger, had just won the Cesarewitch off a mark of eight stone. Julius was made the 10–11 (11–10 on) favourite but in what was apparently one of the most punishing battles ever seen on Newmarket Heath it was Lady Elizabeth who took the prize by inches. Many judges believed that with a kinder campaign Lady Elizabeth could have won the 1868 Derby for the Marquis but her battle with Julius understandably soured her and she was never the same horse again.

Hastings owned another top two-year-old called The Earl but he was prevented from running in the Derby by the machinations of the money lender, Howard Padwick, to whom the desperate Marquis had applied for a loan. All the bookmakers were after Hastings now and he had to resign from the Jockey Club in the face of their inevitable attempts to have him struck off the list of members. There could only be one end though and, worn out and played out, the Marquis finally succumbed to a romantic young man's death on 10 November 1868. 'Hermit's Derby broke my heart,' he confided to a friend just a week before he died. 'But I didn't show it, did I?'

The 1867 Derby may have been the beginning of the end for Hastings, but it represented a famous triumph for Hermit's trainer, a bold and intrepid former cavalry officer by the name of Captain James Machell.

The sight of prosperous and respectable-looking county matrons clutching a few pound coins and queuing up importantly at the Tote windows may be one of the more eccentric images of British racing, but another equally dotty and recurrent emblem are the numbers of chaps with military handles who keep cropping up in diverse capacities, not always those for which they are particularly or ideally suited. There are ex-army officer Stewards, Stewards' Secretaries (especially Stewards' Secretaries), Judges, Starters, Clerks of the Course, Handicappers, so-called Intelligence Officers, even Bouncers, not to mention an inordinate number of former cavalrymen turned trainers, bloodstock agents and amateur riders. This link between horse racing and the army is partly a consequence of the old mounted days when former Hussars and Household wallahs frequently swapped their equestrian expertise in the lines for a career in the training profession, frequently bringing their military manners with them, too. That double-edged connection continues to this day in the shape of the hugely gifted and comically intemperate Major Dick Hern, once of the Hussars but unhappily confined to a wheelchair since a hunting accident in 1984. Hern, who trained with great success for The Queen until he was prematurely 'retired' by her racing manager Lord Carnarvon in 1989, may be known as Dickie by his friends but as far as all lesser ranks and especially the oiks in the racing press are concerned he must be referred to at all times as The Major.

Then there is the enduring social connection between the Turf and the officers' mess. This still thriving overlap was the original reason for our very own Major Tom's introduction to the sport. 'I started going racing because I thought it was the sort of thing that Guards' officers were expected to do socially.' The Major's own military appellation stuck with him once he moved into the bookmaking milieu and is a title, used half-mockingly and half-deferentially by his colleagues, clients and friends, that has never done him any harm.

And there are those other kinds of majors and captains not nearly so pukka as Major Hern and not quite as plausible as Major Tom. In fact, in some cases, they could be described as transparent con-artists and 'non-holding fraudsters' which is not to say that they may not be perfectly charming for all that. This is the sort of category into which one would place such endearing fictional characters as Captain Hamilton-Ricketts, the Terry-Thomas incarnation, who used to drive the school bus for the St Trinian's girls and who would usually while away the time while the nymphets played hockey with an away team by studying the *Sporting Life* over a few pink gins and a couple of Player's Navy Cut in the snug bar of the Dog and Ferret. You think too of Evelyn Waugh's permanently drunk Major in *Vile Bodies* who charms £1,000 out of the naïve Adam Fenwick-Symes, sticks it on a 35–1 winner of the Manchester November Handicap and then scarpers with the boodle.

There is no record of Captain Machell, who was born in Beverley in 1838, ever welshing on anyone. His was an uneventful military life, and he was never the toast of the social salons, but as a gambler he had few equals. He discovered that he had a talent for betting on as well as conditioning horses while he was stationed at the Curragh Camp in Ireland in the early 1860s. His regiment was not fashionable and he had no private or inherited wealth to fall back on so he handed in his papers and quit the service to become a trainer . . . and to punt on his own stable, which he did consistently over the next thirty-odd years with generally quite remarkable success and a seemingly iron nerve. It was the Captain's consummate preparation of Henry Chaplin's Hermit that thwarted the Marquis of Hastings's Marksman gamble in the Derby of 1867. Machell twice won the Grand National with horses owned and trained by himself and in so doing collected enough money from the bookmakers to buy back an estate that his family had owned up in Westmorland more than fifty years before.

For all his gambling triumphs it seems that Machell was not a man who found it easy to enjoy life. It is said that he could be charming but that more often he displayed a grim, narrow and intensely suspicious face to the world. He suffered from periods of manic depression and he was also afflicted by frequent painful outbreaks of gout none of which affected his relish for the ring. He would have taken nearly £180,000 at mid-Victorian rates off the Duke of Hamilton over Hermit's Derby, the young aristocratic mug having offered him 30,000-1 six times several months before the race (which means that Hamilton was sneeringly suggesting that Hermit had a no better than 30-1 chance of winning. Machell accepted those odds and placed six bets of £1,000 each).

On the eve of the contest, Hamilton, the original dim hooray who had thought he could impress everyone by his swagger devil-may-care attitude, was pleading with Machell to write off the bet. The Captain, surprisingly and uncharacteristically, agreed. He was less charitable to the bookmakers one day at old Alexandra Park or 'Ally Pally' racetrack in north London. He asked one what odds he was prepared to lay him about an immature two-year-old he was running in the first. £500 to £400 (5-4) was the best that the bookmaker was going to offer. The Captain was disgusted. 'Five to four about a green youngster,' he's supposed to have thundered. 'Why I'll bet *you* six hundred to four hundred, twice and three times if you like.' The bookie accepted the challenge, wagering a total of £1,200 to win £1,800. (Three bets of £400 at 6-4.) Ten minutes later it was the Captain who was back to collect. His judgement had been completely vindicated. His horse had indeed run 'green', which is to say that due to its immaturity it had been unable to put in a concerted effort, and had been denied by a neck in a driving finish. If the bookie had been more daring and if his original odds had been what Machell had regarded as 'fair' it would have been the layer who collected the £1,200 and, knowing Machell's gambling instincts, probably a bit more besides. Which story perhaps disproves the idea that the only odds-makers ever to have offered a mean set of prices are the ones who have been working for Ladbrokes since 1961.

Captain Machell is buried in Newmarket, in the same cemetery as Fred Archer and countless other immortal names from racing's past. Punters with some sense of the Turf's history still occasionally stop by the Captain's grave today on their way up to the July Course or the Rowley Mile, no doubt hoping that some of the luck (though not the melancholy) that attended his wagering might be psychically imparted to their own.

If Captain James Machell frequently cleaned out the bookies then the bookmakers, banks and libel lawyers conspired in the end to clean out Robert Standish Sievier. Which is not to say that he didn't give them a damn good run as long as he was able to. If you mention Bob Sievier's name to some elderly racing journalists and the more conventional Turf historians they are liable to start muttering darkly and to use words like 'scoundrel' and 'cad' and other quaint epithets found only infrequently outside the speech of the Tote Chairman and *News Of The World* columnist Lord Woodrow Wyatt of Weeford. From these indignant splutterings you can safely conclude that Sievier, while an unlikely candidate for Jockey Club membership or for the Prudential Insurance Company's Good Housekeeper of the Year award, was precisely the kind of fallible, expansive and overreaching personality that instinctively understands the riotous appeal of the Cheltenham Festival where it is considered no sin to have three times more than you can afford on the last and to order up champagne all round, preferably on somebody else's account, before the result is known.

Sievier's life wasn't simply colourful. It was a positive aurora borealis. Legend has it that he was born in the back of a hansom cab in 1860, that his mother was a 'dancer' and that his father was a peer of the realm. 'Lawks a mussy, Lord Bellamy, but we punters love a bit of wrong side of the sheets romancing, don't we,? Mr Hudson?' 'We certainly do, Mrs Bridges.' Sievier, like Helen Vernet, enjoyed a brief early career on the stage and a memorable later career as a witty and acerbic journalist satirising the pretensions of assorted horsy grandees. In between he worked as a bookmaker and owned and gambled on racehorses. Most of Sievier's big money, and he did have some once, was won when he was in his twenties and decided to follow the advice of the American newspaper editor Horace Greeley and 'grow up with the country', only instead of going west and growing up with the American frontier Sievier turned in the opposite direction and travelled down to Australia. When gamblers and racing journalists praise the full-blooded betting and bookmaking culture that exists in that country today, they could do worse than stop for one moment and drink a toast to Bob Sievier's role in bringing about that very desirable system.

When Sievier first arrived in South Australia he found that the on-course bookies at the local tracks only took bets on double events. In other words you had to bet on two races at once and couldn't pick out a single wager of your choice. The bookmakers operated solo without a clerk or a workman and instead of paying out to winning punters after their respective race or races they only dealt with accounts on their own self-appointed settling days. Sievier immediately cut a swathe through all this restrictive nonsense by setting up himself as an on-course layer and accepting bets on single races, employing a clerk to speed up transactions and increase capacity and by paying out straight after the weigh-in. At the end of his first day's trading he was £1,500 up. His success and his audacity made him an instant success with the public and a combination of charm, muscle and bribery enabled him to withstand the initial resentment of his fellow traders, who in any case were not slow to realise the much greater opportunities that now beckoned to them, too, by following his methods. Bookmaking businesses didn't stop booming in the state from that point on.

If Sievier had stayed in Australia and stuck to laying the odds as opposed to taking them (a moral here, perhaps) he might have stayed a rich man. But the gambler in him was eager to try his luck in the ownership stakes back in Britain and as one of nature's original high-rollers he was understandably keen to step out on to a bigger stage than Adelaide could provide.

The turn of the century may seem from a distance like an agreeably relaxed era of ragtime cadences, hock and seltzer and Gaiety Girls in red lace petticoats. But whatever the view from the free side of Epsom Downs the top echelons of the British Turf were dominated by a small group of rich and powerful, aristocratic men. Their personal morals may have been littered with sexual and financial double standards but publicly they insisted on strict adherence to a rigidly narrow social code – especially where the three most important things in life were concerned: money, class and the improvement of the thoroughbred. Races like the Derby, the Oaks and the St Leger were considered the rightful preserve of a small coterie of gentlemen owner-breeders who had all been born into the game. When an ex-colonial adventurer, a former bookmaker would you believe, turned up in their midst and not only started flirting with their wives and daughters but spending large sums of money to try to get his hands on the best bloodstock, their indignation was speedily aroused. Sievier's 'vulgarly commercial' approach drew the same kind of snobbish disapproval that Robert Sangster and, in a slightly different way, the Cockney commodity trader Terry Ramsden incurred many years later.

In 1900 Sievier paid the then unheard-of sum of 10,000 guineas to purchase a filly called Sceptre, by the Prince of Wales's 1896 Derby winner, Persimmon. Bred by the Duke of Westminster and a half-sister to Ormonde, his illustrious Derby victor of 1886, it is unlikely that Sceptre would ever have been available on the open market had it not been for the Duke's death and the subsequent sale of part of his bloodstock interests. With the benefit of hindsight the Westminster family must have regretted their decision to sell as Sceptre became not simply one of the great fillies but one of the finest horses, colt or filly, in the history of British racing. In 1902 she achieved the unprecedented feat of winning four of the five classic races for three-year-olds including both the 2,000 and the 1,000 Guineas back to back. Her only real failure, sadly for Sievier, was in the most important race of all when she managed just fourth place at even money favourite in the Derby.

Over the years Sievier, who had personally taken over the training of his horse at the start of the 1902 season, has frequently been accused of mishandling and even abusing Sceptre and, like the Marquis of Hastings with Lady Elizabeth, of over-racing her to get himself out of a succession of tight financial corners. Whatever the objectivity of these allegations (and if Sievier was a modern jumping trainer winning half a dozen races in a season with the same three-year-old hurdler he would be regarded as a master), Sceptre seemed to prosper well enough under his husbandry. She came back from her Derby defeat to win the Oaks two days later and then the St Leger in September. And in the 1904 Jockey Club Stakes, then run in October, she gave fifteen pounds in weight and a decisive beating to that year's Derby winner, Rock Sand.

Admittedly, Sceptre's first race as a four-year-old had been in the Lincoln Handicap at the very start of the season. In 1903 the Lincoln was one of the biggest ante-post betting events in the calendar but it was not a prestigious level weights classic like the Derby. It was said that Sceptre was only competing in the race due to her owner's pressing need to settle a gambling debt, but because it was a handicap she had to shoulder top weight of nine stone and one pound. She finished fifth. It would be inconceivable to run a modern Guineas winner in such a race. It is still a big betting contest, albeit an annual bookmakers' benefit, but most of the horses competing in it today are mediocrities and quite a few are geldings. The commercial potential of a high-class brood mare would be instantly devalued by mixing in such company.

Later in the summer of 1903 Gentleman Bob, still feeling the heat from the bookmakers, let it be known that both Sceptre and a colt he owned called Duke of Westminster were unofficially up for sale. By craftily asking for a lot more for the Duke than for the infinitely more gifted filly, he created the impression, quite deliberately, that all was not right with Sceptre. His intention was to hook a mug and the plan worked to perfection. One George Faber, then MP for York, was sufficiently taken in to part with 22,000 guineas for Duke of Westminster, which had cost Sievier 5,600 guineas two summers before and which eventually struggled to win a three-horse race at Ascot. Sceptre, the idolised apple of her owner's eye, remained in his care unsold. Alas for Sievier, the Faber scam was just about the limit of his racecourse luck. In 1904, a bare five years after his return from Australia, he was warned off by the Jockey Club, partly for continuing indebtedness and partly as a result of various lawsuits he had been involved in, most of them pertaining to his own or somebody else's money, property or besmirched reputation. It was said that these actions revealed him as not the sort of type to be on the list of registered owners. Lord Wyatt would probably have said that the ex-bookie turned gambler displayed no shame in the extent to which he was prepared to reveal himself as a blackguard. Overtones of Terry Ramsden once again.

Sievier responded to this adversity in some style by promptly starting up his own racing paper called *The Winning Post*, which sold for a penny a time and quickly proved so popular that by the autumn of 1904 it was selling 128,000 copies a week. One aspect of its appeal was that it gave the sporting public the opportunity to read Sievier's invariably shrewd assessments of the relative merits of the leading horses and their chances in the major events coming up. The other substantial part of its attraction was that Sievier mixed this Timeform-style approach with liberal helpings of humour, satire and gossip *à la Private Eye*. The Edwardian racing establishment may have been implacably conservative but when it came to making frank observations about owners, trainers and jockeys some quite mainstream Edwardian racing writers were considerably less supine than one or two of their counterparts today. Sievier took the whole process a stage further (sometimes all the way to the libel courts) and his readership loved him for it.

At the centre of each week's edition of *The Winning Post* was a full-page feature article entitled 'Celebrities in Glass Houses' by 'Tweedledum and Tweedledee' a pseudonym for Sievier, who used his regular column brilliantly to mock and parody a series of prominent and two-faced Turf notables who were generally either open or clandestine gamblers. On Christmas Eve 1904, he turned his guns on to a group of men collectively, if unofficially, known as the Druids Lodge Confederacy. It would be no exaggeration to say that this syndicate of five owners and their Irish trainer (whose full story is well told in Paul Mathieu's fascinating book *The Druids Lodge Confederacy* published by J. A. Allen) plotted, and in most cases pulled off, not only the biggest but some of the most outrageously contrived coups that the English betting ring has ever seen.

Not the least remarkable thing about the Confederates was that they were all archetypal members of the late Victorian and Edwardian governing classes and could in no way be socially marginalised by the establishment as bounders or out and outers like the impudent Sievier. Percy Cunliffe, their chief mastermind, was an Old Etonian City man whose brother was Governor of the Bank of England. His two principal associates, Wilfred Purefoy and Frank Forrester, presented an equally impeccable blue-chip façade to the world. Purefoy, or 'Pure' as his friends called him, was ex-Harrow and the Third Hussars, a wealthy and conventional landowner, who also happened to be a shareholder in Romano's in the Strand and a brace of music-hall theatres. Frank Forrester, another Old Etonian and, like Purefoy, an ex-cavalryman to boot, was Master of that most socially impeccable hunt, the Quorn, whose hounds have been enthusiastically followed by both the Prince of Wales and, until his unfortunate encounter with a concrete water trough, by that noted scourge of the fox, the terrifying Major Dick Hern. Yet, behind their unblinking conservative stance, these men were all dedicated gamblers with a keen interest in horseracing, a fairly elastic moral sense and considerable private resources with which to go to war. They intended, as countless other owners before and since, to gamble on their horses, not purely for the pleasurable diversion but with the express purpose of caning the

129

bookies as they'd never been caned before. To accomplish that objective successfully the Confederacy would have to beat the market. They would have to so fool the layers as to their runners' true abilities that they would be able to get their money on at initially big prices which would be a considerable exaggeration of their actual winning chance, the last part of the game-plan being the essence of Value Betting. What every professional preaches today.

What motive impelled these very proper upper-class men to try their hand in this sphere? To set themselves up as clubland adventurers rather like the heroes of a John Buchan novel such as *The Three Hostages*? Well, they were all so rich that they had no need to work in the mundane sense of the word. So, be it out of idleness, curiosity or compulsion, they had the time and the means to indulge themselves in whatever field they chose. Secondly, the late nineteenth centry was a keenly speculative era with all manner of inventive and enterprising money-making schemes cropping up throughout the British Empire and beyond. Cunliffe and Purefoy had both speculated successfully in the South African gold fields. Purefoy had his spicier show-business investments and Cunliffe was no innocent lamb in the cold-eyed world of the City. There was, therefore, something appropriately in period about this group of ex-officers and gentlemen coming together over the brandy and cigars to hatch an ingenious grand design to try to part unsavoury bookmaking types from their money. Not that Cunliffe and Purefoy intended simply to play the game for the game's sake and let fate have the final say: they were determined to eliminate chance wherever possible and to have as many factors on their side as they possibly could. Even if that would, in effect, mean cheating or not trying with their horses in events prior to their chosen gambling engagement.

The races that the Confederacy were going to make a play for were not the great flat-racing classics like the Derby. They were interested in the big handicaps like the Cambridgeshire where there was a buoyant ante-post betting market and where a crafty and skilful trainer could, by campaigning a horse cleverly, get it into the handicap on a much more lenient mark than its real ability or potential deserved.

Anyone who tells you that this kind of strategy is 'merely corrupt' is being 'merely a prig' or an idiot or both. Carefully planned ante-post touches or 'jobs' have always been a vital and thrilling, if occasionally controversial, part of racing's appeal. And the continuing existence of would-be coups, even in a much weaker betting market, and the public's continuing identification with them, emphatically underlines William Hill's old contention that it is gambling – not prize money, the survival of the Jockey Club or even the improvement of the breed – that is *the* life blood of the Turf.

Cunliffe and Purefoy had no intention of racing horses in a public stable where they would be but one group among many different owners, all competing for the trainer's attentions and all with different and possibly conflicting priorities. They were going to have their own private stableyard where the trainer and his staff worked exclusively for them, where every horse was in differing proportions their personal property, and where they could exercise a tight, not to say paranoid, grip on the passing of information to and from the outside world. To obtain these circumstances they needed premises that were not only well away from the public eye but which would also have gallops that could not be approached without the visitors (and by 'visitors' they really meant touts and bookmakers' men) revealing their identity well in advance. Cunliffe had the perfect place. He owned an extensive estate, sporting and agricultural, high up on Salisbury Plain, and right in the middle of that estate, some two miles south-west of Stonehenge, was an isolated spot occupied only by a couple of cottages and an old pub called the Druids Head. The thick, lush, well-drained turf that surrounded it for miles on either side was a perfect natural training ground for racehorses.

Cunliffe closed the pub and turned the cottages into homes for a trainer and one or two married employees. Then, some hundred yards back from the road, he built a modern red-brick house which he called Druids Lodge and which was for his own and his fellow owners' private use. Next to the house was constructed a U-shaped stable block for forty horses. Cunliffe sank a considerable chunk of his own money, some two and a half million pounds at today's rates, into the project and by all accounts the new stableyard was the Manton (Robert Sangster's private training estate near Marlborough) of its day and the very last word in lavish care and attention to the well-being of its equine inmates. As far as the staff were concerned, Druids Lodge was more of a cross between Dartmoor Prison and the grimmest kind of all-male boarding school. Even Tom Brown and Harry East would probably have found it hard to obtain much masochistic pleasure from its harsh and restrictive regime.

Jack Fallon, the young Irish trainer whom Purefoy hired to run Druids Lodge and who had started out in English racing as a stable boy at John Porter's famous Kingsclere establishment, later described his life up on Salisbury Plain as being about as bleak and lonely as if he had been incarcerated in a fortress in the middle of the Sahara. The buildings must have seemed as gauntly conspicuous: although Cunliffe planted trees and shrubs, which obscure any view of the stable from the A360 road today, at the turn of the century there were no trees and no cover surrounded the house and yard at all. Only mile upon mile of unbroken grass stretching all the way to the horizon. Fallon said that the appearance of even a solitary pony and trap on the skyline was enough to excite the interest and attention of all those confined there.

The stable lads were subjected to a rigid curfew after evening stables and were actually locked into their dormitory at night, encouraging bullying, fist-fighting and all manner of refined tortures. The lads' mail was opened to see who they were writing to and what about and who was corresponding with them. Cunliffe even worried that the numerous immigrants from Tipperary might give away his plans to the parish priest when they were in the confessional. Elaborate subterfuges were put in motion whenever any of the horses that were due to be gambled on were subjected to a serious trial. The lads were never allowed to know how much weight was in their saddle cloths. They would be made suddenly to dismount and swap horses and the riders who participated in the serious timed gallops never knew if it was the 'winner' or the horse behind them that was the real subject of the test. The last thing the Confederates wanted was for any of their staff to start building up groups of private punters (as happened in other stables and as still happens today) and to enter the ante-post market on their own initiative. The lads were all officially forbidden to bet except through their employers' accounts. Purefoy put money on for them when they requested him to and if there were any winnings to come they were added to their wages at the end of each week.

Fallon took charge of Druids Lodge stables in October 1895 but it was some seven years' racing before the Confederates investment really began to pay off. In the meantime several other private gambling stables were at work such as the then Lord Carnarvon's

Whatcombe yard and Captain Bewicke's Grately syndicate, who were also playing duplicitous games with the bookies. Bewicke's men were specialists with the late-telegram device, a scam that, unhappily for the punter, has long since passed into racing history. The modern Big Three off-track bookmaking firms employ sophisticated computer monitoring of a handful of their shops to pick up on emerging betting patterns and to enable them swiftly to contact their representatives on-course to place money accordingly and to restrict and often eliminate their liabilities. Ninety years ago communications systems were not nearly so sophisticated. You could telegram bets to a racecourse and if a telegram was timed as having been sent, or at least filled in, prior to a race's off time then the bookies were expected to pay out if you won. By sending a large number of telegrams at the last minute from a small post office with only one telegraph operative it was possible to ensure that a majority were not received at the track until after the race was over, thus giving the bookies no intelligence of the attempted coup and no time to hedge or contract the gambled-on horse's likely starting price. Bewicke is said to have won himself thousands a week in the 1890s by playing this system but whatever admiration Cunliffe and Purefoy may have had for his guile there was no question of them betting by telegram themselves. The sums that they wanted to get on would have been too large for most understaffed post offices to handle. Their wagering was going to take place ante-post, secretly at first and weeks, if not months, before the intended race.

The Confederates' first big strike came with a horse called Ypsilanti in the 1903 Great Jubilee Handicap at Kempton Park. In contrast to some of their later coups, Ypsilanti had been trained quite openly and his chance was there for all to see. He had started the season with a third place in the Lincoln under seven stone nine. The professional gambler Charlie 'Old England' Hannam, a punter of some courage and acumen, confided to Fallon that Ypsilanti might just about have won up at the straight Carholme course if he'd been able to take an 'easy' half-way through the race. Hannam's advice was to run the colt next time out around a racetrack with a turn. The Jubilee, a big ante-post betting race taking place around right-handed Kempton six weeks after the Lincoln and in which Ypsilanti had been allotted the not overly severe burden of eight stone one, seemed the ideal contest. Fallon was able to get the horse in better mental and physical condition than ever before. The stable stepped in at 25–1 as soon as the first prices were issued and by the Monday before the race Ypsilanti was down to 8's. More public money on the course sent him off the 7–2 clear favourite. His Irish jockey, Ben Dillon, pushed him to the front after the first quarter mile, took a pull before the turn into the straight and cantered home by one-and-a-half lengths. According to Paul Mathieu's research, Jack Fallon had some £350,000 in modern money to come from the layers while the owners were estimated to have cleared the equivalent of a staggering £4 million. And Ypsilanti was only the beginning.

The Great Jubilee, now sadly relegated to the status of just another handicap, may once have been a natural plungers' contest but even in 1903 it could not compare to the Cambridgeshire which in the early nineteenth century was run on the last, as opposed to the first, Saturday in October. This famous nine-furlong handicap, this cavalry charge up the wide-open Rowley Mile with its huge fields and extensive ante-post betting possibilities, was one of the top gambling events in the calendar, an irresistible attraction to both bookies and punters alike. When the bookmakers' first list of prices for the 1903 Cambridgeshire was issued at the beginning of September there were several entries from the Druids Lodge stable. The Confederates' 'intended' was a three-year-old filly called Hackler's Pride that Fallon, on the owners' instructions, had deliberately been running down the field over shorter distances in top midsummer six-furlong races like the Wokingham Stakes at Ascot and the Stewards Cup at Goodwood. As a result the handicapper had allotted Hackler's Pride a meagre seven stone one for the Newmarket race which Fallon believed wildly underestimated her actual ability. He would have given her more like eight stone seven which meant she had a breathtaking twenty pounds in hand.

Cunliffe, Purefoy, Forrester and the other syndicate members had already begun backing Hackler's Pride long before her name started to crop up in the ante-post lists in mid-October. Like Alex Bird fifty years later, Purefoy had numerous private commissioning agents, most of them untraceable to the Confederates and some of them located as far away as Australia and South Africa. Not to be outdone this time, Fallon managed to escape long enough from his employers' relentless observation to set up a network of his own punters. Included among them were such diverse characters as the station master at Birmingham New Street and an Irish friend of the station master who happened to be a local parish priest. Cunliffe and Purefoy were livid when they discovered that Fallon had been gambling in his own right and not through the Confederacy but on this occasion they had to let it pass.

The owners carried on staking deceptive sums on each of their other two Cambridgeshire entries and it was only when all of the big private commissions had gone on that they started showing their hand at the public call overs. Four nights before the race, one individual bet was placed on Hackler's Pride to win the modern equivalent of nearly £500,000 at 11–1. The bookies and the racing press could now see which of the Druids Lodge horses was 'expected'. Come exercise on Newmarket Heath on the morning of the race, 30 October 1903, it was apparent to every observer that Hackler's Pride had been trained to the minute and was virtually a different animal from the also-ran at Goodwood in August. As the Turf paper the *Sporting Luck* put it: 'The murder was out.'

Having had a first public quote of 25 – 1, the filly was sent off at 6 – 1 on the day. But such were the huge amounts of money wagered on racing in that era, much of it on course, long before a few big betting-shop chains could dominate the market, that not even this colossal gamble was enough to make Hackler's Pride start favourite. That distinction went to a colt of Lord Howard de Walden's called Kilglass who was returned at 9 –2.

It is very easy in hindsight to make a famous gamble seem natural, inevitable and assured. It is never quite like that at the time. The experience of directly partaking in a betting coup is rarely a tidy one and usually involves as much high comedy as high drama with fear, self-doubt, excitement and absurdity mixing freely in roughly equal measure. Of course, Cunliffe and Purefoy would probably have disdained such feelings but then they were archetypal 'control' punters, rich and powerful men who, like Kerry Packer in one of his casino binges (or Hemingway when he confronted his charging lions and bulls), need to face the risk of great loss to prove to themselves and the world just how powerfully in control they really are.

For most of us, it is not too easy to seem effortlessly calm and composed if you are standing on Newmarket Heath on a typically cold and rainswept autumn afternoon, wishing in God's name that you had some cover over your head, that you'd brought your waterproof trenchcoat as opposed to the one that just looks good, feeling your shirt sticking to your ribcage with nervous perspiration and wondering just what you are going to do, how you are going to explain and where you are going to run to if the horse doesn't win.

Strictly according to the record books, Hackler's Pride's 1903 victory was not that sort of experience. Far from it. It seems that the race was every bit as painless as Ypsilanti's win at Kempton. Fast away and in front after four furlongs, the further the filly went the more she seemed to be enjoying it and, unmarked by Ben Dillon's whip, she positively cruised home by three lengths. But the other runners, not to mention the handicapper, were made to look fools and this time the punters and the press didn't like it. Angry mutterings were heard about the stark contrast between this race and the Hackler's Pride of earlier in the year. Then there were the attempts to put the public off the scent by making them think that the stable was backing their other two runners instead. That was decidedly crafty but not illegal. For the clear evidence of 'inspired' betting and the marked improvement in form, the trainer and jockey – and the owners too – were astonishingly lucky not to face a Stewards Enquiry. But what did they care? The racing history books have always said that the Druids Lodge Confederates collected £250,000 in old money from the 1903 Cambridgeshire. On the Mathieu convertible scale, that comes out at an incredible £10.5 million in today's currency, making it the biggest recorded betting coup in the history of the British Turf. Mathieu believes that Fallon himself must have drawn the equivalent of £1.39 million and no doubt the station master and the priest had their celebrations too. And, not the least extraordinary aspect, at least by modern standards, was that all of the bookmakers seem to have paid up without complaining, one or two with smarting faces and pumping hearts, no doubt, but without anybody attempting to have the race invalidated or declared a fraud.

Twelve months later the stable pulled off another momentous stroke when Hackler's Pride succeeded in winning the Cambridgeshire for a second year. This time she carried eight stone ten and only just got home by a neck giving thirty pounds to the runner-up. Once again, her final pre-Newmarket run, an apparently disappointing performance at Doncaster, had been a crafty deception. Once again, her owners deliberately backed one of their other entries from 25–1 to 100–7 to fool the market. Hackler's Pride opened at 33's, dropped to 20–1 and then actually went back out again to 25's. The syndicate moved in again and supported her down to 7–1 on the eve of the race. Her eventual SP was 7–2 joint favourite. Whether or not they no longer minded this chicanery, or whether they were just happy to have joined in the punt on-course, most members of the racing public were the mare's friends this time. Her true racing qualities, it was said, had been courageously displayed and her worth was no longer in doubt even if her trainer's methods had again made a mockery of the form book.

For all the rigid secrecy that continued to be enforced up on Salisbury Plain, everybody in racing now talked of what the Druids Lodge team had done, were doing and might do next, and their possible long-range plans for the big ante-post betting races were discussed and pored over as avidly as Lester Piggott's likely Derby mount was in the 1970s and 1980s. It was at this point that Bob Sievier made his memorable entry into the controversy with his *Winning Post* – Tweedledum and Tweedledee – lampoon of Cunliffe. Throughout the article he went out of his way to pay tribute to the owner and his colleagues' great honesty, to their public-spiritedness, their open-handed relations with the press and their generally unimpeachable concept of fair play. Of course, the real inference of the article was that it was exactly these qualities that Cunliffe and his partners so conspicuously lacked. The following March, Sievier added an equally biting satire of Purefoy, printed with a superb cartoon by The Snark depicting the Mr Inscrutable of polite society wearing his racing colours and a dancer's tutu (a jokey reference to his interest in music halls and chorus girls) with a halo, framed out of a riding crop, over his head. The jokes and the parodies had a telling effect and while the Establishment still had no time for Bob Sievier they responded to the prevailing mood. From now on the Druids Lodge owners found that their horses, whatever their previous form, were being allotted stiffer and stiffer burdens in the big gambling handicaps. There were to be no twenty-pound weight advantages again.

Jack Fallon's run at Druids Lodge did not last much longer. Purefoy held him personally responsible for the defeat of his cherished home-bred chestnut colt Lally (named after his favourite actress, Lily Else) in the 1906 Derby. Plenty of experienced judges were convinced that it was simply a dislike of the firm ground on which the race was run coupled with the effect of a rigorous early-season campaign, dictated by the owner, that brought about the colt's downfall. And this was, after all, the Derby, at the time still

the premier thoroughbred horserace in the world, not some glori-
fied twelve-furlong handicap where you could 'cook' your chosen
representative and try to make mugs of the bookies. But Purefoy,
blinded to the horse's true merits like countless other rich and
obsessional owners before and since, was convinced that Fallon
had negligently over-trained the horse or possibly even had him
stopped as a result of some conspiratorial alliance with the layers.
The sourness in the relationship between the trainer and his
bosses, which had surfaced before Hackler's Pride's first
Cambridgeshire win three years before, had never really cleared
up. In spite of having delivered the goods to the extent of 280
winners and a whole string of successful gambles, Fallon, who was
probably happy to get out anyway, paid for this one painful and
expensive loss with his job.

In 1913 Percy Cunliffe succeeded where Purefoy had failed
when his colt Aboyeur, trained by Fallon's replacement, fellow
Irishman Tommy Lewis, triumphed in that year's Derby, albeit as a
result of the controversial Stewards Enquiry that threw out the
official first past the post, Craganour. It was in every way a
sensational race as it also featured the death of the suffragette
Emily Davidson beneath the heels of the King's horse, Anmer,
while Cunliffe, who, one imagines, would have been an unlikely
supporter of women's rights, had a thumping touch on his colt,
considered a rank outsider on form, of £250 at 100 – 1. Ladbrokes'
profits on the race were said to have been wiped out at a stroke
thanks entirely to this one, unhedged, wager.

The First World War initiated the break-up of the Druids Lodge
Confederacy. The army took over the estate and many of the lads
joined up. By the time racing in Britain resumed, most of the
original staff were either dead or had gone far away. The owners,
too, had seen their comfortable Edwardian fortunes somewhat
reduced as a result of overseas investments lost during the fighting. In 1934 Cunliffe sold out to Mr J. V. Rank, the non-betting,
non-drinking Quaker founder of Rank Hovis Macdougall whose
wife Pat was the furious gambler and whose brother J. Arthur was
to launch the careers of several generations of English movie stars.
After Rank's death in 1952 the place passed on briefly to a couple of
other racing magnates and then on to an agri-business company
who ploughed up the gallops to plant potatoes. The stables are still
in use today as a livery yard though the estate's current proprietor,
a Sussex landowner, is said to have plans to turn the whole

property into a golf course and conference-centre-cum-luxury-hotel.

Purefoy, Cunliffe and Forrester were all very rich men when they set up their syndicate and, the privations of war aside, they were still paper millionaires when they died. Purefoy left an estate valued at the equivalent of £1.1 million in 1930 and on their deaths twelve years later his two old associates were said to be worth nearly £2.5 million apiece by the same computations. Others were not so fortunate. Jack Fallon swiftly dissipated the profits he made while training at Druids Lodge, most of it on a series of badly researched racing and farming ventures and in entertaining his family and friends on both sides of the Irish Sea. For a while in the 1920s he trained for the flamboyant financier and punter Jimmy White at his Foxhill stables near Swindon. White had a particular enthusiasm for drinking champagne that had been stored in chalk so Fallon and his staff used to spend an inordinate amount of time burying bottles of Mumm and Pol Roger in the surrounding Wiltshire downland and then digging them out again when White, his friends and their floosies made one of their regular Sunday-morning visits. In 1927 White's businesses collapsed and their stricken founder subsequently poisoned himself. His downfall seems to have caused as much pain and distress to the investment portfolios of one or two prominent racing figures in the twenties as the collapse of the Charles St George-led Lloyd Insurance syndicates did to similar individuals sixty years on.

Fallon ended his life trying to bum money off old racing acquaintances at the entrances to the major tracks. In 1935 a group of sympathisers led by the jockey Steve Donoghue and the *Sporting Life* journalist Meyrick Good were sufficiently moved by his plight to start up a fund to try to provide for his wife and children. The family, no doubt, appreciated it but it was too late for the trainer. He died flat broke the following summer.

Three years later it was Gentleman Bob Sievier, the acerbic scourge of Purefoy, Cunliffe and others, who, in John Betjeman's immortal phrase, also 'paid the final entrance fee' and ascended to the great Members' Enclosure – or would it have been Tattersalls for Sievier? – in the sky. The once wild colonial adventurer turned bookmaker, gambler, owner, journalist and warned-off mocker of the rest was also said to have been utterly penniless at his death.

Cunliffe and Purefoy never showed their emotions. At least not in public. We assume that they savoured the great coups that they landed but they would never have visibly displayed their feelings while alive any more than they can do so in death. One or two of their fellows were rather more demonstrative. If Fallon and Sievier could talk back from the grave they would surely say that theirs was a good life and that like countless other faces, chancers and plungers, past and present, they were never happier than when gambling money on the racetrack. But what, you may ask, about the pain and suffering that their profligate addiction caused to those people who loved and depended on them? Wives, children, lovers, partners, friends. Would their recollections be quite so romantic? It must be doubtful. Then again, who wants to be too pharisaical about the all-too-human faults and failings of basically sympathetic characters who are no longer around to speak up for themselves? Certainly no contemporary 'railbird' or betting-shop habitué, or indeed anyone who has ever been intoxicated by the glorious thrill of winning easy money on the horses and who has got in over their head as a result, can afford to criticise. They ought to be ' ... t to know that it is very much a case of 'There but for the gra.. d go I.'

CHAPTER ELEVEN

A Better Class of Investor

AT THE turn of the century on-course betting on horse-racing was a nationwide passion. It survived the Depression, and it survived the Austerity Age, when almost all outdoor spectator sports drew much bigger crowds than they do today, and when more ordinary penny-ante punters than ever before sought to escape from the drabness of rationing and shortages by making weekly visits to the horse and greyhound tracks.

The forties and fifties were also the age of numerous extravagant individual gamblers, both men and women. Some of them, like Miss Dorothy Paget and the Aly Khan, had inherited money, others, like Mrs Pat Rank, had married it or had made money out of the war or the rebuilding period that followed. Laurie Wallis's client, the Lincolnshire farmer Frank Dennis, had amassed a fortune in cash which he kept stored in a box under the bed. All of these punters had their day but very few consistently made a profit at their bookmaker's expense. One of them consistently lost. Alex Bird, whose own career as a professional gambler began during this period, has always maintained that the greatest mug punter of all time was the Manchester architect and surveyor, Joe Sunlight, who was active on the tracks for nearly forty years between the late thirties and his death in 1979.

Sunlight Joe was a Russian émigré, like the parents of the Stein Brothers, and he apparently displayed the same kind of commercial acumen in building up a fortune through property development as Snouty and Max, and then Snouty's boy Cyril, were to demonstrate in their mastery of the bookmaking business. He both owned and designed the Sunlight House office block in

Manchester city centre, once one of the tallest, though by no means the most beautiful, buildings in the country and his real-estate empire extended right across the north of England. Yet Joe's relationship with the bookies was characterised far more by naïvety than brains. For the best part of twenty-five years he used to have a bet on virtually every horse-race every day of the week, frequently backing two or more runners in each contest. His daily turnover often exceeded £10,000 in early post-war money. It never seemed to dawn on him that even if he sometimes won – and Joe didn't win often – his scattergun staking methods were bound to result in a consistent overall percentage loss.

What was so extraordinary about his indiscriminate approach to betting was that in all other respects Sunlight counted the pennies religiously. When visiting a racecourse in his distinctive grey over-coat with the olive-green velvet collar, he always insisted on travelling inconspicuously by second-class train or bus (hardly de luxe modes of conveyance in the ration-book era) even though he had a Rolls-Royce Silver Ghost sitting in his garage at home. Old book-making hands say that he only paid off his betting bills once a year, and even then they'd be lucky to get as much as 50 per cent of what he owed them. It was partly for this reason that bookmakers like William Hill used to regard Sunlight as a 'top of the book' client, which means that they regularly discarded his bets when calculating the element of profit or loss that would obtain to them on a particular race. Joe's disinclination to pay up, coupled with his parsimonious private housekeeping, obviously counterbalanced his gambling habit in the long run because when he died he still managed to leave a personal fortune worth over £5 million.

Another colossal punter of the pre- and post-war years was Miss Dorothy Paget. She owned the truly immortal Golden Miller, the five-times Cheltenham Gold Cup winner and also 1934 Grand National victor (completing the Gold Cup-Aintree double in the same season) who, even by the debased standards of racecourse superlatives, was an unquestionably great racehorse and one of the two or three finest steeplechasers of the century.

Dorothy Paget's father was an English peer and her mother was a member of America's stupendously wealthy Whitney family. Not surprisingly, therefore, money was no object to the lady who enjoyed a substantial private income which she believed was there to be spent and preferably to be gambled on racehorses. Yet, although she occasionally hit the mark in style, it is said that her outlay regularly outstripped her winnings by four or five times to one. She was an intensely superstitious punter and always made her trips to the races in a coat of the same colour and style as she had worn on a previously successful expedition. If someone rang her up on the morning of a big race day and their telephone number was 3403 she would want exactly £3,403 on one of her horses that afternoon. It's a matter of opinion as to whether or not she ever realised how much of a mark she was for the craftier bookmakers: Ron Pollard has revealed how William Hill would sometimes cynically lay a trap for her by bribing the jockey of a fancied horse on which she had invested heavily to 'part company' in the country or otherwise throw the race, thus ensuring that Miss Paget's bet was a loser even before the flag went up.

Those who knew or remember Dorothy Paget well say that she yielded to no one in the area of eccentric personal characteristics. A large, rather galumphing-looking woman, modelled more on the lines of Gertrude Stein than the chic and petite Helen Vernet, she was hugely selfish although by no means unamusing company and clearly not used to being denied. She liked to ring up her trainers in the middle of the night to discuss running plans and after one of Golden Miller's Gold Cup wins she presented her trainer and jockey with a life-size statuette of the horse. Made of chocolate. She depended heavily on her long-suffering private secretary, Ruth Charlton, who was married to the top flat-race jockey, Charlie Smirke. Ruth was also a good friend of Geoffrey Hamlyn's, the then youthful SP correspondent, who would often assist in placing assorted of Miss Paget's four- and five-figure wagers with the rails giants of the time such as Hill, Parker, Preston and Laurie Wallis. In return Mrs Charlie would sometimes arrange lifts for Hamlyn in the capacious Paget motor to some of the early post-war race meetings when public transport was still hard to find. It seems that these car journeys were frequently incident-packed adventures. On one occasion Miss Paget responded to a breakdown by commandeering another motorist's car and ordering the driver and his passenger to abandon their journey and take a back seat while she drove at breakneck speed to Manchester races. Another scenario involved her not only in requisitioning somebody else's vehicle but forcing them to sit it out with Ruth in her own stranded Humber, waiting for the breakdown van to arrive, while she set off, in Silverstone fashion once again, for Cheltenham. It was the first day of the Festival, after all.

Dorothy Paget was not the only remarkable high-octane female gambler of the forties and fifties. There was also the obsessive and totally fearless Mrs J. V. 'Pat' Rank, wife of the later owner of Purefoy's and Cunliffe's Druids Lodge stables. Jimmy Rank was reputedly one of the wealthiest men of his age – which was just as well because it is said that his wife used to gamble what was mainly his money with reckless abandon. According to contemporary odds-makers, she staked and lost at least ten times more than she ever won. And, according to Jim Dreaper, son of the late Tom who trained Jimmy Rank's Prince Regent to win the 1946 Cheltenham Gold Cup, the non-gambling Quaker owner had to resort to buying his own bookmaking business – without his wife realising it – to try to have all of her bets passed through that agency in an attempt to impose some control on her gambling and to give him some chance of regaining at least a fraction of his losses. A richly bejewelled and scented chain-smoker, Pat Rank must have struck the sort of theatrical image regrettably seen less frequently on British racecourses today but which you can still find sometimes sitting alone and betting heavily at the top roulette and blackjack tables in Crockfords and the International Sporting Club or in the Grand Salle at Monte Carlo.

High stakes and occasional substantial losses were both familiar experiences to Prince Aly Khan – although partly through adopting Joe Sunlight's policy of paying the bookies as infrequently as possible he rarely tasted anything as vulgar as the ashes of defeat. The Aly enjoyed such an abundance of good cards anyway, from fabulous wealth to good looks, charm and considerable sexual magnetism (not to mention two stables of top-class racehorses) that walking away a winner in the betting stakes was hardly essential for him and certainly didn't affect his theoretical ability to pay his tailor's bill each quarter.

The Aly was born in 1912 right into the élite tier of European flat racing and was always destined totally and irrevocably to be a part of it. His father 'the old Aga Khan', as people still refer to him today, began his family's massive but always shrewd investment in bloodstock in 1921 and when he died in 1957 left two-fifths of his racing stock and property to his philandering son. The Aly bought out his two co-heirs and by the time of his own death three years later had the world of European racing and breeding at his feet. In 1958 he won the French 1,000 Guineas, the Irish Oaks and two of France's four championship events for two-year-olds. In 1959 his colours carried everything before them, winning the Arc, the Eclipse Stakes and the 2,000 Guineas as well as the French 1,000 Guineas for a second time. Most famously of all, he saw his scintillating filly Petite Etoile go through the season unbeaten with a run of six Blue Riband victories that included the 1,000 Guineas, the Oaks, the Sussex Stakes, the Yorkshire Oaks and the Champion Stakes. It was entirely appropriate that these magnificent thoroughbreds were all trained and conditioned by two of the finest horsemen that the European game has ever known: Noel Murless in England and Alec Head in France.

When the Aly Khan died in a car crash in Paris on 12 May 1960 at the age of forty-eight his friends and associates found it hard to believe that such a brilliant personality could have been so violently and prematurely extinguished. 'He was too alive to die,' said a friend, and it seemed an appropriate phrase to try to describe the character of a man who, outwardly at least, had always been the consummate charmer and playboy of his generation. Like many an expansive host, he could apparently be petulant and selfish when his own desires were thwarted but most people were prepared to forgive these little 'outbursts' and to accept his dictates and the panache with which they were expressed and bask in the glow of his undoubted charm. Perhaps this is why his name still instantly recalls those famous black-and-white photographs of him in his morning dress at Epsom just after the war. Top hat and tails, silk stock, binoculars, cigarette holder and, draped ravishingly on one arm, the impossibly lovely figure of Rita Hayworth. Yet, if you believe the many salacious stories about the Aly's private life, this same handsome and outrageously blessed individual, married at the time to one of the most sexually desirable women in the world, was also possessed of a tawdry Kennedyesque appetite and craving for casual sex with other women on a weekly, daily and even hourly basis.

Talk of the Aly's sexual exploits inevitably hovers perilously close to the sort of tacky and prurient revelations that should be no part of an essentially sympathetic book about the bookmaking and betting fraternity. But some psychiatrists cannot make enough of the connections between sex and gambling – and the Aly was a man who seemed to devote himself to both activities almost addictively. There is no denying that the feeling of omnipotence and self-affirmation that comes from being a big winner is not so very far removed in some minds from the emotions of a triumphant sexual conquest. And if some women find you more attractive the more you win (and the more that you are prepared to risk losing as you attempt to win) from gambling on the horses, the Aly may conceivably also have felt that the more women he 'had' then the more women would want to be had by him.

The notion of the predatory male sating his lust wherever his fancy takes him doesn't sit easily today when attitudes towards women and sexuality are so different, but it is, perhaps, not hard to understand why some women found him so attractive. It was a potent, erotic mixture of his seductive aura as an exotic Middle Eastern prince, his charm and that he had so much money to throw around. Bored society wives in the forties and fifties apparently boasted publicly that they had been to bed with him, even if only once for half an hour between races. Even their husbands – typical passionless Englishmen presumably – were supposed to have been secretly proud that they had been cuckolded by the Aly and not that absolute ass Carruthers at the FO. But was he really such a great and prodigious lover? One woman who ought to know says that he kept a permanently filled ice-bucket beside his bed into which he intermittently plunged his right hand – and perhaps more than that – in order to prolong the moments of passion. But was this simply a ruse to extend the ecstasy or an essential ma-noeuvre if there was to be any ecstasy at all? Whatever the case, it is legitimate to say that it is the sort of thing that positively enthralls gambling 'experts' intrigued by the psychological subtext.

According to Dr Marvin Steinberg, executive director of the Connecticut Council on Gambling, speaking to the International Conference on Risk and Gambling in London in 1990, some 15 per cent of compulsive gamblers are also sex addicts but 'they gener-ally look on sex as fulfilling a biological need rather than as a sensuous experience'. Steinberg declared that heavy-duty punters 'often don't know how to cuddle because they were deprived of that type of contact as a child. Many have no concept of non-genital contact. They are generally impatient with foreplay because it takes too long and the shorter the foreplay the less intense the orgasm. Sex is often a brief experience for the dedicated gambler.' Well, well, well. Did Prince Aly Khan really get less sensual pleasure from making love with Rita Hayworth than he did from watching Petite Etoile and Lester Piggott win the Oaks?

The Aly split most of his gambling business between Ladbrokes, the charismatically named 'Beau' Goldsmith who traded on the rails as Jack Wilson & Co. and William Hill. It was Hill who eventually tried to put a stop to the Aly's practice of letting his losing accounts run on unsettled until the time came when he backed a few big winners again – when he sent round a representative to the bookmaker's offices to collect a cheque.

One day in 1954 one of the Aly's emissaries came round to Hill's office wanting a payment of £9,000. Instead of handing over the nine grand, Hill asked the associate to sit down and wait while he drafted a letter explaining to the Aly that he was putting the £9,000 to his credit and adding a further £5,000 giving him a limit of £14,000 to bet up to. This way he hoped to make a profit out of him for a change. Geoffrey Hamlyn tells of a fascinating unscheduled and unannounced visit that the Aly subsequently paid to Hill at his home in Albion Gate. It was hardly the done thing in the early fifties for a suave and cosmopolitan Ismaili Prince to mix socially with a bookmaker of lowly origins on his own territory. The Aly obviously intended to try to charm Hill, to flatter him with his attentions and consequently to seduce him into allowing him to continue betting and paying as he wished. The older man mixed cocktails for his distinguished visitor and they chatted agreeably about general racing topics for over an hour. But Hill was a hard man too and equally determined not to give way on a point of principle. He explained to the Aly why he had acted as he had and insisted that theirs could only be a normal bookmaker–punter relationship in the future. The result was something of a stand-off between these two powerful egos. The Aly went a full season without having a single bet with Hill's firm and at the end of the year Hill sent him a cheque for £9,000 and closed his account.

The Aly's otherwise expansive lifestyle has not been adopted by his son. The old Aga had decided that the Aly was too shiftless and irresponsible to inherit the non-racing side of his empire so he passed that on to his grandson, the Aly's son and current Aga Khan, Karim. No dilettante punter he!

Nobody ever described Alex Bird as a dilettante. Obsessional, yes. Cold, unemotional. Boring, even. But never with even a trace of frivolity. Bird understandably took pride in that although he started betting in the late thirties and was at Epsom in the year of Rita Hayworth's visit to the Derby in 1948 (when he was allegedly too busy with 'business' to waste time stargazing), he survived for over fifty years as one of that small and select band of genuinely successful professional punters.

Bird was born to play a part in the gambling industry. His father's ostensible occupation was that of a coal merchant in the semi-rural suburb of Newton Heath, north of Manchester. The real hub of his life though, the enterprise closest to his heart, was his necessarily secretive operation as the local street bookie. His son became fascinated at an early age with the closed world that was directed from a set of attic rooms behind a panelled door on the top floor of his father's offices. He was intrigued by the panoply of bookies' runners and clocked betting bags going back and forth to the local factories to allow the hapless workers – unable, in 1925, to bet by phone on credit like a toff and prohibited by law until 1961 from betting legally off-course in cash – the harmless pleasure of a wager.

When he was fifteen Bird left school to work in his father's business. Slowly it dawned on him that real money might be made from backing horses as well as laying them if a punter studied the form book carefully enough. Accordingly, he equipped himself with all the relevant literature and proceeded to devote several years' painstaking effort to passing his O and A levels in racing. His first big win came when he netted £410 on the 1938 Grand National and over the next fifteen to twenty years in particular he cleaned up on that race applying regular systematic study – in those days the fences were much stiffer than they are now – to weeding out the horses that could be guaranteed to jump and stay from the faint-hearts and mediocrities. He was also quick to pick up on Phil Bull's pioneering use of times as an aid to backing two-year-olds. His most consistent supply of winners, though, followed his discovery that as the result of an optical illusion created by racehorses passing the winning post at speed it frequently appeared that the horse on the far side had triumphed in a photo-finish whereas more often than not it was the other way round.

The racecourse bookmakers always bet on the outcome of a photo. Sometimes it takes several minutes before the result is announced while the print is developed or the judge calls for a second print to enable him to make his decision. The odds on the horses concerned in the photo can fluctuate dramatically during that time.

In the 1940s there were no television pictures or camera patrol films providing on-course racegoers and bookmakers – via their tic-tac operatives – with live coverage or a replay of the action. Bird used to position himself by the line, keep his head absolutely still and use his eyes as a kind of human camera lens. He found that from this vantage point if he thought that the horse farthest away had won it *had* won. But from time to time his on-the-spot 'camera' would suggest to him that the horse on the nearside had triumphed: Bird discovered that he was able to make a substantial profit by backing his judgement in this way.

There can be no doubt that at the peak of his powers Bird was an impressively shrewd and disciplined player whose bets were only accepted with some trepidation by the major bookmaking firms. Sometimes his accounts were closed and on several occasions his requests to open a new account were turned down. For this reason he frequently made use of a brilliantly organised network of commissioning agents, *à la* Purefoy, who could get his money on, often at the last minute, without the layers being able to detect the source of the investment. Yet the more successful and established he became, so an ever-increasing pomposity began to creep into his demeanour.

In 1953, by which point he had a gambling turnover of several million pounds a year, he became a Lloyds underwriter and from then on, this arch traditionalist, who said that his favourite racing moment was the Royal Procession at Ascot, insisted on being referred to not as a gambler but as an 'investor'. It was as if he believed that the latter word with its connotations of the City and high finance might somehow impart to his activities an aura of superiority and class. Perhaps it also helped him to single himself out from the mugs and gulls who had contributed to his father's housekeeping bills thirty years before.

The truth was that with his large cigars, his sheepskin jackets and his fawn-coloured coats, Bird was beginning to remind some racing correspondents of those rather boring, self-made and self-promoting Mancunian and North Western businessmen for whom Harold Wilson displayed such a fondness during his premiership. Like all professional gamblers, who regard their betting as a higher calling demanding the same kind of clinical precision and skill that it takes to become a brain surgeon, Bird had always been anxious to dissociate himself from the public image of the punter as a halfwit in a pub or betting shop forever bad-mouthing the most recent losing favourite. But, whether as a result of this underlying insecurity or simply out of a desire to impress, he sometimes talked about other leading figures in the racing industry as if he had always been on the most intimate terms with them all.

'Oh, thank you, Mr Bird, for your wise and professional advice about what I should ride in this year's Derby.'

'That's all right, Lester. I'm always happy to put a young fellow to rights. Remind me to send you another crate of champagne next Christmas.'

Alex Bird may well have been a close personal friend of many top jockeys and trainers but this playing up of flattering notions of cosy familiarity could strike a note not so very dissimilar to the preposterously bogus claims of some of the telephone hot-line tipping services.

Ironically, or perhaps appropriately, there were occasions when Bird's judgement was proved as spectacularly and embarrassingly wrong as that of even the humblest tipster or mug. In the spring of 1979 he was sitting on a number of attractive ante-post bets about a horse called Tromos that he had backed at the end of the previous flat-racing season to win the 1979 2,000 Guineas. Tromos was scheduled to have a prep race for the Guineas in the Craven Stakes at Newmarket in early April. Before the race Bird, unusually for a professional gambler, allowed himself to be interviewed on television by the terrier-like Bruffscott. He not only boasted about how many thousands he would make from his 'investments' when, not if, Tromos won the 2,000 but also publicly assured the viewers that Tromos would definitely win the Craven by at least three lengths. From the overweening certainty with which he announced this news you'd have thought that he was reporting that Christmas Day falls on 25 December. Tromos finished second, beaten a comfortable two-and-a-half lengths in a three-horse race. He subsequently went down with the cough, which means that he developed a virus and never even ran in the Guineas. One bookmaker crudely declared that the sound of Bird's ante-post vouchers being flushed down the lavatory echoed around the betting ring for the rest of the afternoon.

Four years later Bird was caught out again. This time he was convinced that a particularly promising two-year-old colt called Gorytus, who had won his first two races in style, would prove invincible in both the Dewhurst Stakes at Newmarket and the following year's 2,000 Guineas and Derby. Once again he invested with confidence, expecting to win himself a five-figure sum. Once again the racecourse and the racing press were alive with the details of his wagering but once again the horse ran as if under a spell. To be fair to Gorytus he ran so badly in the Dewhurst, in which he trailed home a distant last of four, that it was obvious to everyone that something was seriously amiss. The Jockey Club's forensic scientists were never able to find any conclusive evidence that might have proved that the horse had been doped, but Bird remains convinced that Gorytus was got at and in very much the same way as Pinturischio was nobbled in 1961.

One recounts these old racing stories not from a desire to discredit Alex Bird but to underscore the truism, so obvious but so often overlooked, that there is no such thing as a certainty on the track. Nothing can make a fool of you more quickly or comprehensively than a racehorse and therefore the notion that you can somehow get round this by calling yourself an 'investor' rather than a punter is a non-starter. The very act of putting large sums of money on a horse instead of investing it in Ladbrokes shares declares you to be a fundamentally reckless rather than prudent individual. To be fair again to Bird the great majority of his bets, the winning ones, were never splashed over the front pages of the trade papers and were always determined by strict adherence to the principal of value. Yet even that indisputably wise doctrine must occasionally be applied with discretion as Alex Bird found to his cost.

In 1986 he was one of a number of betting and racing observers who asserted that Europe's champion racehorse, Dancing Brave, was virtually unbeatable in that year's Breeders Cup Turf at Santa Anita in Southern California. A more sober consideration of the facts would have warned them that Dancing Brave had everything against him: the track, the weather conditions, the 3,400 mile journey from Sussex and not least that he was competing for the eighth time that season, four weeks after winning a vintage Prix de l'Arc de Triomphe and nearly seven months after making his three-year-old début on a wet spring day at Newmarket. He finished fifth. Undeterred Bird stepped into the Breeders Cup debate again two years later, sending commissioning agents to Las Vegas to obtain what he considered to be false and over-generous American prices about two of the English horses, Warning and Indian Skimmer, who were running in that year's Breeders Cup Mile and Breeders Cup Turf in Louisville, Kentucky.

You may have only the featureless PMU windows to bet with at an American racetrack but in Las Vegas you'll find no shortage of the real thing, once-met-never-to-be-forgotten characters like Jimmy 'The Chief' Shapiro, Big Paul Sardi and Walter Ganz. They'll give you all the action you can handle. Not surprisingly,

Vegas is still the place to get a really big bet on because the overall surfeit of money in the city means that no serious bookmaker should ever go short of custom. The Las Vegas bookies call the odds on American racing every day of the year but you can only bet with them in cash if you are present in their offices in the big hotels in Vegas itself or Reno or elsewhere in Nevada or in Atlantic City, New Jersey. Out-of-state punters have to bet in credit on the telephone in the same way that one does with Stephen Little and Victor Chandler in Britain.

The Vegas bookies aren't the only odds-makers to offer ante-post prices about the Breeders Cup. Given the large number of European runners that go over for the contests and the ever-increasing European interest in the event, the big British bookmaking firms run ante-post and race-day lists of their own. Inevitably their prices about the English and French horses, whose form and connections they know well, are rarely generous (even though until 1991 only one British trained runner had ever won a Breeders Cup flat race). The American odds about the European challengers are usually much bigger. A perfect opportunity, you might think, for a spot of value betting.

In 1988 Alex Bird correctly deduced that the US bookies, in common with large sections of the American racing press (most of whom are as pathetically ignorant of European racing as we are of the sport in America and Australia), were being patronising and dismissive about the English representatives. Bird believed that the Americans' opening odds of around 6 and 8–1 for Warning and Indian Skimmer were an insult. Both horses had won top class Group One races in Europe and were coming out of the élite stables of Guy Harwood and Henry Cecil. In fact, Warning was representing the same owner–trainer–jockey combination of Saudi Arabian Prince Khalid Abdulla, Harwood and Pat Eddery that had been associated with Dancing Brave. Which, in the light of his performance in the Breeders Cup, might have been seen as a worrying omen, at least by the superstitious.

Alex Bird wasn't interested in superstition but his first big mistake was to forget that the races were taking place not in Britain but in Kentucky. At Ascot maybe Warning would have been able to beat the American opposition with his two hind legs tied together but out in Louisville the English pair were going to have to contend with many of the same inherent disadvantages that had confronted Dancing Brave two years before. The weather this time was sympathetically cold and wet but the new Matt Winn turf track that had been laid inside the existing Churchill Downs dirt track and had never been raced on before was exceptionally tight with sharp American turns and a slippery sand base in place of lush grass and galloping English undulations. You might have thought that any serious professional gambler would have wanted to take a look at the racecourse first before making his 'investments'. In the circumstances it was surely one thing for a smart player to take 'an interest' at the inflated American odds but quite another to talk about the English duo's chances, as some were doing, as an opportunity to buy money.

Alex Bird's second big mistake was fatally to underestimate the American layers. Jimmy and Paul may not know a lot about English racing but they haven't survived in business for so long in a city like Las Vegas by being altogether dumb. In local parlance, 'they've got all the smarts'. They knew that the visitors were totally unproven on a tight turning track and that they'd had to fly across the Atlantic and go through quarantine to take part. They also knew that the Brits record in the Breeders Cup series to date had been less than overwhelming. And that's why they priced them so high.

In the days leading up to the contests some members of the attendant British press corps continued to talk up the chances of Warning in particular as if he was the reincarnated essence of Eclipse and Nijinsky combined. His trainer Guy Harwood hardly inspired that kind of confidence. He spent the build-up period stamping around the training compound in a flat cap and Barbour refusing to talk to journalists and looking like a bad-tempered Sussex farmer at a Bank Holiday Monday point-to-point. For Harwood, and for all the rest of Warning's supporters, the action on the track when it came was a sobering experience.

Indian Skimmer put up a courageous show in the Breeders Cup Turf but still could finish no better than third. Her jockey lost ground on the bends and the testing surface sapped her stamina. Warning was routed. He finished a humiliating last but one. Those European racing enthusiasts lucky enough to be there will never forget that 1988 Breeders Cup Mile. We'll never forget the brilliance of the winner, the French-trained filly Miesque, or the inspired riding of her much-maligned jockey, Freddie Head. He broke fast from the stalls, he was right on the heels of the leaders going down the back stretch and he made his move on the turn into the home straight. By comparison Pat Eddery's performance on Warning was incomprehensible. He seemed to be trying to settle his mount at the rear early on, as if he was riding around Sandown or York, whereas the pace is so fast from the outset in American racing that it is usually vital to get a good position at the first bend, exactly as if you were competing in a greyhound race at Wembley or Wimbledon. Get too far behind early on and you'll rarely make the ground up later. Eddery gave away so much in the first quarter-mile that his chances of victory were negligible well before half-way. The British were devastated. After the race Warning's trainer and jockey blamed the track, the conditions, the Americans, the draw, everything. Afterwards was too late for Alex Bird.

The veteran gambler was disgusted by the 1988 Breeders Cup. Disgusted by the tight course and disgusted that the American runners, like the five-year-old gelding, Great Communicator, who won the Breeders Cup Turf, were able to run on pain-killing medications prohibited in Europe (another fact that had been widely known and argued over in advance). Bird was so distressed that he vowed he would never bet on the Breeders Cup races again. Yet, only twelve months later, his men were back in Las Vegas.

In the autumn of 1989 Bird's agents were sent out to take a price about Zilzal, the much-hyped Michael-Stoute-trained colt, which was contesting that year's Breeders Cup Mile, also taking place far from Newmarket around another razor-sharp track in the intense heat and humidity of Gulfstream Park, Miami. Zilzal was undoubtedly a horse with terrific speed and class who, like Warning, had put up a couple of brilliant performances over a mile in England. But, as well as all the usual problems, Zilzal, even when supposedly relaxed, was a coiled spring of nervous intensity who was liable to snap at any moment. His jockey, Walter 'The Choirboy' Swinburn, had to take him down to the start early and alone in order to contain him. And he was drawn on the wide outside. The champion American trainer, D. Wayne Lukas, remarked that if he was Michael Stoute he'd scratch. Lukas was talking a good fight in advance as usual but, not for the first time, his prognostication turned out to be brutally accurate.

'Tell us, Walter,' enthused the ubiquitous Bruffscott, interviewing Swinburn the day before the race, 'does it make you feel nervous to have so much responsibility resting on your shoulders?'

'Well, Brough,' replied the nonchalant Choirboy. 'If I was nearly forty-eight and I'd never ridden a Breeders Cup winner I might be nervous.'

'Well, I'm nearly forty-eight and I've never ridden a Breeders Cup winner and I don't mind admitting that I'm extremely nervous,' responded the terrier.

'Exactly,' said Walter.

Zilzal finished fifth.

At the 1990 Breeders Cup meeting at Belmont Park, New York, the not-so-wise-old Bird almost got his money back when the blindingly fast Dayjur, trained by none other than Major Dick Hern, a veritable redcoat among the Yankees, came agonisingly close to winning the Breeders Cup Sprint on dirt. Dayjur only lost because he attempted to jump a shadow in the dying stages of the race. It cost him the spoils by a neck. It cost Alex Bird a payout of £250,000.

In 1991 the Breeders Cup returned to Kentucky but this time Bird was not recorded as placing a bet. Unluckily for him, 1991 was the year when the champion French two-year-old-colt Arazi, who would have started at odds-on in Europe, won the Breeders Cup Juvenile on dirt and was returned at just over 2–1 on the track. And England's Sheikh Albadou, trained by Major Hern's one-time assistant, Alex Scott, won the Sprint at odds of over 25–1. Who ever said that gambling on horses was easy?

The intriguing thing about Alex Bird's Breeders Cup record to date is the question of whether any bookmaker or trust-fund manager analysing his bets in the series would have regarded them as the careful placements of an investor – shrewd, sagacious and impartial – or as the bold though repetitive habits of a clever but fallible gambler?

Bird could justifiably have retorted by pointing to the lifestyle that his gambling – the Tromos and Breeders Cup embarrassments aside – earned him over the years: the 'mansion' in Cheshire, a private plane, de-luxe motors and smokes. And regular luxurious winter holidays in the sun. Alex Bird died after a short illness in December 1991. Fifteen months earlier he and his partner Peter Hirst had pulled off an old-fashioned coup in the Ayr Gold Cup with a horse that they backed down from 40–1 to 14–1 and who was called, appropriately enough, Final Touch.

In the final year of his life the dogged old player became the honorary vice-president of the National Association for the Protection of Punters, a splendid and long overdue organisation that seeks to steer us confirmed mugs away from the rocks and in the direction of customer satisfaction and even prosperity. The only problem, as Bird himself would have been the first to agree, is that most of us tend to listen to and then forget or even pointedly ignore any kind of wise counsel, sometimes taking an almost perverse pleasure in going down roads that we'd be much better advised to pass by. How else can you explain how you managed to end up throwing your money away on a bunch of equine nonentities in a thick sea fog at a gaff track on a humid Monday afternoon?

CHAPTER TWELVE

Brighton Rock

THE IDEA that, like the Aly Khan, you are giving life a good run for its money, uttering a debonair cry of 'Turn the wheel, maestro, and let fortune do its worst', is not the sort of notion that comes instantly to mind when you are standing on the crowded concourse of Victoria Station on a hot, sultry midsummer morning. Understandably, the mostly elderly American tourists, gathering in the queue by the ticket barrier for the Orient Express departure for Folkestone, were gazing around them with a mixture of bewilderment and despair. What is this, you could see them thinking, and where the hell are we? Where is the age-old glamour of the Continent? The mystery and romance of European travel?

The closest approximation to old European glamour were the Tourist Board beefeater images that adorned the wall posters next to the red-and-brown frontage of WH Smiths. The teeming flow of arriving and departing domestic passengers mainly conformed to the familiar leisure-wear images of the contemporary homogenised mass: lots of T-shirts and shorts, backpacks on frames, parties of scurrying school kids, lads with cans, lads with *Just William* haircuts, late-to-work secretaries trying to manage their too sticky apricot croissants and away-daying pensioners struggling with their splintering very English baguettes and Styrofoam cups of spilling-out mud-coloured coffee. The automatic train announcement board kept clattering away in the background signalling the next departure to such exotic destinations as Streatham Common, Norbury and Thornton Heath. And hanging over everything was that sickly inescapable aroma, so familiar to regular visitors to the Cheltenham Festival, that potent combination of fast-food burger fumes and rancid sweat.

Yet once upon a time some excitement, some romance and some *frisson* of danger pertained to this place, for from beneath these former yellow- and green-painted train-shed roofs of the old London and South Eastern Railway, dark green Southern Electric trains and brown-and-cream steam-hauled Pullmans once left the capital for the Kent and Sussex coast, for Brighton and the sea. And on these platforms, by these ticket barriers, signs were posted on Brighton bank holiday racedays saying, 'Don't play cards with strangers.' Some did. Some were cleaned out, too. Other less foolish or less adventurous souls, on their way down to Worthing and Bognor or returning home to Coulsdon, Merstham and Purley Oaks, sat back respectably and watched – and, no doubt, secretly trembled just a little with the illicit thrill of it all.

Years later the mods and the scooter boys followed the same route, at least, those who were without scooters or just temporarily *hors de combat*. 'Out of their brain' to the sound of Pete Townsend and 'going down, going down, on the very first train from town'. Looking for bother, excitement, thrills and pills by the sea.

All these characters, the card sharps and the race gangs, the mods and the rockers, the off-duty villains and the weekend lovers, whatever their generation, whatever their game, were either consciously intent on, or subconsciously drawn in, to shaping their destinies in the same still seedy but prosperous, sensual and timeless town where, even in the age of sexual restraint, shopping malls and the hideous, hermetically sealed executive suites of the Ramada Renaissance Hotel, there still remains something in the very ozone that beckons of warm chip papers and afternoon lust, of half-a-dozen oysters and a bottle of splash, and of sunlight glinting on a cut-throat razor and melting the pink outer coating of a stick of Brighton Rock.

But reflections on this fascinating side of our social history are not the stuff with which it is easy to hold the attention of committed and paid-up horse players like John Moynahan and A. J. Kincaid – at least not in advance of an afternoon's gambling. The two of them were waiting for me in a first-class compartment towards the front end of the 12.05 p.m. departure from Victoria to Brighton. Our destination was not, of course, the pier or the prom or the Ramada but the faintly barmy, increasingly tatty and still irresistible racecourse.

Neither was this to be an ordinary Brighton race meeting. This was the mid-June Monday of Royal Ascot week, the day before the start of the second great on-course gambling festival of the year, and our main intention in conducting this visit to the coast was to try to launch a pre-emptive strike against the bookmakers, to provide ourselves with some much-needed pocket money for the big occasion coming up. Moynahan was confident that success would be ours and a few days beforehand had predicted three certainties at least.

Not that a day out at Brighton races ever really needs justifying, be it as a springboard to Ascot or as a certain opportunity to buy money. Cheltenham in March is a wild and passionate fixture: a combination of the *fiesta* at Pamplona and a semi-religious event where half the congregation are on speed. Ascot is an intense and overwhelming betting occasion but it has less than a third of Cheltenham's freewheeling atmosphere and the people who run the racecourse, in particular the gatemen who guard the enclosures, regularly do their best to make you feel as if you've wandered uninvited into a private party. By comparison with the other two, Brighton is the basement. Like Hackney Saturday morning dogs. Like writing off whole days at a time in your local betting office. It can be life-enhancing, it can be seedy, but it never fails to reacquaint you with the rough, ordinary, day-to-day essence of racing and gambling.

When it comes to the history of bookmaking and the place of the bookie and punter in the nation's affections, Brighton has had an intriguing if slightly obtuse role to play in that development. Not that you can talk about these things to John Moynahan. Well, not on his way down to the racecourse. He had quickly settled himself into a corner seat with his briefcase open by his side. He had his head in his form books and further manuals, guides, Timeform cards and sheets of form were spread out all around. It wasn't immediately possible to converse with A. J. Kincaid either. He was totting up his losses on the US Open Golf Championship and the Stella Artois tennis while considering taking prices about Cash and Sabatini for Wimbledon and England for Lords. But from the look of Kincaid – crumpled linen suit, smouldering cigar, eyes searching for the next drink – you could tell that here was a sympathetic soul who might be prepared at some later stage if not to digress entirely, then at least to think beyond the entries in the fifth race at Yarmouth.

As the train rattled off across the Thames and sped through

Clapham Junction my own and Kincaid's thoughts turned swiftly to the prospect of refreshments. To alcohol, cholesterol and fat. To all but the most relentlessly professional gamblers, or to those peculiarly ascetic souls like our accompanying journalist, the appeal of going racing is not simply that it represents a chance to beat the market and have a bet at decent prices. The whole adventure also affords an opportunity to indulge in the sort of deliciously irresponsible behaviour perceived to be directly at odds with the oppressive routine of everyday life. A day trip to Brighton may hardly compare with the spectacular hedonism of the Cheltenham Festival but it offers its own more modest attractions. Getting drunk, or at least pleasantly loaded, in the train on the way down is certainly one of them.

'What about a drink?' asked Kincaid on cue.

'And what about a mid-morning snack?' I suggested.

'No, thank you,' replied Moynahan, not even bothering to look up. 'I enjoyed a very satisfying breakfast before setting out.' We knew what that meant. An early morning run, a bowl of muesli and another solitary two hours with the Timeform *Black Book*, habits that were frequently dismissed as pure affectation by Kincaid who insisted that a man in Moynahan's position ought to have enough contacts and inside information to be able to dispense with this slavish study. For his part, the journalist liked to retort that all inside information was nothing but illusory gossip guaranteed to prise even more money out of mugs like Kincaid. 'I think we can do ourselves a great deal of good by avoiding the favourite in the first,' he announced, his eyes still glued to the Brighton form in the *Racing Post* like Sherlock Holmes studying a relief map of the Great Grimpen Mire.

'Yes, yes, yes,' replied Kincaid impatiently. 'We've been through that argument already.'

The modern, under an hour service from London to Brighton and the coast, may have none of the sumptuously painted, tinder spark and rouched-curtain glamour of the old Brighton Belle but does have a reasonably congenial buffet car situated just behind the forward first-class carriages, well known to regular racetrack visitors to Plumpton and Fontwell in winter and to Brighton during the rest of the year. The buffet-car attendant, on this stiflingly humid and overcast day, was a short, spruce, grey-haired party who was sweating it out in a little blue-and-red jacket with gold epaulettes on the shoulders, which made him look as if he should have been mixing cocktails for the American tourists on the Orient Express. Instead he was turning out a popular line in toasted bacon-and-cheese sandwiches. For some inexplicable reason, you are never allowed to buy these on other British Rail lines but they are a standing order with the Sussex-bound punters and card players, like the trio of familiar faces who had taken up residence at one of the plastic, grey-and-white check buffet car tables.

The kaluki, bragg and gin rummy games remembered on the Brighton line by the likes of Arthur J. Sarl, who as 'Larry the Lynx' was the racing correspondent of *The People* for more than thirty years before the Second World War, may be thought to have died out with the age of steam but some pared-down semblance of that atmosphere can still be found on these trains today. The pots are usually bigger on the way back when some of the London boys with Epsom information are celebrating the nice touch they had on the Ron Smyth or John Sutcliffe thing in the big one (Smyth and Sutcliffe being well-known gambling trainers). Or alternatively, if things didn't quite work out according to plan, are commiserating with the Bell's miniatures and foully lambasting the same horse. 'That fucking pig. It couldn't win first prize in an abbattoir.'

These days the hard core of bookmakers who still ride the rails rarely join in the card schools and you would be equally unlikely to find any seriously high-rolling or disciplined punters among the players either. But winter or summer there is one group of leathery old denizens of the betting ring who you will always find tucked up in the buffet car on the coast-bound race trains. This very morning four of them were occupying the facing seats just across from the card game. These mainly ageing and diminutive gents, Sidneys and Morries, Tommys and Stans, are the Tattersalls' boards bookmakers' workmen or clerks. It is their job to record all of their bosses' transactions, mainly in pencil, in the big ledgers that they hold while constantly keeping the guv'nors' abreast of the balance of their book and absorbing information from the tic-tac men and runners as to the fluctuations in the odds on the other pitches. The major share of this business is usually conducted in a frantic ten-minute surge of trading before the off. Time and progress have not yet been able to replace or improve upon the dextrous skill and years of accumulated knowledge of racing, odds-making and numbers that these wise old hands possess. Sidney, Morrie, Tommy and Stan. Old native East Enders, most of them, East-End Jewish and proud of it. Mickey Fletcher may be brimming with contemptuous disdain for the boards bookmakers but it is difficult to feel any active dislike for their clerks. These veteran workmen have met characters like the Asparagus Kid before. They have seen all the big players come and go, layers and punters – the big villains too, coming round the pitches and asking for protection money especially down at Brighton and Epsom, in the fabled days of on-course gambling before and after the Second World War. Sidney, Morrie, Tommy and Stan, smoking their fags, sipping their coffee and eating their bacon sarnies while discussing the form for the day's card, which must be about the twenty or thirty thousandth of their careers. By the look of one or two of them, with their bloodshot oyster eyes and the veins protruding over their temples, you feel that it may very nearly be their last one too.

Having had no time for 'a satisfactory breakfast before setting out' both Kincaid and I filled up with double toasted bacon and cheese, washed down with liberal amounts of junk coffee and double gin and tonic. Throughout this repast we enjoyed a lively discussion with the Morries and Stans about the merits of passing on the favourite in the first, Willie Carson's overall record at Brighton, and whether John Sutcliffe had deliberately laid one out for the following day's Ascot Stakes.

Watching Kincaid arguing each point with enthusiasm I was reminded, not for the first time, that it never seemed to be any problem for him to escape from the responsibilities of work to slip off for a day's racing and gambling. He says little about his business which is connected with the manufacture and distribution of strong alcoholic beverages from the West Highlands of Scotland. We sometimes try to imagine him at work in the mysterious office which we are never allowed to see but which we know to be located up some narrow Dickensian alley off Leadenhall Street. One imagines he hardly ever attends this address on a constant round-the-clock basis. More likely he only stops off there briefly, one or two mornings a week, before setting off on one of his riotous tours of betting offices, restaurants, clubs, casinos and private rooms. What an enviable existence, less well-heeled fellow punters might say, son and heir to an old family firm, a concern that seems capable not only of sustaining him in the role of a sort of part-time executive director but of withstanding both the pressures and fashions of an aggressive boom and the ravages of a fearful slump, thus guaranteeing the future distillery owner a seemingly inexhaustible line of credit, quite invaluable for betting purposes especially at the start of such a week of dramatic all-racing, non-working action as this. Could life possibly be more ideal?

The Network Express swept on past Gatwick Airport and then lurched out over the Balcombe viaduct. The deep green Sussex Weald, with its red-brick and weatherboard farms, its oaks and its oasthouse conversions, stretched away gently on either side. After Haywards Heath we ordered more drinks, a couple of beers this time as well as gin and tonic, for Kincaid was determined to tempt Moynahan at least into tasting something before the train reached the sea. As we made our way back along the narrow corridor, clutching our cans and plastic cups – two of which were already half empty – the train began to bump and roll even more violently than usual causing the fizzed-up alcohol to splash over our jackets and shoes. The next thing we knew we were out of the grey daylight and racing into the coal-black darkness of the Clayton Tunnel beneath the downs.

As the wind roared in through the open corridor windows, enhancing the mood of fleeting Hitchcockian melodrama, we momentarily lost our balance and half fell in through an open compartment door. Sitting on his own was a well-known punter and face. A sleek smartly dressed professional who originally made his fortune from speculating in the northern house-building and property market in the sixties and seventies. This punter and sometime bookie, let us call him Mr Bolger, aroused from his form book study by our sudden intrusion into his first-class fastness, looked around lazily, turning his head up towards ours as if in slow motion. The expression on his face was cold, impassive and menacing. The noise of the train reverberating against the tunnel walls made any attempt at conversation impossible. Lights flashed past us at intervals in the dark and from the open windows came the smell of electricity and pitch as tangible and intense as the hamburger fumes at Cheltenham. For a few brief seconds, eyeball to eyeball with Bolger beneath the compartment's overhead bulb, it was easy to imagine him not as a powerful well-built fifty-year-old in a 1990s velvet collar coat but as a rather different kind of face from another era – in a snap-brim trilby and a chalk-stripe suit with a tailored shirt and a naked lady patterned tie, with perhaps a pearl-handled razor just visible in his inside pocket. With only a little more imaginative effort I could picture him getting slowly to his feet and then breaking into a soft shoe shuffle while miming expertly to Al Bowlly *à la* Dennis Potter. With Sidney, Morrie, Tommy and Stan appearing on banjo, washboard, triangle and ukelele in the background.

Then, as suddenly as it had started, the roaring, darkness and flashing lights cut out. The train, now unnaturally smooth and quiet, was out of the tunnel and pattering on across a valley of houses and fields. We excused ourselves to Bolger, who said nothing, and quickly regained the tranquil silence of our own compartment a few doors down. Moynahan's seat was empty. His papers, annuals and Timeform guides had all been neatly packed away back into his briefcase. We each took a stiff drink of gin, sank back into our own seats and shut our eyes. I was just beginning to dream of sharing a nightmare day at the races with Jack Spot, Prince Monolulu and the Brighton Trunk Murderer when the compartment door opened and shut noisily and we both opened our eyes with a jolt.

'Drunk already?' enquired Moynahan, returning briskly to his seat and cracking open one of the lager cans.

'Not at all,' replied Kincaid loudly.

'Not at all,' I echoed. 'I was just thinking . . .'

'Did you know . . .' began the form book specialist, brushing some cigarette ash off the trousers of his lightweight suit, '. . . that in the 1947 flat-racing season Towser Gosden had a strike rate of nearly 40 per cent at the Sussex tracks. That included a dozen individual winners at Brighton and only one of them was odds-on. He always knew precisely how good his horses were and when they were ready to move up in class. The bookmakers were always one step behind him.'

'Fascinating.'

'Fascinating.' Which it was. But the other fascinating thing about a run down to Brighton is that as well as bringing back memories of some of the great old respectable names of Turf history it also brings on thoughts of one of the darker and less palatable periods in racing and bookmaking's past, when low-life characters walked tall around Brighton racecourse and not always in the shadows, an era vividly evoked in *Brighton Rock*, the best and most famous of all novels about the town and particularly by its unforgettable opening line: 'Hale knew, before he had been in Brighton three hours, that they meant to murder him.' Of course Graham Greene's story isn't solely about the race gangs, but images of gangsterism (and in particular of pre-war betting-oriented protection rackets) form a constant backdrop to the riveting saga of the teenage hoodlum, Pinkie Brown, and of his gradual descent into hell.

Greene didn't invent this seemingly melodramatic background. At the end of the First World War a number of top London villains relocated their rackets on the south coast, especially in Brighton. Rich pickings were to be had there from running night clubs, amusement arcades and dance halls and, in those far-off days long before legalised off-course cash gambling, from extorting protection money from both the illicit street bookies and the legitimate on-course layers.

Even after the rumble on Lewes racecourse in 1936, the subsequent trials and draconian prison sentences, a detectable sense of danger, now embodied in the national folklore, continued to cling to the places where bookies and punters gathered to do business. And that element of danger and risk, along with its natural accomplice, the indulgent spend-now-pay-later mentality, which Brighton has traditionally catered to for more than a century, continues to play a seductive and by no means negligible part in persuading people to go to a racetrack and gamble on horses. It is also connected with that intoxicating but usually harmless boost to the virility that comes from being a winner, a bragging, self-affirmative statement, particularly attractive to men, that says, 'Look at me. I'm Jack the Lad with cash to burn. I'll have three monkeys on the 5–1 shot, bubbly all round and a new suit, a suite at the Grand and a new and fabulously glamorous lover before tea.' Not the least entertaining aspect of a jaunt up onto the Downs is that, even after the passage of more than forty cleaned-up years including thirty of legitimate off-course gambling, some real sense of spivvery and guile, if not of physical danger, still remains.

'Hale knew, before he had been in Brighton three hours, that they meant to murder him.' As our taxi swung out of the station forecourt and pulled away down Queens Road we glanced back over our shoulders at the Victorian station façade. But unlike those superbly atmospheric opening scenes in the 1948 black-and-white film version of *Brighton Rock* we could see no chipper William Hartnell spying watchfully from beneath the clock. Neither was there any sign of his fellow actor, Nigel Stock, lounging indolently in a pub doorway or about to jump on one of the special buses up to the course. At that point we felt that our lives were in greater danger from the weather than from a razor blade or a cosh.

Greene's Brighton raceweek opened against a background of sun-drenched blue-sky summer with short brown grass, dust dry chalk on the Downs and old yellowing Tote tickets lying abandoned in the sun amid the plantains of the south coast bungalow gardens. This June morning there was no sun and no blue sky, only horrendous fog-like cloud and exhausting humidity. I had asked the cab driver not to take the usual shortcut up to the track but to follow Hale's route down to the front. As we trickled along slowly in the traffic, past 'Sergeant Yorke's Casino', the offices of 'Casa Sorrento: Apartments To Let' and past all the little chip fryers, pubs and cafés between the station and the clock tower, drops of warm rain started to spit down from the grey sky. Even with the cab windows open we all felt as if someone was wrapping a hot thick towel very tightly around our heads.

Greene described a band playing on the pavement by the Old Steyne and 'a negro wearing a bright striped tie', sitting on a bench in the Pavilion garden smoking a cigar. We saw only a pair of gaunt-looking charity collectors standing either side of a large billboard proclaiming grim details of AIDS deaths worldwide accompanied with a warning to Brighton's epidemic population of hard drug-users never to inject with a dirty needle and never to share a fellow addict's syringe.

It is a steep climb from the Pavilion up through Kemptown past the cheerless American Express headquarters and on to the racecourse above Whitehawk Bottom. No overcrowded trams surged up the hill in our wake, no Packards or Morrises or little scarlet racing models with brasses perched fetchingly on the driver's knee. At the top of Freshfield Road we paid off the monosyllabic cab driver and as the hot showers continued to drip down from the grey-green sky, Moynahan flashed his metal press badge, Kincaid and I bought the usual Members' Enclosure passes and then we all ducked in through the panelled doorway that leads on to the course. 'In the first race the runners are as on your racecard,' declaimed a blocked-nosed loudspeaker announcement in the background. We were on home territory once again.

The back of the main stand at Brighton, which was erected in 1965, looks like a hideous grey pebble-dash and breeze-block National Car Park blot on the landscape, the kind of thing that would drive The Prince of Wales to talk to a whole flowerbed of geraniums. It's not much better on the inside. Amazingly, the firm that designed and built it, Sir Alfred McAlpine Ltd, are shameless enough to allow their identity to be displayed for all the race-going world to see via a plaque commemorating their 'achievements' in the foyer leading to the Tote betting hall on the ground floor.

If the view from the back of the stand is bleak then the view from the front, from the terracing and Members' Lawn, is of an apparently absurd and implausible racecourse where you would think that any chance of consistently turning up a profit ought to be 100 – 1 at least. Brighton is constructed on the Epsom principle, which roughly translates into 'Let's all scramble around the rim of the Downs and the first one to reach the winning post without falling over is the winner.' The track is a dead ringer for Epsom and once upon a more adventurous time they ran an influential Derby trial there each May. Not any more: these days the municipally owned course, with its sliding turns and perilous descent – a jockey was killed there in a fall in 1981 – is firmly in the fourth division of the quality league. But, for all that, its regular summertime cards of selling races, claiming races and low-grade handicaps, few of them offering much in the way of prize money and most attracting the poorest level of competition, provide splendidly entertaining opportunities for jobs, touches and general raffish no-goodery. The biggest problem is trying to guess which of the supposed batch of non-triers in the two-year-old race or the six-furlong three-year-old handicap are really 'not off' and which one has been prepared by his crafty trainer to hoodwink the rest. If it is already something of a challenge for the mug punter to make money, if they insist on backing horses who may or may not be trying and who are in any case racing around a switchback circuit it's harder still to distinguish the lean from the overwrought, and the seriously committed from those carrying an off-games note, when the racetrack is partly shrouded, as it still was this early Monday afternoon, in a shifting blanket of sea mist and fog.

While Moynahan went off to get the latest information from the weighing room, which he insisted would be of a different calibre from the whispered champagne-bar advices now being canvassed by A. J. Kincaid, I climbed right up to the top of the terracing beneath the roof of the stand. It was 1.50 p.m. on a June Monday and the lights were all on in the Palace Pier. Even so I could only make out the Channel as a block of flat, wet, clammy-looking greyness with no clearly delineated horizon. I could just see a red-and-cream double-decker bus trailing through the murk down the road from Rottingdean away beyond the mile-and-a-quarter start.

Closer to hand the mist had cleared briefly to reveal the blocks of mini high-rise flats and the little rows of post-war housing beneath the edge of the Downs and the rows of caravans parked along the infield rail. But the colour of the turf between the seven- and the two-furlong marker was a mystery.

Not that everything was quiet on the gambling front. Far from it. Down in the ring the scattering of on-course bookies appeared to be doing some lively business as the runners cantered down before the first. Which you could say underlines the point that most punters are even more dumb than they look and will still go on betting even when they can make out little more than the ears and tails of the objects of their speculation. Thoughtful gamblers, even if they have already placed their bets ante-post or by phone, will invariably want to study their selection in the paddock before a race. There are certain tell-tale signs to look out for, well known to the habitual race-goer. Everybody wants to back a calm, relaxed and unflustered horse who is not so completely asleep that he seems unprepared for the challenge ahead but who is not playing up unduly or fretting and sweating his chance away before the start. If it's a particularly chilly afternoon in mid-April a three-year-old thoroughbred filly may not yet have come into her summer coat and may not quite be ready to do herself justice. Conversely if the race is taking place in late October, the same filly may have already 'gone' in her coat or grown her woolly, winter covering, a sign that she might be over the top for the season. You don't have to have been racing very often to be able to spot these differences, or to be able to distinguish between a sleek and rippling athlete ready to race and a skinny little ferret with its ribs peeping through or a lumbering and overweight plodder. But the one thing you absolutely have to have if you are going to make a proper assessment is a close-up view of the horses. Betting blind at a fourth-rate venue like Brighton is not a guaranteed way to make money.

But part of the crack about a day down at Brighton, and there is plenty of crack to be had for all the concrete and pebble-dash and sea-fret gloom, is the crowd, the company, the players. Brighton racecourse, like Epsom, is still as it always has been (and here an atmospheric connection with Greene's era if not with the razor blades still persists), a home from home for the Good Fellas of the betting and racing community – for Cheltenham Tony, for Barry and Tel, for double-glazing barons and kings of the motor trade, for South London and South Coast Del Boys and Trevs, who just might, no disrespect, be not entirely on the up. Even the equine participants seem to reflect some of the characteristics of the onlookers in the stand and in the ring: fly, wide, rough, hard, perhaps not entirely to be trusted. Their names, too, are usually more suggestive of Catford or Hackney dog stadium than of Ascot Heath: on this very programme we would be watching such blue-blooded athletes as Sharlie's Wimpy, Calvanne Miss, Hightown Executive and Chin the Ref.

'Willie'll win this,' opined one tasty-looking punter about the first race, his grazed knuckles and broken nose suggesting that he might have done a bit of ref-chinning himself in his time – possibly quite recently.

'Trevor says he nailed on,' agreed a friend, as he chomped his way stoically through a dry-looking white-bread sandwich.

Willie, Carson naturally, may not always feel flattered to be so heavily identified with by the ordinary non-Timeform punters but they are his most devoted admirers and they make up the majority of race-goers at every Brighton meeting. They perceive Carson, not entirely accurately, to be their kind of jockey. A hard-riding unpretentious 'little man'. A cheeky Scots chappie who may be one of the highest-paid riders in the world but still gives his all every time. And who probably reads the same paper they do. 'Go on, Willie. Go on, my son.'

As it was, Willie didn't win the first, a five-furlong two-year-old dash worth two grand to the winner. He was on a striking-looking chestnut débutante, saddled by the Newmarket-based Cockney-Australian trainer, Mick Ryan, who resembles a cross between Rupert Murdoch and Bill Sykes. This popular combination, sent off the 11–4 second favourite by the crowd, were turned over by a skinny little wired-up beast from the Epsom stables of the crafty seventy-two-year-old handler, Ron Smyth. Tasty, the ref-chinner, was not at all pleased and even removed his unflattering short-sleeved shirt in disgust.

'Trevor,' he bellowed to his mate down below, 'you abomination.' Trevor, who had been attempting to lurk interestingly by the winning post, turned round with a start. When he saw Tasty he broke into a sheepish grin. Tasty waved a muscular arm back again, his naked and pungent armpits taking no prisoners among those punters unfortunate enough to be standing nearest to him.

Remembering Moynahan's wise advice about the favourite I had decided to pass on the first race altogether. Kincaid, the true gambler, had also passed on the favourite and placed instead a couple of expensive forecast bets on two of the other runners, who unfortunately finished third and fourth. Sidling down along the rails afterwards in our swanky dark glasses, a rather pointless accessory in the prevailing hot cloud, Kincaid and I tried to take a leaf out of Trevor's book by lounging nonchalantly next to the Victor Chandler pitch. What, I wondered, did the other punters make of us? Did we look like big-time faces? Did we have sufficient cool? I didn't like to ask Kincaid how much he'd just lost but he certainly looked the part of a high-roller especially as he chose this moment to light up an enormous Monte Cristo cigar. So is effrontery all? Were the bookies taken in? And if the bluff is big enough will you always be treated as a four-figure winner even if you are nothing of the sort?

The second race and the next challenge to our own and John Moynahan's judgement was a mile-and-a-quarter maiden event for three-year-olds and up. Now, the gospel according to the professional gambler is that, if you want to win at racing, you must know not only when to bet but also when not to bet. As this maiden race was such a mediocre contest and as the bookmakers were offering only very cramped prices about the two possible winners, our form and value expert insisted that we should not bet on this competition at all. Tasty and Trevor were altogether bolder. They were convinced that Willie would definitely be their man this time and they and their brothers in the ring plied his mount with enough handfuls of cash to send it off as the 6–5 favourite in a field of ten with only one serious rival to beat. And in beating it our Willie applied to his mount some of his own distinctive brand of physical assistance, especially when the rival refused to give in with a furlong to run. 'Go on, Willie. Give it some,' roared the lads in the stands and little Willie most certainly did give it some, seeming to turn round in the saddle and select his spot before applying half-a-dozen four-square whip-cracking smacks to the three-year-old's velveteen quarters. 'He runs for the whip,' Moynahan sagely informed us afterwards, whereas it may have been equally true that the horse ran as gamely as it did to get away from the wretched thing and from the midget sadist perched on its back. But whatever the horse's pain barrier he stayed on to such effect that he managed to get his nose over the line a split second ahead of his rival. The cheering broke out, the hugging and thumping took over and fresh drinks were ordered in the cheap

BRIGHTON ROCK

seats for an on-course gamble triumphantly brought off. Kincaid
was cheering. He had backed the winner so at least he had something to celebrate, even though there was not a lot of profit to come
as he'd also gone in hard with another losing forecast bet.
Moynahan and myself, J. P. McManus's little known second and
third cousins twice removed, had nothing to come. We were both
much too smart to bet on anything.

Next on the card was a seven-furlong seller, but Moynahan,
now flushed with non-playing superiority, like someone who takes
you out to lunch and orders two salads after watching you choose
lobster, filet béarnaise and crème brûlée, was adamant that we
should pass on this too. 'How can you expect to make a profit
backing fourth-rate horses in a selling race in semi-fog at Brighton?'
he reasoned, making something of a mockery of his supposed
preference for egg-and-spoon races at the gaff tracks. 'Follow the
money,' would be the traditional small-time punter's response but
we were supposed to be above such clichéd truisms. Let the
common folk believe it if they wished, but we were no suckers. Of
course, we were no winners either because the money very much
followed the eventual victor, MCA Below The Line (owned,
according to the racecard, by an all-class outfit by the name of Mike
Clyne Associates) who was backed in from 6s to 3–1 and who
pissed up by three lengths with Chin The Ref trailing in sixth,
leaving Moynahan still triumphantly and uncommonly smug,
even with no apparent reason, and leaving Kincaid and me, three
races down, no richer and beginning to feel like peabrains and
prunes. This was not the sort of afternoon we had bargained for.

A modest portion of the crowd, some backers of the winner,
some losers, some disinterested parties like ourselves, trooped
around the corner to watch the subsequent auction in the unsaddling enclosure. The auctioneer, a suave rather foxy-looking type
in senior-partner country-solicitor gear, opened the proceedings
on an inadvisably smug note. 'Fifteen hundred guineas, ladies and
gentlemen. Fifteen hundred guineas for this decent-looking prospective sprint handicapper. Already a winner. Fifteen hundred
guineas. At fifteen hundred guineas, ladies and gentlemen. Who's
coming in with me at fifteen hundred guineas?' Pause. Silence.
'Who's coming in? Are you all coming in? Who's coming in? Who's
coming in with me to have a chance of this attractive south coast
specialist. At fifteen hundred guineas, ladies and gentlemen. At
fifteen hundred. Who's coming in?' Pause. Silence. 'Who's coming

in with me at fifteen hundred guineas? Well?' Pause. Silence. No one was coming in by the look of it. Not a single solitary professional or amateur, regular or casual, trainer's or knacker's arm was raised in response. Perhaps some prospective bidders were puzzled by the auctioneer's rather arch manner and phraseology. 'Who's coming in with *me*?' Did that mean that he had already bought two legs and the tail himself and would be at least a joint partner in the venture? A matey chum to share the training bills with and someone who could be relied upon to buy the champagne next time out? Anyone would have thought that he'd already arranged for the gelding (yes, it was only a gelding and a pretty manky-looking one at that) to be transferred from Hambleton trainer Bill Pearce to Luca Cumani or Michael Stoute. Perhaps he had only just had Lester on the phone or had booked Pat Eddery for the Stewards Cup. Perhaps . . . but not very likely and the crowd, not so unsophisticated for once, weren't having any of it. They may not all have been bloodstock agents but they could definitely tell the difference between Mill Reef and this slice of potential hamburger meat. 'Who's coming in?' continued the auctioneer. 'Who's coming in with me at fifteen hundred guineas? Who's coming in?' Pause. Silence. 'Is there anyone coming in? Is there any bid at all?' People started to turn their heads away in embarrassment, to stare intently at their shoes or at their racecards or at the runners' and riders' board for the next. But the auctioneer's humiliation was not yet complete. 'Well . . . *is* there any bid?' He ploughed on, trying to make us feel suitably ashamed as if in our craven lack of enterprise we had personally let him down. 'Any bid?' He turned to a plump and blushingly red-faced official standing nearby. 'Why won't they bid?' The official grinned at him stupidly. 'We won't bid my cocker,' explained a *basso profondo* Millwall voice from the front of the crowd, 'because the race was a piece of piss, the horse is probably a dog and you are definitely a plonker.' Cruel, ribald laughter ran around the edges of the ring. The auctioneer blanched and a pained expression crossed his face as if he had just sat on the wrong end of a shooting stick. *His* gamble had come entirely unstuck.

Craning our necks with the rest to try to discover the identity of the speaker we discovered him to be none other than Tasty the refchinner who had assumed an authoritative pose by the rail with Trevor and the sandwich eater on either side. Tasty's intervention brought the 'sale' to an inglorious end. The auctioneer's mumbled finale of, 'Unsold,' was barely heard over the continuing laughter. His brief moment of authority, his temporary command of the stage had been blown away and as the horse was led out Moynahan, Kincaid and myself, in common with assorted other sniggering and mainly proletarian onlookers, turned our backs on the scene and headed once more for the ring.

The fourth race, a mile-and-a-half handicap and the most valuable event on the card, finally presented us with the kind of opening we'd been looking for, a modest opportunity for value betting. Our selection was a three-times Brighton-course winner who had been comprehensively beaten last time out on soft ground at Epsom, but who was now back running over his favoured fast surface and who would have William Hunter Carson's assistance in the saddle. He had been allotted the welter burden, as the form scribes like to call it, of ten stone, four pounds more than any winning weight he had ever carried before. But this was only a three-horse race and we reckoned that he only had one other horse to beat, a light and hard-trained-looking three-year-old, who on his previous outing had won a more valuable Newbury handicap, heavily gambled on, by four lengths. The three-year-old was expected to start favourite but with not a lot to choose between the pair. Moynahan estimated that evens would not be an unattractive price about ours and that even a single percentage point better than that would be value all the way.

Kincaid and I duly got on at 11–10 on the rails and then saw office money push the price right through evens to 10–11 (11–10 on) at which point there was still some demand. And who on earth at that daft but exhilarating moment of triumph could possibly have preferred to bet with a Tote monopoly where you don't know the exact odds of your runner until after the race and where you cannot shop around for a price?

The race, though brimming with tension for those of us with an interest, was about as nailbiting as an average edition of *A Question of Sport*. The three-year-old, who was sweating in front of as well as behind the saddle, went straight to the head of things with Willie tucked in on the rails a few lengths behind him and the outsider or 'rag' three lengths in arrears. And that's the way they stayed for the first two thirds of the contest. Three minute, semi-luminous shapes, blurs in the still not completely cleared mist, edging along the rails beside the ice-cream vans, school buses and semi-detached houses beneath what might as well have been the edge of

173

the world. Then, just below the distance, which means with just over a furlong to run, Carson drew alongside the long-time leader.

'No danger, Willie. No danger,' yelled a heavyweight professional punter in front of us.

'Yeah. No danger, Willie. You little Scots git,' enjoined an uncomplimentary associate. They were both right, though. With less than half a furlong still to go the 'little Scots git' just shook the reins up and down a few times and without the slightest recourse to the whip stylishly and cleverly nudged his mount over the line by what looked like a margin of three-quarters of a length (but which the judge, who must have been prematurely celebrating his own winning bet, instantly declared to be a clear two lengths).

We cheered. Commonly, vulgarly and not all like suave, unemotional high-rollers. In fact it would be no exaggeration to say that we cheered our heads off. 'Go on, Willie. Go on, my son. Go on, my beauty.' Then with one quick, grateful look up at the heavens above, illuminated by sunshine for the first time all day, we bounded back down the concrete terracing, collecting Moynahan on the way who informed us very smugly that he had 'invested at twos' and then raced over the tarmac and grass and swung in through the doors of the Winning Post bar. We'd had enough of Moynahan's rules and self-discipline and were emphatic that this occasion should be devoted to the observance of a slightly different, less ascetic rule. The maxim of the rarely winning, usually imprudent but determinedly high-spirited punter: 'Don't ever pay the bank manager until you've slaked your thirst.'

CHAPTER THIRTEEN

Two Time Losers

Brighton's Winning Post bar, which is a drinking joint on the ground floor of the Members' Enclosure and is indeed opposite the finishing line, looks from the outside like a sort of 1930s to 1950s grey pebble-dash suburban bay window.

But, no matter how drearily unimposing the exterior may be or how grey the day or how frustrating your betting and gaming experiences, the atmosphere inside the Winning Post is always an immediate lift to the spirits. This is because one of the great joys about a track like Brighton is that, in keeping with the prevailing theme, the punters, drinkers and race-goers you meet in the Members' are exactly the sort of low-life diamonds who would be steered in the direction of Tatts or even the Silver Ring at Ascot. And the gentlemen among them, be they young or old, in the construction business or the motor trade, gold bullion or a VAT racket, invariably find it essential to attend the races in the company of notably vampish female companions, who tend to wink, smile and look knowingly at you while leaving slightly more lipstick than might seem necessary around the rims of their champagne glasses.

Suitably reinvigorated, not to mention rapidly overheated, by a combination of these heady surroundings and several large gins we settled down gratefully at a table in the window. We were just about to pool our ideas about the next when our attention was abruptly snatched away from our racing papers and pages of form by a large, heavily jewelled hand slamming down on Kincaid's back. The hand was connected to a dark-blue designer suit, a smart silk tie and a smiling, shaggy but well-coiffured head. It was our very own Terry Ramsden *manqué*. Cheltenham Tony.

'You dog. You crafty dog.'

'Tony,' laughed Kincaid, cheerfully enough.

'Tony.' We laughed too, somewhat insincerely in Moynahan's case. Tony pulled a chair up to the table.

'Coming down to Brighton on the sly. Doing a little runner with the rent money. And you don't even think to count me in. Shame on you. Shame on you.' He was grinning hugely, one arm still clasped around Kincaid's shoulder. In his other hand he was holding a glass of champagne.

'I thought you were still away in Spain, to be honest,' said Kincaid.

'In Spain? Me? Mañuel Santana at a time like this?' He took a drink from his glass. 'Actually, I got back last Friday. Just in time to brush up the old top hat. I'd never stop in Spain during Royal Ascot week, Alexander. You know that. And what better way to start the ball rolling than with a little casual relaxation at my favourite track?'

'This is your favourite track, is it, Tony?' asked Moynahan innocently.

'Well, one of my favourites. My dad used to work here once upon a time. Jockeys' valet. Back in the fifties. Lester. Scobie. Harry Carr. He knew them all. Get us some more glasses, will you, Maurice.' Maurice, an older, bespectacled and curly-haired associate who'd been hovering at Tony's elbow and who must have been boiling in his grey overcoat with the black velvet collar, departed to the bar as ordered. He returned with three extra champagne flutes and an ice-bucket containing a bottle of chilled something or other. Tony poured us all a glass and then replaced the bottle in the ice bucket which Maurice had put down on the table between himself and Kincaid.

'Here's to it, gentlemen. Happy days and all that bollocks.'

'Here's to it,' we responded.

'Any particular fancies then, Tony?'

'Fancies? Round this place? You must be joking. Got a few lined up for tomorrow, though. And the next day. And the day after that. And just you wait until Friday.' He leaned forward conspiratorially across the table. 'And that's not an Ascot job at all. Which is something I need to talk to you about, A. J.'

'Ah. Well, I'm not too sure about that.' Was there just a faintly detectable note of alarm in his voice? 'I don't think I'll be all that much involved this week. It's been a bit of a bad time for me lately.'

'Well, we both know the truth about that one, don't we?' Tony winked at Kincaid and then turned to share the joke with the rest of us. 'Haven't I still got little bits of paper from Cheltenham, Liverpool and Newmarket? Markers I believe they call them. IOUs. Burning little holes in my suit pockets. But does the boy call me?' He was talking to Maurice now. 'Does he ring? Does he invite me for a day out at the races?'

'You know what it's like when you hit a bad run.'

'Of course I know. But do you think I only want to talk to you about debts? Who do you think I am? The bleeding bank manager?'

'He's very careless with his friends,' said Moynahan.

'No, he's not,' said Tony giving A. J.'s arm another squeeze. 'He's just a bold and irrepressible punter, that's all. And he could be a lucky one too. If he plays his cards right Friday.'

'What's so special about Friday?' I asked him. Tony put a finger to his lips. Then he brought out his silver fountain pen, tore a piece of paper off the top of the *Sporting Life*, wrote something on it and pushed the piece of paper over to Moynahan and myself. It said just one word. *Redcar*. We looked at Tony again but he still had his finger up to his mouth. Then he took back the piece of paper, screwed it up and threw it away. 'Now then, gents,' he said breezily. 'Any way I can assist you this sporting afternoon? Tennis? Cricket? The away meeting? What's your pleasure? What's your choice? All sums considered. Large or small. Cash . . . or credit.' Here he was, brazenly offering to lay us bets even in such a conspicuously public place. He had dropped his voice down marginally but it was only a small concession.

'What do you know about the fifth race at Yarmouth?' asked Kincaid, exhaling a fresh cloud of cigar smoke.

'They say that the Julie Cecil thing has been working very well.' Tony took a quick look over his shoulder and then dropped his voice a few semi-tones. 'They say . . . that she could be a Group Three horse in a month or two's time.'

'I heard that,' said Kincaid.

'She's also got a temperament problem,' said Moynahan. 'She doesn't like passing other animals. Something of a problem for a racehorse.'

'Temperament problem,' scoffed Tony. 'She could be a paranoid schizophrenic and still beat that lot. It's only a maiden, after all. And because Mrs Cecil is not yet as fashionable a trainer as her former husband we ought to get a decent price. 7–2. 4s even. What do you want on, A. J.?'

'Well, I'd like to back it to win, me . . . I'm not sure . . .'

'Think of a number.'

'A couple of grand?'

'I tell you what I'll do. I'll put you down for a monkey at 4s.' He wrote the bet down in his racecard. 'How does that sound?'

'Let's do it.'

'Now that's more like it. Maurice? Get us another bottle.' Maurice scuttled back up to the bar. 'Well then, everybody. What do we all think about the next?'

'I think the favourite's nailed on,' said Kincaid.

'The favourite looks hot,' agreed Tony.

'I'd want to see him going down first,' said Moynahan. 'He looked pretty hard trained at Goodwood.'

'I've already got a nice little forecast bet with Victor,' declared Tony, presumably making a chummy reference to Victor Chandler. 'I always get the better of him with my little forecasts.'

'I'm going off to watch them going down,' announced Moynahan, getting impatiently to his feet.

'Yes, indeed,' said Kincaid. 'The battleground beckons once again.'

'Shall we meet back here then after the next?' suggested Tony affably.

'After the next,' agreed Kincaid.

'Or after the last,' added Moynahan in character. Maurice was left to leave the new champagne bottle in the care of the barmaid who wrote Tony's name on it and placed it in its own ice-bucket on the counter behind the bar. Socialising was over for the moment and once again the real, serious business of horse-racing was at hand.

Kincaid's first priority was to get some more money on the Julie Cecil thing in the fifth at Yarmouth but he didn't want to incur any further liabilities with Tony. We found out from John Henwood's man on the rails that the filly had opened up at twos – proving that one or two other faces had been privy to Tony's information – but had then drifted out to 11–4. In spite of this apparent easiness in the market we decided to take that price and also to couple her with the favourite and top weight in the next, another second-rate handicap, at Brighton. We then dodged, slipped and elbowed our way back up through the crowd and pushed open the heavy glass doors of the concrete and pebbledash Tote Betting Hall wherein we knew we would be able to watch the Yarmouth race live on satellite TV.

Around twenty or thirty other desultory-looking punters, watery-eyed losers you'd have said at a glance, were standing around staring at the SIS screen. As usual some racecourse official had turned the sound down too low and although the caption said 'Yarmouth 4.0' the pictures could just as easily have been coming from Bangor or Downpatrick or Steerebeck or countless other venues that most punters have heard mentioned hundreds of times in their local betting offices but have never been anywhere near. We recognised the gorse and broom along the golf course in-field and more importantly we could see stall number ten, our stall and when the stalls crashed open we could see Willie Ryan coming out of it wearing Sheikh Mohammed's second colours.

Ryan noticeably tried to steady his filly early on and to settle her towards the rear of the field. Steve Cauthen riding one for John Gosden and wearing the Sheikh Mohammed first colours made the running followed by Muis Roberts, Bryn Crossley and Frankie Dettori. Everything was going smoothly, it seemed. As they took the first bend the Julie Cecil filly was travelling comfortably on the bridle and Ryan looked as if he would have no trouble getting a run when he was ready to make his move. Then all of a sudden, with just over three-and-a-half furlongs of this eight furlong race still to cover, something awful happened. Ryan's mount stumbled – so badly that she was nearly on her knees. There was no evidence that she didn't want to pass other horses as Moynahan had predicted. The accident probably came about for no other reason than that she momentarily lost her footing on the fast green grass.

It was at this juncture precisely that the full volume returned on the commentary. 'Stumbled number six. Princess Farida,' announced the commentator loudly and enthusiastically. And that was just about it, at least as far as we were concerned. Steve Cauthen stayed in the lead all the way to the line. Muis, Bryn and Frankie followed him home at a respectable distance and Ryan, well, Willie, ever the considerate horseman naturally, eased his filly right down, allowed her to regain her balance in her own time and just coasted in quietly at the rear of the field. In tenth place actually. Tenth out of fourteen. Which was quite something considering the stumble but scarcely any consolation when you've just dropped your entire roll. We looked across at the other TV screen just in time to see Richard Quinn triumphantly booting home the top weight and favourite in the handicap at Brighton. So why, oh why, hadn't we just backed that horse? Why hadn't we stuck with the action where we were actually racing? Instead of being clever – clever inside faces and posting our money three hundred miles away to the edges of the North Sea, investing it, what's more, on a fourteen-runner eight-furlong maiden race for three-year-old fillies which, as any experienced horse player will tell you, is just about the riskiest betting medium in which you can speculate. Of course, the reason for our folly was that we were both total, unreconstructed mugs, losers and nerds. But were we going to leave it at that? Were we going to be puny and take our defeat lying down? Well, we weren't quite sure.

At first the omens for any further successes didn't seem encouraging. Beginning to feel decidedly hungry we toyed briefly with the idea of finding some kind of high-fat cholesterol-rich snack that we could stuff into our systems to boost our blood-sugar levels and assuage the rather hollow, sickly feeling in our stomachs, understandable after our loss but hardly conducive, we felt, to a rewarding form book study of the last. Turning into the euphemistically entitled 'Teas, Coffees and Light Refreshments Bar' at the far end of the Tote Hall we saw the usual unappetising row of doughnuts, sausage rolls and jam turnovers sitting under a glass cover on top of the counter. But displayed next to them, inhabiting and infecting the same airspace, was such a grotesque and stomach-heaving sight that even our normal buccaneering indifference to racecourse junk had to be reconsidered on the spot. Two four-ounce pieces of sick-looking red meat were sitting on a plate in their own blood up at one corner of the shelf display next door to the jam doughnuts. 'Try one of our delicious steak-in-a-bap sandwiches. Only £5.95', trilled a green-and-white caterer's pronouncement in the background. Only £5.95? They looked as if they should have come with an on-the-spot enrolment-form for a lavish private-health insurance scheme plus a prominent damages lawyer's daytime telephone number. The 'steaks' looked ill and we felt ill looking at them. How long had they been there? There was plenty of gore on the plate and we were coming up to the 4.30 p.m. race. Suppose there had been no takers for the entire afternoon and these two pieces of suppurating mad cow had been sitting out here in the stale Tea Bar air since at least 1 p.m.?

Two men in stained white coats were clearing up empty boxes

and dirty glasses behind the, no doubt, entirely blameless and innocent cashier who was perched up high on a stool by the coffee machine. They looked like a cross between dustmen and abattoir attendants. Perhaps they'd delivered the meat for the baps straight from the slaughterhouse that morning? Perhaps they were waiting to cart away the dead meat punters from the betting ring – like ourselves, dare one say it? – after the last? We both felt faint. Our appetites dwindled in a second. Who needed food now, anyway? What we really wanted was a strong alcoholic pick-me-up. But we couldn't face the Winning Post again. Not yet. The atmosphere there would have been inappropriately effervescent. At Cheltenham there had been no alternative to staying within the smog-like fumes of the hamburger van to get a drink. But here there *was* an alternative. We turned our heads and, without looking back, walked smartly away out of the 'Teas, Coffees and Light Refreshments Bar' and strode quickly up to the other end of the Tote Betting Hall. To the NARBOL (National Association of Racecourse Betting Office Licensees) cash-betting office with bar adjacent which was situated underneath and to the rear end of the cheap enclosure seating in Tatts.

The NARBOL 'Bet Here' windows were doing a brisk trade on the dogs meeting at Bristol, pictures of which were freely available thanks to the eternally active TV screens of SIS. Groups of muscle-bound, crop-haired punters in Tasty the ref-chinner short-sleeved leisure-wear shirts were piling high the cans and choking out the fag ash on to the Formica-top tables and the linoleum floor. If Pinkie Brown or the Hoxton Mob were to return to Brighton in 1992 then this is surely the part of the racecourse that they would choose for their razor fights.

We downed a couple of large Scotches standing up at the bar next door to the jellied eels, whelks and mussels stall where non-Members'-Enclosure-sized portions of prawn and crab were also available in little pale-blue tubs with plastic forks. But for all the imitation tridents and fish-net décor trawled across the back wall these watery-looking offerings did not excite, perhaps because the pervasive smell – the surrounding beer, cigarette and sweat fumes notwithstanding – was reminiscent less of the English Channel than of the public conveniences situated along the front.

'What we need,' declared Kincaid gravely as he started to leaf through the pages of his red plastic-bound Raceform Notebook, 'is a nice third or fourth favourite at 6–1 or up. It can't always be the market leader.' Now it has to be said that you wouldn't have thought it would be hard for the favourite to win this concluding six-furlong handicap, given that the level of competition was not high and – appropriately enough as the cries of 'Go On You One Dog' echoed in our ears from the crowd gathered around the TV sets on our left – that the names of most of the contestants could once again have walked out of the kennels at Hackney: Sharlie's Wimpy, Calvanne Miss, Grown at Rowan, Cut Up Rough. The jockeys were an altogether more pedigree bunch and included for the fourth and final time this Monday afternoon the resplendent Willie, who was teamed up with the most likely market choice. But did we want a favourite? Did we want a market choice even at a surprisingly generous 7–2? What about something like Calvanne Miss? 'Go on, Calvanne. Go on, you Whiskas Supermeat.' A nice safe each-way bet at 5– or 6–1. That's what we wanted. Or was it? 'Give up, son,' croaked a cheery old voice, his remark directed at A. J. Kincaid and his Raceform. 'If they really knew the winners do you think they'd still be writing that book every week?' This little gem of wisdom came from a friendly old cove in flat cap and glasses who looked as if he had been sitting at the same Formica-top table since they opened up the stand. Kincaid was just about to enter into some merry badinage when the bronchitic old-timer spoilt it all somewhat by adding, unnecessarily one felt, this telling observation. 'Once a loser, always a loser. Eh? Once a loser . . .'

'Yes, yes, yes,' responded Kincaid tetchily. 'Thanks very much. Tell everyone, won't you? I mean, feel free.' In an effort to try to salvage some dignity and the necessary ice-cool nerve of a face we decided to leave this low-grade bar forthwith and head for the ring.

'Calvanne Miss. Calvanne Miss,' Kincaid kept repeating as we stopped off in the gents. 'Calvanne Miss. A good sensible each-way bet. They'll never keep her out of the frame. Stands to reason. Calvanne Miss. Tyrone Williams. A good jockey. Well . . . a jockey. What the hell's that?' Something wet and unpleasant had just started dripping down on to our heads. Looking up indignantly we discovered that we were standing directly underneath a large white Twyfords Civic Lavatory cistern which looked as if it was about to leak some more globules of insanitary liquid onto our hair at any moment. 'No, thank you very much,' said Kincaid, ducking swiftly out of the way and, in the manner of the final afternoon of the Cheltenham Festival, nearly pissing on his foot in the process. 'This won't do at all. We must think positive. We must think self-belief. I think I am a winner . . . therefore I *am* a winner.' He sounded as if he almost believed it. 'We must go outside now and incisively, yes, that's the word, incisively, carry off this last.'

As so often happens, there seemed to be more activity in the ring before this final event than there had been for any of the previous five. Regan, Binns, Gibbs, Mendoza, Louis Levy, Sam Harris and Dave Saphir. All they had to do was make an orderly queue as a bobbing tide of mugs, serious mugs and mugs like ourselves, who at least hoped that they were faces streamed up and down between the rows of pitches, in among the chalk and the outstretched arms, the abandoned betting tickets and discarded tissues from the earlier events.

After making a quick tour of the rails and sounding out the views of one or two 'sources' and 'informants' who were working for the books, the newly incisive Kincaid returned in an agitated state.

'Nobody fancies this Calvanne thing at all,' he reported. 'And you know the fate of all good each-way bets?'

'They finish fourth,' answered John Moynahan, who had appeared suddenly at Kincaid's elbow.

'Exactly. And that way you do your money twice. We should be putting it on the nose. On the favourite. Carson's mount. Down there they're saying it can't lose.'

'You'd have to be worried about this Welsh thing, though,' said Moynahan. Kincaid and I both looked down at our racecards. Welsh thing? What Welsh thing? What on earth could he be talking about? 'Number thirteen,' said Moynahan helpfully. 'With the apprentice riding. He's come on a 300-mile round trip from Gwent. Won well last week at Chepstow and gets in here without a penalty.' (Meaning that there had not yet been time for him to be rehandicapped with the result that he was remarkably 'well in' at the weights.)

'Yes, but this isn't Chepstow, is it?' responded Kincaid unconvincingly. 'It's a completely different kind of track. A different kind of race.'

'It's certainly a different kind of track,' agreed Moynahan.

'No, no, no. Carson's is the business again here. Everyone agrees. It's obvious.'

Looking up and down the rows of boards bookies' pitches and trying to monitor and analyse the market moves in these crucial moments before the off, I felt that Kincaid probably had a point.

183

Calvanne Miss, our original each-way certainty, surely couldn't win? She was positively friendless and everywhere on the slide having opened up at 5s and gone out rapidly to 13–2 and even 7s in places . . . There was some money for the Welsh-trained runner at 6–1 but the confidence in Carson's mount was infectious. Even as we stood there we could see most of the front row boards bookmakers cutting its odds from 3–1 to 11–4 and even 5–2.

'The runners are going behind,' we heard the commentator declare, meaning that they were going behind the starting stalls and would soon be loaded up and on their way. Kincaid and I, our minds working in unison, lurched simultaneously down the rails in the usual, frantic, last-minute attempt to get a price. It was with unimaginable gratitude that we were able to get on at 3–1 with John Pegley who accepted our two cash bets of £300 to £100 without hesitation.

Marvellously inflated by this heroic attainment of better odds than the next man we scrambled back onto the terracing to watch. To watch what? Well, not exactly a race, more a snatched, frenetic and intermittently clear picture of coloured silks, chestnut horse-flesh and fragile equine legs changing, stretching and galloping down the hill. The course commentator, who even in the clearing light must have been possessed of almost magical and visionary powers, assured us that for the first half mile at least there was only one horse in it and, if this was true, we were right out of luck. Because, according to the commentary, that first half mile was all – Calvanne Miss. And comfortably too. Calvanne by one. Calvanne by two. Calvanne by three at the three-furlong pole. But just as we were looking round for a small, private little hole to crawl away and be sick in, our pride, our happiness, our day out by the sea was suddenly made whole again by receiving the sweetest of all possible news, coming, admittedly, via a rather rapid *volte-face* from the commentator. 'But as they run towards the final quarter mile now it looks as if this leader may just have shot her bolt.' Great cheers from the sportsmen in the crowd. 'And it's Martinovsky now who's making rapid headway from Sharlie's Wimpy and Grown at Rowan and also coming with a strong late-run on the stands side-rail is the favourite number one, Green Dollar.' And that was when the crowd really erupted – the Tasty the ref-chinners, with no shirts and strong armpits, and the bla-zered young executives who had just finished their racecourse caterers' £5.95-a-head traditional cream teas. Together their battle-cry nearly lifted the roof off the McAlpine stand. 'Go on, Willie. Give it some!' What a slogan to go to war with! Several thousand partially intoxicated, highly motivated, desirous for cash, fun-punting lads and chaps roaring their hero – well, their selection – home. 'Go on, Willie. Give it some!' And once again, on cue, our Willie most certainly did give it some. Even with the din being made by his supporters you could still hear his own and the other jockeys' 'persuaders' snapping viciously through the air. The favourite shot forward, as well he might. One well-timed thwack like that for the rest of us and we would have reached the Palace Pier in a single move. But it did the business all right. Whip back down again and head down too and those arms, legs, elbows and boots – yes, we have to say it here – characteristically pumping and driving away, little Willie and the favourite, in spite of conceding over two stone to their nearest challenger, the ten-year-old Sharlie's Wimpy, took what was surely going to prove a decisive advantage.

'Go on, Willie. Go on, my son. You've done it. You've done it,' we shouted, already starting to make our way back down the terraces. But he hadn't done it. Sometimes the closing stages of a horse-race, even a fast-run six-furlong sprint, seem to extend and elongate before your very eyes. And to substitute defeat at the precise moment of victory. That was the case here. With what could only have been fifty or sixty yards still to go, a bay-coloured streak of greased lightning suddenly appeared up the inside rail. It was bearing the number thirteen cloth: the 'visitor' from Wales. At that same instant Carson's mount seemed to falter and lose momentum. You could practically see the horse's legs tying up beneath him. The bay only got its head in front a few strides before the line but it was staying on to such effect that a few strides after the post it had gone a length clear.

The Judge called for a photograph but we knew our fate. Down in the ring the boards bookies were betting 10–1 on (1–10) that the bay would get the race. Sure enough the result came through quickly with a neck quoted as the official winning distance. Hardly a crushing or ignominious defeat for Carson and the favourite but, for us, that narrow margin made all the difference (as all experienced punters will understand) between feeling like a couple of prize-chump chimps and relaxed, debonair and most gracious winners. We had arrived in Brighton with some cash in our pockets. We had been up after the fourth. Then we had done all our profit on the Yarmouth fiasco. And now we had blown the remains of our 'float' on a losing 3–1 favourite in the last. So much for our stated ambition of raising a little pocket money for Ascot. So much for playing the horses.

We found John Moynahan standing on the small patch of Members' Lawn. Inevitably he had backed the Welsh-trained winner and, as he had promised us in advance, it had been his third such victory of the afternoon. He didn't crow about it. He just smiled. Tony and Maurice were waiting for us in the Winning Post bar.

'That was an unfortunate reversal in the last, A. J.,' said Tony, quickly. 'I saw you both punching the air with delight. Prematurely as it turned out. And what a shame about the Yarmouth mishap.'

'What a shame,' said Kincaid.

'It does make such a difference when you get out on the last,' continued Tony, making a calculation in the margin of his racecard. 'I always say that if you can just get out. I should think that if it hadn't been for those two big losers you'd have had an almost winning day.'

'That's what I always seem to have,' said Kincaid with just a hint of emotion. 'An almost winning day.'

We saw off the unfinished bottle of champagne though, unsurprisingly, the caterers' best vintage – or whatever it was that Tony was treating us to – didn't taste quite so good now as it had before the stumbling disaster of the Yarmouth filly. Neither did the atmosphere of the bar seem quite as convivial as it had earlier in the afternoon.

When the Winning Post finally closed Tony and Maurice headed off to their Mercedes and we walked through the Members' gate out into the sea-breeze, fish-batter and cut-grass-after-the-rain smells of a Brighton summer evening. The fog had cleared and the humidity with it. The sun was shining and the sky was a deepest blue. We picked up a handful of copies of the *Brighton and Evening Argus* containing tomorrow's declared runners for Royal Ascot and to lift our spirits there was actually a free taxi waiting by the kerb.

Taking the short cut this time we rolled back down the steep incline through Kemptown past the pinched little roads of pre- and post-war villas. The cab driver had his radio on full volume and it was tuned to a sixties revival show. And that's how it was that the plangent sound of Martha Reeves and the Vandellas drifted out of the open taxi windows and away over the rooftops and TV aerials and Sky satellite dishes of the seaside town. As we turned right up the hill towards the railway viaduct, beneath which Pinkie and Dallow had walked in the dark to 'cut' Brewer the slow-paying bookie while a slow goods to Lewes belched smoke into the black sky above.

CHAPTER FOURTEEN

Optimists and Faces

LOSING ISN'T nearly as much fun as winning and yet most punters lose most of the time. Why do we persevere with our betting? What is the psychology of gambling?

There are so many different types of horse players, all of them betting for their own reasons, that it is extremely difficult to generalise about the typical punter. You could be referring just as easily to the Queen Mother as to Barney Curley or an old-age pensioner in a betting office in Penge. Most punters, if asked, would probably say that they bet for no more complicated reason than that they enjoy it and that they love the risk and the excitement of gambling slightly more than they can afford to lose – and tend to be understandably resentful of what they regard as pretentious psychological explanations of their 'condition'. Nevertheless, it would not be wholly unfair or inaccurate to say that the great majority of gamblers on horse-racing are motivated by some mixture of escapism, optimism, masochism and greed, the four qualities being present in different measure in each individual.

If you disregard the twice-a-year punters on the Grand National and the Derby and the occasional visitors to a point-to-point, the optimists and escapists are by far the largest and most distinctive group of players on the horses. The optimists are always convinced that tomorrow, some day, one day, soon, will be their big break, genuinely believing that they can harness luck to their cause, as if it were a spirit that can be called up and enlisted on anyone's behalf, providing you know the correct incantation. Most bookmakers, cynical and pessimistic characters by nature, will tell you that all optimists are mugs and that 99 per cent of betting-shop customers are complete mugs. Professionals despair of making the lay punter realise that the generally meagre level of concentration and analysis that they apply to their betting means that the odds will always be stacked heavily against them. What the professionals fail to realise in their turn is that not all enthusiastic amateurs are self-deluding fantasists into the bargain. Many of them deliberately eschew the relentless form book study and self-discipline of the Timeform Organisation because to adopt it would mean turning their gambling into a form of work. They want to keep it as a pleasurable pastime and light-hearted relaxation. Their Saturday-afternoon Yankees and racecourse jackpots, their many 'desperately near' misses and very occasional winners, light up dull days and mundane routines and often supply the only moments of sheer excitement and adrenalin in otherwise barren lives. These bits-and-pieces punters may be mugs in the narrowest sense of the word but they are hardly out of control and don't deserve to be berated for their vice or character weakness any more than the average recreational drinker.

The second recognisable group of distinctive types, for whom optimism is also an essential prop, are the racing insiders and faces who bet as a regular habit to try and improve on the income that they make from the racing industry. These insider dealers are a lot more crafty and guileful than the armchair and betting-shop optimists and mugs. They include owners, trainers, speculative individual bookmakers and large numbers of underpaid stable lads (the latter probably comprising one of the biggest gambling constituencies in the country).

The insider's betting patterns depend on them knowing something or thinking they know something of which the bookies and the rest of the gambling community are not aware. This 'information' frequently turns out to be as hopelessly wide of the mark as the ignorant prejudices of the taproom bore but from time to time successful strokes are still pulled on the British Turf and there remain plenty of owners and trainers who will happily cheat with their horses, in the manner of the Druids Lodge Confederacy, if they can see a way of making a profit as a result.

In an altogether different class from the ordinary inside faces is the little band of high-rolling professional gamblers, the successors to Charlie Hannam and Alex Bird. The professionals, who probably have a gambling turnover of at least £2 million a year, bet much more selectively and much less frequently than the inferior optimist or face. They, too, pride themselves on their access to inside information but they never get involved merely as a consequence of racecourse rumour or the opinions of others. Neither do they want to be associated with fixed races or doping scandals. Horse-racing is their livelihood and they don't want to swap it for any other. They sometimes try to engineer betting coups when they want to beat the market without revealing themselves to the layers and they still employ teams of unattributable punters and agents, like Purefoy and Bird, but they are not interested in stopping a favourite for a few thousand pounds.

The fourth and most distressing group of recognisable punters are the compulsive and self-destructive gamblers, kin to the chronic losers in the casinos and at the card tables, who may include any of the other three types who have gone seriously and comprehensively off the rails. They come in all ages and from all backgrounds and together they add up to the bleakest, most depressing side of betting on horse-racing.

The truly compulsive gambler *is* a masochist. They know that their betting continuously and unfailingly places them in a situation where they experience pain, humiliation and loss but still they continue. A compulsive gambler may be a fallen high-roller who has worked his way through millions but whose ego cannot survive without the gratification and feeling of omnipotence that his betting provides, or may be a truant teenager who has ruined themselves over £200 in a Ladbrokes' office or a housewife with half a dozen secret credit-betting accounts who has mortgaged her home and her life to subsidise her habit. Psychiatrists like Dr Steinberg would say that many compulsive punters are suffering from an illness or affliction and that they are no longer able to think of or face a way out of their predicament. Some self-destructive players are pathologically selfish and indifferent to the effect of their betting on others who may love and depend on them. The end of the line for the compulsive and masochistic punter can be bankruptcy, divorce, vagrancy, prison, even death. Alternatively they may find the strength or encouragement to confront their addiction and seek the help of Gamblers Anonymous.

One of the most determinedly optimistic forms of gambling on horse-racing is ante-post betting. This is never more popular than at the start of the new flat-racing season each spring, which is when both the committed and occasional punters play the annual game of trying to guess which of the winter and pre-season favourites for the first flat-racing classics have trained on, and have some realistic prospect of success at Newmarket in early May. And which of them have had 'a little minor setback' or 'trod on a stone at morning exercise' or 'not quite gone through with it in their faster work' or any of the other standard excuses wheeled out by evasive trainers to try to conceal that their latest blue-blooded talking horse has about as much chance of winning the 2,000 Guineas as the Queen's Royal Ascot representative, Sir Piers Bengough, riding side-saddle on a donkey.

Back in the nineteenth and early twentieth centuries many of the top flat-racing trainers like Jack Fallon and James Machell were bold and inveterate gamblers liable to erupt in understandable rage if the identity of their best three-year-old or their laid-out 'job' for the Royal Hunt Cup or the Cambridgeshire was revealed prematurely by the press. One hundred years later only the Lambourn-based Barry Hills among the first division of flat-racing 'handlers' will openly admit to being a gambler. The top Newmarket yards try to insist that they are too busy or too dedicated or just too frightfully ascetic even to think of having a bet while still refusing to give away little more than their name, rank and serial number when confronted by an interviewer. Cynics suggest that for them the real gamble is not with the bookmakers but in the bloodstock market and that they are too craftily adept at calculating their own and their owners' potential end-of-season stallion shares to blow prematurely the reputation of a marketable commodity. Which is one reason why they race some of these pampered individuals so sparingly, if they can get away with it.

These same trainers have taken to attacking the bookies and the racing press for supposedly hyping up various of their unexposed prospects and hoisting them undeservedly to the top of the ante-post lists. The scenario that the trainers have in mind involves some journalist with a column to fill ruminating in print about, say, a handsome but unraced Nijinsky colt in a top trainer's stable, said colt being a half brother to a former classic winner and due to make his own race-course début in a leading classic trial in a few weeks' time, etc. Such comments can indeed be enough to make some punters pick up the telephone and dial their bookmaker. And there have certainly been instances of bookmakers' public relations representatives attempting to exploit the subsequent media interest by appearing to talk up the size and amount of the bets struck on what, at the time of the 'gamble', will still be a strictly morning glory with nothing in the way of concrete form or achievements to back up its home reputation.

The bookies defend this practice by saying that there has to be at least some semblance of public demand for a horse's odds to contract, that hype alone cannot persuade the punters to bet and that if these market moves are generally dependent on a surplus of speculation over hard evidence it is not always the fault of the layers. Neither do racing journalists and gallops watchers feel that they deserve to be crucified simply for trying to give the betting public some idea of which horses are developing and at what pace. They believe that you could as easily blame the hype on the trainers themselves, who are increasingly seen to be ducking the established pattern of top two-year-old races especially with their colts and sending out their B and C teams instead. Their best juveniles, who will run once at two if they're lucky, are more likely to be hidden away in assorted back-end maiden events at Nottingham and Leicester.

The Italian born Luca Cumani, a tremendously skilful and immensely crafty trainer, has perfected the art of winning major second-season races, both Group events and handicaps, with 'dark' or unexposed three-year-olds. The equally gifted but equally cagey Michael Stoute has frequently trumped the classic pack with a late-developing top-class colt or filly such as the 1988 2,000 Guineas winner Doyoun, the 1989 Oaks winner Aliysa and the same season's champion miler Zilzal, Alex Bird's Gulfstream Park 'investment', who was unraced at two but who then progressed from winning a maiden race to the Group One Sussex Stakes in little more than two months.

Nobody decries the trainers for these artful demonstrations of their talent and ability but having set the precedent of hanging on to their best cards until well into the game they can hardly be surprised that bookies, punters and journalists annually try to beat the trainer and the market to it by attempting to guess in advance which each season's unexposed stars will be. Betting long range, ante-post, for all its undoubted hazards can be hugely profitable if you get it right, which is where all the phone-line touts and faces and every other inside expert from Timeform to Channel 4's Derek Thompson come in with their news direct from the horse's mouth. Everybody wants to be wise after the event. When a horse like Shergar wins the Derby by ten lengths there is instant agreement that he's so patently brilliant that his success was a foregone conclusion. You'll hardly have made much money out of him though if you backed him at his official starting price of 10–11 or 11–10 on. But if you were sufficiently far-sighted or well informed or just plain crafty enough to have 'bought' Shergar at 25 – 1 during the winter then you'll be enjoying a massive ego-inflating boost of pride and delight. Similarly, if you get on what you think is going to be Michael Stoute's 1,000 Guineas filly or Cecil's 2,000 Guineas colt at 33–1 in January and then you watch its price drop steadily to 8–1 by the first week of April, the rush of excitement is every bit as spine-tingling and egotistically satisfying as the emotions experienced by any other speculative futures or commodity trader in any other marketplace.

Suppose you are able actually to go up to Newmarket and wheedle your way in among the other moles, touts and connections as the colt has a trial spin on the Limekilns gallop one chilly Wednesday morning. Pat Eddery is there in his purple and green satin Breeders Cup jacket, having flown up especially in his private plane to partner the horse. Pat's agent is there. The owner is there. The owner's racing manager is there. The trainer is there, naturally. Mike Dillon of Ladbrokes is there, too. ('What's it got to do with Mike Dillon of Ladbrokes?' asks a naïve observer.) And after it's all over and the horse has breezed through the dewy mist at a high and apparently effortless cruising speed, you manage to overhear Pat's post-work chat, at once monosyllabic and swagger, with Stoutie or Henry, the Prince or the Sheikh. And you see the nodding and the twitching and you hear the muttered exclamations of 'Good. Good. OK then. Good,' and all of a sudden you feel for yourself the wonderful virile buzz of actually being there, of being on the inside, of being a player and you think, Oh, yes. Yes, please. I'll buy him again to win me another four grand at eights. Or, perhaps alternatively, you decide to hedge and make a backer's book by acting as a private bookmaker and laying off a piece of your 33 –1 bet at a few points over the current 8 –1 odds to other punters, not insiders, who didn't get on at the bigger price and who are now desperate to get a slice of the action.

Come the day of the race, if the filly or colt manages to win or even to run second or third at your fat, each-way price, you again experience a great surge of affirmative triumph. Your fur has been stroked. Your cool professional's insight into the game has been confirmed to everyone around you. If the horse loses or finishes out of the frame, oh well, obsessional character that you no doubt are, you still manage to convince yourself that if only the ground had been better or the spring warmer or the pace stronger and if only Pat, Willie or Steve had delayed their challenge just a little bit longer you'd have ended up the rightful winner, after all. And in that mood it's odds-on that you'll be taking ante-post prices about the following year's Guineas by mid-July while first going in seriously over Cecil's or Cumani's Derby horse in advance of its public trial at York two weeks after Newmarket. And on it goes.

There is never any shortage of long-range and credit-account wagering on the Derby although the bewildering proliferation of ante-post favourites for the race in recent years has left most punters dazed and confused. Some journalists see in these exchanges little more than the crafty machinations of the publicity departments of the big bookmaking firms. If you are an ante-post bookie, though, you'd again be entitled to lay at least a part of the blame at the doors of those same Newmarket trainers who are as reluctant to expose the true abilities of their potential middle-distance horses as they are of their Guineas colts. And for all the suspicion of easy money and the conviction that when the Big Three talk about 'significant backing' they are dealing in chicken feed by Australian and American standards, even the big companies can lose in the ante-post market which is why their accountants wouldn't weep over its passing. A move that any gambler worthy of the name should strenuously resist.

Trying to get the lowdown on Henry Cecil's or Michael Stoute's likely Derby horse may feel like a search for the inside track but at least the investigative punter is gambling on one known and proven commodity. A trainer whose unblemished record is there for all to see. The other kind of insider trading, the inspired gamble based on information known only to an intimate few, tends to be far more conspiratorial and close knit and may involve the punter in having to trust a trainer or jockey whose record is not quite so black and white.

Henry Cecil's clients are not the sort of people who need to bet to make money but the vast majority of racehorse owners, not being Arab sheikhs or Japanese or American multi-millionaires and knowing that they have a negligible chance of ever winning the Derby, enthusiastically bet on their horses in the infinitely less valuable contests in which they generally run whenever their trainers give them the green light. Their occasional triumphs, rarely to bank-breaking sums for the bookies, give pleasure and encouragement to everybody else. The controversies begin when trainers try to nudge things their way by giving their runners an 'easy' when the money's not down or issuing instructions of 'not off' or 'not today' to their jockeys.

There is a constituency within the racing establishment and press which likes to believe that the sport has never been straighter, that corruption is a thing of the past and that our jockeys are all shining white knights on horseback. It's certainly true that the huge retainers and contracts now paid to the leading riders make it scarcely worth their while to take bribes or favours from corrupt bookmakers or other powerful gambling individuals in the style of William Hill's hired hands over forty years ago. A less generous view has it that some jockeys on the flat and over the jumps, partly as a result of their long struggle up the ladder and their numbing years of hard stable labour, are preternaturally disposed to looking kindly on wads of fivers handed over in sealed manilla envelopes. And so it was and ever more shall be.

This is, again, not to say that modern betting-oriented corruption is always as clumsy or overt as in the bad old days or as lurid and unbelievable as in the plots of the average Dick Francis novel. The revelation in September 1990 that two horses had been doped at Doncaster and another at Yarmouth came as a genuine surprise even to the hardballs in the betting ring because there had been no proven dopings (the Gorytus and other allegations aside) since Pinturischio and the idea of stopping horses in such a heavy-handed fashion had seemed a thing of the past. Wandering around a stable yard with a syringe in your hand seems as obvious a way of drawing attention to yourself as hanging about outside a bank in a striped shirt and a black mask carrying a bag marked Swag. (Similarly, the camera patrol film makes it much harder for a rider accidentally-on-purpose to fall off at the open ditch on the far side than it might have been in 1949.)

At the time of writing no one has been charged with the Doncaster and Yarmouth dopings. The police and horse-racing's own internal police force, Racecourse Security Services, claim that they think they know who was responsible but that they couldn't get enough evidence to prosecute. Predictably, the security divisions of the Big Three bookmaking firms are quite sure that *they* know who was responsible and weren't surprised by the names and identities that swam into the frame. A desperate punter trying to beat a losing streak, an on- and off-course Yorkshire bookmaker with a reputation and a warned-off ex-trainer at the end of the line. The bookie was interesting but the punter and trainer were perceived to be second- and third-rate cheapies and losers, not major players at all. And in spite of the rumoured death threats that were said to have been circulating after the dopings no dead bodies have as yet been found floating in the Fontwell water jump as in Francis's thriller *Dead Cert* and nobody has come forward to tell of jockeys being recruited to assassinate other jockeys by helping them onto a row of spiked railings on the run-up to Becher's Brook.

Even some of the scores of 'non-triers' that the rails bookie John Pegley claims to see on the track every week may not always be as suspicious as they seem. Sometimes a trainer will be keen to give a backward or immature horse a quiet introduction to what will be required of it on the racecourse in future. Sometimes the horse may have been difficult to get fit on the gallops or be returning from injury in which case too strenuous an effort would be inappropriate first time out.

But when the exonerations have been exhausted and the excuses have been wheeled out, every experienced daily observer of the racecourse and the betting ring (and that doesn't just mean losers speaking through their pockets) knows that John Pegley is substantially correct and that there are countless instances of trainers and jockeys actively conniving at running unfit horses or horses that are not intended to win – *not* for veterinary or precautionary reasons but because they are trying to fool the bookies and the punters and get those horses dropped down the handicap so that they are allotted a lenient weight for a chosen gambling engagement next time out. As a consequence of this practice, other horses pop up, well backed and showing a remarkable improvement in or reversal of form in events that their most recent efforts apparently gave them no right to win.

When successful betting coups take place, the reaction of the Big Three bookmakers can be distinctly variable. Sometimes the leading firms are only too pleased to release copious details of the supposedly audacious touches pulled off at their expense in their own sponsored hurdle races and big flat-racing handicaps. The actual amounts staked in some of these bets may be little more than £500 or £1,000 a time and even if the bookies have to pay out a couple of winners at 33–1 they have probably made a profit of two or three times that amount on their overall book on the race. But given that the betting-shop owners are forbidden by law from stimulating demand by direct advertising these so-called big winners, often written up generously in the tabloid press, provide them with marvellous free publicity. The notion is put about that the firm in question is everybody's friendly and accommodating bookmaker, that they take risks and that sometimes they really do lose, thus encouraging the average not especially clued-up reader to pop down to his or her Ladbrokes, Hills or Coral office and fill in a betting slip to see if they can become big winners too. One or two easy-going racing journalists, who happily receive sides of smoked salmon and crates of champagne from bookmaking companies' agreeable public relations representatives each Christmas, know exactly how the wheels go round.

When a really big gamble pays off – the participants win serious money and the big bookmakers' profit margins are genuinely hit by the scam – the experience of some players is that these self-same accommodating betting-shop chains are usually the first to cry, 'Fraud' and 'Stop thief' or 'Will you wait and take a cheque next January?' But when an attempted betting coup goes down, then even if the layers who accepted the bets realise that the horse at the centre of the stroke was a set-up job they will still happily pocket all the stake money and you won't hear a word about police investigations or the bets being cancelled and the race declared void.

If you manage to land a touch and succeed in getting paid, you may still have to weather the disapproval of the 'beaks'. This may seem a childish expression to use about the racing authorities but the Jockey Club have comported themselves for so long as a cross between Avery Brundage's International Olympic Committee and a board of public-school governors *circa Tom Brown's Schooldays*, that it seems an appropriate word. Generally speaking, the lower a trainer is down the racing pyramid, the more likely they are to be penalised for too openly or successfully 'having it off'. A small permit holder (maybe a farmer with a few horse boxes) on the Welsh Borders who scoops £12,000–15,000 desperately needed pounds from a stroke in a selling hurdle at Bangor-on-Dee, thus managing to pay off at least some of the murderous interest on his overdraft for that year, may end up being carpeted by the Jockey Club at their Portman Square head offices. If they deem that something underhand has taken place and that the result was inconsistent with the horse's previous efforts, the club's disciplinary committee may conceivably fine him a substantial portion of his winnings and ban him and his jockey for the next three months of the season. On the other hand, a more prominent trainer with good social connections and a prestigious list of owners can cheat rotten with a horse by running it twice over the wrong trip or in the wrong class and then clean up with it when the conditions are right in a valuable handicap at Ascot or Goodwood. Instead of being asked to explain the apparent improvement in form he will find everyone falling over themselves to congratulate him on his judgement and skill.

If you are a full-time racing writer it is usually considered to be bad form to draw too much attention to these variable standards. It is not just that access to tips and information may quickly dry up: you may be told that it just doesn't do to give the mugs in the street the idea that racing isn't entirely on the level. Where will the future employment of countless breeders, trainers, jockeys, stable lads and selfless racing correspondents be then? Yet from time to time, and in spite of these blandishments, some of the more serious, frustrated or less reverent souls in the press room try to blow the whistle on those they regard as the most blatant two-timers. (Just as some of their predecessors endeavoured to do in Purefoy's and Cunliffe's time.) What kind of racing future will there be for anyone, they argue, if punters in betting shops are being daily mocked and abused? And why is officialdom so spineless that it refuses to tackle the worst of the culprits?

With the honourable exception of the *Independent* and the Paul Haigh column in the *Racing Post*, there is all too little irony or bile in the mainstream racing press. But while it can only be healthy to satirise the more hypocritical owners and trainers (as Sievier satirised the Confederacy in 1904) and to tip the wink that you are on to their more outrageous 'outfitting' dodges, it is not always necessary to be too prim about it – or to plead the interests of the punter as the justification for your disapproval. Punters today, if they confine themselves to a betting office, may find it much harder to strike a decent bet at a decent price than their ancestors did, but when it comes to the availability of helpful information they are vastly better off than their counterparts of ninety years ago. This generation of race-horse gamblers can read up about possible non-triers who may be 'off' next time out in countless form books, trade paper Pricewise pages and periodicals and then have the same information underlined or amplified by telephone hot-lines, tipsters, television and video pictures and their betting shop's daily satellite racing service, SIS. There are plenty of illuminating signs there *if* you make the effort to look for them.

Where, anyway, would racing be if everything was always blandly open and above board? If every racehorse competed regularly and interminably on its merits? Take away the betting and take away that hint of chicanery that goes with it and most race meetings would become about as compulsively exciting as the Badminton three-day event. And if British racing ever does decide to do away with the bookmakers and to compress all its betting turnover through the Tote or PMU windows it will have to take the risk that some fixtures at Ascot and Newmarket may become as flat and antiseptic as some afternoons at Longchamp, Maisons Lafitte and St Cloud in Paris, where even on Group One classic race days (outside the Prix de l'Arc de Triomphe) there is sometimes less tangible atmosphere and about as many paying spectators as turn up at Plumpton on a November Monday.

Needless to say, the big bookmaking firms employ a wide-ranging intelligence service to enable them to get wind of any possible strokes at a very early stage, affording them sufficient time and opportunity to flush out the protagonists and head 'em off at the pass. One midweek summer's day in 1990 an English-based jockey who was riding regularly for a top Irish stable at the time was passing through Dublin airport on his way back to London. As he went through the checking-in formalities a friendly Aer Lingus operative, who recognised his face and said that he liked racing, asked him innocently if he had anything good coming up. The jockey wasn't specific but he did say that he was hoping for a rather good time at Kempton Park that evening. After he had passed through onto his plane, the same Aer Lingus officer picked up a phone and dialled a special contact number in Dublin city. The number was the Irish connection of a leading British bookmaking firm. The Aer Lingus officer dials this number regularly whenever he might have something for them. He reported his conversation and particularly what the jockey had said about his Kempton engagements. He was thanked for his information and assured of some payment in the usual way if anything came of it.

The bookmakers' Dublin office then called their principal London number and the London end quickly took a look at the jockey's booked mounts at the Middlesex track. He had four: three of them well exposed and of no great account but the fourth was a three-year-old colt from a small Hampshire stable, beaten on its seasonal reappearance, but now dropping back to sprinting distances for the first time since winning over that trip as a two-year-old. The bookmaking firm had no contacts in the Hampshire yard but by getting on to their contacts in other southern stables, some of whom knew the other stable lads, they were able to establish, inside an hour, that the connections of the colt were convinced that it couldn't possibly lose at Kempton and that they were going to try and win a tidy sum on it. The main opposition in the race was to be provided by the easy winner of a five-furlong Newbury handicap who had disappointed in a Group race in Ireland last time out but who was now to have the assistance of Pat Eddery. Eddery's mount was expected to start favourite and the Hampshire colt's anticipated starting price was around 5–2. By getting their on-track representatives to back the horse at the start of the evening, the bookmakers were able to ensure that its opening price on the boards was a niggardly 4–6. To give credit to the on-course betting market the odds drifted out to 7–4 at the off as the course layers tried to loosen up betting exchanges and get some money for the favourite in their satchels. The three-year-old broke fast, went straight to the front and was never headed. The connections had their winner all right but not at the odds they had hoped for. From the moment the first show went up they must have realised that something was awry. What they didn't know was that it was their jockey's momentary indiscretion at the airport that had ditched all their hopes of a killing.

Loose or indiscriminate talk is not the gambler's only obstacle to success. Attractive ante-post prices may vanish at a stroke if 'the right men' begin to apply – another bookmaking euphemism for the shrewdest gambling owners, trainers and their associates. These faces, if they contact the more paranoid bookmaking firms direct, are often likely to find themselves bargained with and offered only a portion of their money at the officially advertised odds. On 23 March 1990, a horse called Daring Times landed some tidy wagers in the six-furlong Shaftesbury Handicap at Doncaster. Daring Times was trained up in North Yorkshire by Lynda Ramsden who along with her immensely shrewd gambling husband Jack (who placed the horses and organised the commissions), was running the most successful betting-centred stable in the country at the time. The owner of Daring Times was one of Jack's regular partners, the frighteningly sharp rails bookmaker Mr Colin Webster, himself also a punter of note.

Some sections of the press described the Daring Times race as a spectacular betting coup that had supposedly resulted in huge liabilities for Ladbrokes, who were reported to have laid the horse at all prices from 33–1 down to 5s. The connections, while admitting that they had pulled off a nice little touch, scoffed at these stories as mere bookmaker-inspired hype. 'I think the cleaning lady must have beaten us to the 33–1 at a minute past nine this morning,' joked the silver-haired Webster. 'The Lord of the Ring', as some of his fellow bookmakers have nicknamed him, was referring to the regular punter's standard complaint that when you ring your local office at opening time to try to take advantage of an advertised price, you are frequently informed by the shop manager that those odds have already gone and that the new prices, surprise, surprise, are considerably shorter. 'I know someone who tried to take the 33s about Daring Times with Ladbrokes and were offered 14s,' said the bookie.

Jack Ramsden, who got on at 16–1, declared, 'That 33–1 is a lot of window dressing for the bookmakers. They're just a lot of bloody whingers. I couldn't get that price and no one else could have tried because no one else knew about it.' Webster admitted to getting on at 16–1, 14–1, 10–1 and 8–1. 'I think at the end of the day we averaged about 8–1 to our money,' he said.

To be fair to Ladbrokes, since September 1990 they have been running a new guarantee scheme whereby their betting-shop punters are promised that they can back any horse to take out a maximum of £250 until 10.30 a.m. each day. Well-known credit-account clients may be allowed to stake more. So there we are. And £250, eh? Phew. These bookmakers, they take some risks. Unfair? Well, not entirely, but it is important to keep one thing in perspective. There is all the difference in the world between exceptionally well-informed professionals like Webster and Ramsden and the ordinary, casual, weekday and Saturday betting-shop loafers. The top gambling trainers, their punters and connections are not engaged in a purely sporting or diversionary activity. They are trying quite ruthlessly to win large sums of the bookmakers' money (and if bookmakers didn't exist they would be dealing with illicit bookies rather than trying to win it off the Tote). And though it may not be J. P. McManus's or Barney Curley's style, most punters, great or small, love nothing better than to talk up their triumphs real or imaginary and further verbally to rubbish the always cowering bookies. And if their bets go down, their later embellished report of the transactions will still make clear that more than anything it was the undeserving layers who brought about their luckless defeat. By refusing to pay a quarter the odds a place, by refusing anything less than £10 bets, by refusing to go better than odds-on the favourite in the third. Even when the bookmaker loses he can still be cast satisfactorily as the villain.

Yet for all the instances of both bookie and punter mendacity, and for all the regrettable shortage of characters, risk-takers and pound notes compared with half a century ago, gambling trainers as well as maverick gambling individuals still occasionally get past the enemy and carry off a stroke in style. Lynda Ramsden had Daring Times exactly right for his run for the money and two other trainers with few peers at laying out a horse for one specific target are the one-time stable lad Barry Hills, formerly of Robert Sangster's Manton estate but now back at South Bank, Lambourn, and the ex-jump jockey Jimmy FitzGerald, born in the inimitably named Irish village of Horse and Jockey (actually a flat featureless crossroads five miles outside Thurles in County Tipperary) but who trains up at Malton in Yorkshire.

Barry Hills is a man who really enjoys betting. He has a positive appetite for it like James Machell. He also has an appetite for the major Festival flat-race meetings from Chester in May to Royal Ascot in June, Newmarket in July and so on. Being involved on those stellar occasions, both as a competitor for the most sought-after prizes and as a participant in the socialising that goes on before and afterwards, is to a man like Hills the *raison d'être* of a trainer. But it is an expensive lifestyle to maintain, especially when you throw in mid-season trips to the international bloodstock sales and flat-racing's traditional long winter holidays in the Caribbean. And while Hills certainly doesn't need to rely on whatever income he may make from his gambling it is a valuable supplement none the less. Some betting trainers don't inspire by their appearance: they seem either too gaudy and flash or too flushed and played out. Barry Hills looks the part in every way. He's small and hard, always sharply but smartly turned out and he has a penchant for the biggest and most expensive cigars. Fledgeling racing correspondents all learn early on the story of how Hills was able to start up in business on his own from the money that he won when a horse called Frankincense, from the Newmarket stable of John

Oxley for whom he was travelling head lad at the time, won the 1968 Lincoln at Doncaster. It's his ability, learnt during his period as a lad, rarely to overestimate his horses but to know exactly the potential of what is passing through his hands that has made Barry Hills so invaluable an ally to an enthusiastic betting owner like Sangster, his long-time patron and friend.

The two men combined to execute a stroke made in heaven in the 1990 Cambridgeshire at Newmarket (still as popular and as treacherous a betting race as it was in the era of Hackler's Pride). The object of their gamble was an improving three-year-old colt called Risen Moon. The easy winner of a seven-furlong race at Doncaster in September, some doubted whether Risen Moon would last out the stiff nine furlongs at Newmarket. Hills had few fears, the colt's home work at Manton having convinced him that stamina would not be a problem. Rarely has his judgement been better vindicated. Ridden with quite alarming self-confidence by Steve Cauthen and sent off the 7–1 favourite in a field of forty, the son of Hawaiian Sound didn't begin to make a challenge until well inside the final furlong but still managed to win going away by a length and a half. Hills revealed afterwards that he had started backing the horse at 16–1 in early September and had then stepped in again at 8–1 on the eve of the contest. 'Barry Hills doesn't bet in bus fares,' observed one journalist. Robert Sangster, a cheerful, enthusiastic, though by no means always winning punter, had a double reason to celebrate as his wife Susan had given birth to their second child that morning.

Two weeks later Hills was back at Newmarket to try to scoop the second leg of the Autumn Double, the two-and-a-quarter mile Cesarewitch, with that year's Ebor Handicap winner, Further Flight. He came close – astonishingly close, when you think that no trainer had completed the double for several decades – but not quite close enough. Two and a half furlongs out, Steve Cauthen went for home with most of the opposition apparently beaten off. But not all of them. At the distance Further Flight was picked up effortlessly by another lightly raced and improving three-year-old by the name of Trainglot, ridden by Willie Carson and laid out for the race with great deliberation by the crafty Irish-born trainer . . . Jimmy FitzGerald.

In his last race before the Cesarewitch, a two-mile handicap at Thirsk, Trainglot had nudged home by a head under nine stone ten. Yet Fitzy had somehow managed to get him into the

Newmarket weights on seven stone twelve and not surprisingly the horse responded as if he had been turned out into his paddock without a saddle. He won so easily it was almost laughable, strolling home by six lengths from Further Flight who had another ten lengths to spare over the third. 'Mike Dillon won't be pleased,' joked Carson as he dismounted afterwards and for once it seemed evident that publicity-conscious Ladbrokes had indeed been taken for what racing correspondents like to refer to as 'an old-fashioned gamble'. Trainglot was reported by the SP correspondents to have taken more than £130,000 out of the ring in recorded four-figure bets alone although, of course, all the connections' money had gone on in advance and by phone. Fitzgerald admitted having 'had a nice bet at 16s and again at 10s' but he wasn't about to disclose the full scale of his success any more than Hills had a fortnight before.

Not the least entertaining aspect of an enquiring chat with Fitz is the suspicion that the slight deafness in his right ear appears to get worse whenever you ask him a leading question about a possible future gamble, though when it comes to assumptions of incredulous innocence the Irishman would be the first to agree that he is still only an amateur compared to the skill regularly displayed by two other northern-based trainers, the authentic Tykes, Peter and Mick Easterby. Over the years the Easterbys have perfected the role of dumb uncouth Yorkshiremen – the sort of plain-speaking farmers who use string to keep their trousers up – especially in response to questions about any jobs being hatched in their Great Habton and Sheriff Hutton yards. Some of the best betting and racing fun of the year comes when you study the entries for a big ante-post betting race like the Ladbrokes Ayr Gold Cup, the £75,000 six-furlong handicap run on the third day of Ayr's Western Meeting in September. Each Easterby has won the Cup but, understandably, they keep trying to win it again. Such is the nature of the race and the record of their stables that any nominations they make arouse instant excitement or, possibly, if you are making an ante-post book for the sponsors, instant alarm.

Suppose that one of Mick's tentative runners is a horse that was 'an unlucky loser' in a race over the distance at Beverley in July, some time before the weights for the Cup were compiled and whose only run since has been in a two-furlongs longer contest, also at Beverley two weeks before the big one. On that occasion, the form book tells you, the Easterby representative was 'well up

with the pace early on but found a couple too good in the las
quarter mile. Sure to be better for the race.' A-ha, you think.
You've found it. This is it. A laid-out Mick Easterby job who was
patently having an easy after an eight-week gap and for whom the
money will be down when he's back over the right trip on 21
September. 'Off for its life,' you could say, to use another rather
sinister racing expression. The excitement mounts. The adrenalin
begins to flow. Especially when you make a series of important
phone calls to your bookmaker. The only snag is that, come the
day of the race when you scrutinise the field of thirty-two, you
realise that there are thirty-one other horses in the line-up who
appear to have been given an identical preparation.

Hills, FitzGerald and the Easterbys may have had their days in
these gambling handicaps but serious professional gamblers, while
possibly appreciating the crack of a helicopter ride to Ayr, disdain
them as a medium for investment. They regard them as fly traps
for the mugs.

The professionals prefer non-handicap races with no more than
ten or twelve runners, where the horses are competing at level
weights or the accepted standard weights for the best of their age
and where the over-round in the bookies' favour will be nearer
single figures than Ladbrokes 1991 Ayr Gold Cup book of '28. It is
by exercising this kind of self-control that the professionals aim not
only to save their money in September but to ensure that they
won't end up kicking their heels around the gaff tracks in the
dreary mid-winter period after Christmas. Which is when every
professional gambler worthy of the name expects to be enjoying
the same Barbados sunshine and sharing the same exclusive
beaches as Victor Chandler and Mickey Fletcher.

CHAPTER FIFTEEN

The Luck of the Irish

IT IS extremely hard to square any notions of masochism and pain with the way that men like J. P. McManus and Barney Curley, the two punters that the bookmakers fear the most, approach their betting. Some determined psychologist might be able to detect certain masochistic threads in the habits of the two Irishmen, citing their conceivably guilt-ridden Catholic education as evidence, and Curley did after all once train for the priesthood. But degradation is not a word that their lives and demeanours instantly bring to mind. Discipline, yes, the carefully learnt self-discipline that tells them when to bet and when not to bet, but definitely no visible glimpses of birch twigs.

Watch J. P. McManus on the balcony of the large, comfortable box that he rents out each March high up in the modern part of the Cheltenham stand and there's no question of him being run by an uncontrollable addiction. We have his word for it that he is moved deeply by the emotion of the Festival. It is his most cherished event of the year but on the outside, like a true poker player, a Las Vegas champion, he betrays absolutely nothing.

One of the most frequently asked questions about any major gambler is whether they were born or made. John Patrick McManus was born to a modest Limerick farming family in 1951 and his first, gainful post-school employment involved working thirteen-hour shifts on the land, operating a bulldozer and apparently discovering at first hand the difficulties of keeping going through heavy ground. He remembers his wages in those far-off late-sixties' days as being in the region of £10 a week and he spent most of that pay packet in the Limerick City betting shops. By his early twenties he had become a devoted student of the form book and, with something of a bank behind him now as a result of his first speculative touches, he decided that it was time to take his destiny into his own hands. Instead of snooker, boxing or Gaelic football, his chosen medium would be gambling on the horses.

It is important to remember, especially when bombarded with some of the wilder and more exaggerated stories of J. P.'s betting, that he established himself in racing and laid the basis for his perfectly respectable annual income not as a punter but as an on-course bookmaker and he still plays that role on the rails in Ireland today. In 1975, though, when he made his first appearance in the ring at Cheltenham it was indeed in the guise of the lean and hungry gambler right out of Western legend. And, if the English layers had been in the dark about him prior to that date they got to know him pretty well in the following few years.

The Irish have had to put up with a great deal of patronising drivel being written about them in connection with the National Hunt Festival. A certain type of middle-aged, very English racing writer will assure you that the Irish punters are always 'twinkling eyed' and 'jabbering' and 'jigging about' with excitement. They launch into choruses of 'Danny Boy' and 'Rose of Tralee' between races and they are all so ignorant of the form book that they only ever back the Irish-trained horses in every Festival contest, regardless of their odds or ability.

Irish breeders, horse-dealers, owners, trainers, jockeys, bookies, punters and ordinary race-goers have indeed contributed a rich seam of emotion and affection to the National Hunt meeting and the occasion would never have attained its unique blend of poetry and passion without them. But Irish racing people, like the Irish in general, are not one-dimensional stereotypes but distinctive individuals from all walks of life and from both Northern and Southern parts of the island. The great beauty of Irish racing is that it is much less formal and stratified than its English counterpart and Irish racing enthusiasts have a natural disinclination to bow and scrape before titled stewards in a bowler hat. Their example of how to enjoy yourself on a racecourse has militated against Cheltenham's old preponderance of stuffy shire and ex-army types and has brought thousands of new race-goers to the Festival from towns and cities and areas of British life far removed from the demesne of the horse.

The excellence of Irish-bred steeplechasers and hurdlers goes back as far as the birth of horse-racing. The flood of Irish-trained winners at Cheltenham began with Vincent O'Brien's extraordinary run at the meeting in the late forties and early fifties and continued through the achievements of men like Tom Dreaper who, as well as Arkle's three Gold Cup victories, sent out the winners of twenty-three other Festival prizes. These days, the best Irish chasers frequently end up in English stables due to the greater purchasing power of British trainers but from the mid seventies to the early eighties the Irish challenge at Cheltenham was still at its zenith.

The big Irish talking horse or hyped-up fancy at the 1975 Cheltenham Festival was an animal called Kilmakilloge who was trained at Ballnonty in County Tipperary by Edward O'Grady, the then twenty-eight-year-old Irish horseman who had prepared Gay Future to land its part of one of the most audacious betting coups of all time at Cartmel the previous year. All winter long this young novice hurdler had been built up by the press as a kind of 'son of Arkle' (and how many times have we all done our brains by chasing that fantasy) and it was suggested that he only had to turn up at the start in one piece to collect. The original plan was to run him in the two-and-a-half-mile novices' hurdle on the opening day of the meeting but the weather had one of its old archetypal pre-Cheltenham fits. A deluge descended and there was no racing at all on the Tuesday afternoon. The two-and-a-half-mile contest was put off until the Thursday but the second day's extended programme opened with the half-mile shorter novice event. O'Grady decided that in view of the heavier than expected ground, Kilmakilloge should run in that race instead. The McManus wad was all riding on his back along with the savings of a good many English journalists who, convinced that they had foreseen another Irish Pegasus, had tipped the horse virtually to a man.

The only trouble was that one or two other Irish horses were running in the race as well. One of them was an equally promising young chasing type called Bannow Rambler who had been sent over from the Wexford yard of the celebrated horse-dealer Padge Berry and was to be ridden by the Irish champion jockey, Padge's son Frank. The night before the race some of the Bannow Rambler connections were partying in a pub near Stow-on-the-Wold. Around one o'clock in the morning, with the festivities still in full swing and the bar doors firmly locked to keep out prying representatives of the law, one of the company produced a hold-all which he then proudly opened for the landlord's inspection. It contained more than £20,000 cash in sterling, all of it destined to be spread in small stakes around Gloucestershire's betting offices the following morning.

In the paddock before the race Kilmakilloge looked rather light and hard-trained and O'Grady was privately worried that he might have become dehydrated and not taken the journey to England as well as he had hoped. He was still sent off a red hot 11–10 favourite but the weight of office money for Bannow Rambler forced his price down from an expected 8–1 to 9–2 at the off. As they started down the hill towards the second last hurdle Kilmakilloge, who had been in the first five throughout, was poised on the inner on the heels of the leaders and appeared to hold every chance. But Bannow Rambler was beginning to close on the outside. Less than a furlong later Kilmakilloge had 'gone'. And the enormous cheer that went up from many of the Irish punters in the stand as Bannow Rambler was called in front for the first time left nobody present in any doubt that the English had been sold another dummy pass and that plenty of the smart money had gone for the other one.

Two years later Bannow Rambler came back to Cheltenham for the Gold Cup. This time the McManus cash was riding on his back and he started favourite. He was still going well within himself when he was brought down at the tenth fence when the former Champion Hurdler, Lanzarote, fell tragically and fatally in front of him.

J. P. may have been knocked back but he was not knocked out by these expensive defeats. He got some of his Bannow Rambler losses back on the O'Grady-trained Rusty Tears who won that year's champion hunter chase and in the summer of 1977 he positively cleaned up on Vincent O'Brien's flat racers during the Ballydoyle stable's record-breaking European season. At Royal Ascot his string of successful five-figure wagers, three of them on the Piggott–O'Brien–Sangster combine, rocked the English bookmakers to the roots. McManus has been a good friend of the Ballydoyle–Coolmore Stud entourage ever since and it is not hard to detect a similarity between the bookmaker-punter's poker-faced style and the canny manner and native intuition of O'Brien himself. Very few of Vincent's and Robert Sangster's great classic and Group One successes of the late seventies and early eighties went without substantial ante-post support from 'the man down the road'. One of the most famous instances of those collective victories was the devastating triumph of El Gran Señor in the 1984 2,000 Guineas at Newmarket. That race made all of Tipperary rich and half of Cork and Limerick too, though J. P. was by no means the only punter to have most of his profit margin blown away when El Gran Señor was subsequently turned over in the Derby.

In March 1977 McManus went for another seriously big touch in the Cotswolds, this time on his own horse, Deep Gale, again trained by O'Grady, who had been laid out since the beginning of the season for the four-mile amateur rider National Hunt Chase. He, too, was only cruising on the bridle when Deep Gale got unsighted at the twenty-first fence and fell. His jockey, Boots Madden, was convinced that he was going so well at the time that if he could just have caught the horse and remounted they would still have won. Undaunted they brought Deep Gale back to the Festival in 1980 to contest the opening two-mile novice hurdle. Once again the big money went on but once again it went astray. Deep Gale ran well but too freely and had nothing left when he was tackled at the penultimate flight by the speedy ex-flat racer Slaney Idol and the former bumper champion Daring Run, the two of them leading home an Irish monopoly of the first five places.

The betting ring has not been the only medium of a McManus Cheltenham gamble. Up until the late seventies he used to spend the Festival week in the Queen's Hotel in the centre of the town where he was a regular winning feature of the big backgammon games that often used to see out the night in the hotel's back room. Then one year the new THF management decided inexplicably to crack down on the gambling sessions and pretty soon both the bar bills and the gamblers went elsewhere. These days the race crowd at the Queen's has gone progressively down market and J. P. himself has long since decamped to the more comfortable, stockbroker ambience of the Lygon Arms in Broadway.

Up to and including the 1991 Festival the 'Sundance Kid' had seen his colours carried at the meeting on no fewer than fifteen different occasions but in spite of the twin Deep Gale plunges it's a pure fiction to imagine that he always bets heavily on his own horses. Jack of Trumps, sent off a ridiculous 8–11 favourite for the 1978 National Hunt Chase, carried little of his owner's money and none at all when he ran in the 1980 and 1981 Cheltenham Gold Cups. And when Bit of a Skite finally carried off the elusive amateur's prize in 1983 the bookie-gambler didn't have a penny on him, as O'Grady had warned him beforehand that although the horse probably had one good day in him he was also liable to go lame at any time so it would be unwise to get seriously involved.

The wilder and more far-fetched accounts of these episodes, in which the owner risks a million every time, have been built up partly because a lot of ordinary punters love to identify with J. P. and with his real or imagined exploits. The more spectacularly cavalier they can make him out to be, the more courage and encouragement it imparts to them. There is no trace of smugness about McManus. He has never flaunted his wealth or cast himself as a superior mortal to the rest of us day-to-day losers. But it adds spice to his legend that his associates include that crafty, skilful and infinitely charismatic group of Southern Irishmen sometimes collectively if light-heartedly referred to as the Cork Mafia and including the likes of the mighty cattle barons John and Jim Horgan, Lord Killanin's son, the slow-burning trainer, the Honourable Michael 'Mouse' Morris, the bloodstock tycoon Timmy Hyde of Castle Hyde Stud (whose father Tim won the 1946 Cheltenham Gold Cup on Prince Regent for Tom Dreaper) and the Coolmoore supremo John Magnier – and that exiled Irish horseman across the water and most popular Corkman of them all, Jonjo O'Neill. These men, humorous, guileful and impossible to dislike (providing you don't take too censorious a view of the Gay Future saga) are vastly more interesting than the two-dimensional stereotypes of good and evil who inhabit the betting ring in most fictitious racing and gambling scenarios. Betting, to men like the Horgan brothers, is not merely a numerical or cerebral exercise. It is a gesture at once passionate and calculated that sums up a whole approach to life.

At the 1986 Cheltenham Festival, the meeting made unforgettable by the mare Dawn Run's emotional victory in the Gold Cup, there was a widespread belief that Ireland's Bobsline, already a Cheltenham winner, couldn't lose the two-mile champion chase. He had been a desperately unlucky faller twelve months before and 1986 was going to be the year when he belatedly assumed his rightful title. McManus didn't fancy him. He didn't believe that the horse had ever recovered 100 per cent fitness after his mishap the previous March. He fancied another Irish-trained horse, Buck House, also a previous Festival winner, who was being sent over from the Fethard stable of Mouse Morris down in the same fertile Tipperary countryside as Eddie O'Grady's yard seven miles away.

J. P. believed Buck House to be an out-and-out two-mile chaser, who would relish the fast ground and who was being ridden by the best jockey in the race, the Irish Cheltenham specialist Tommy Carmody. He laid Bobsline to other high-rollers at a point or two over the odds and backed Buck House. Buck House won by four lengths and J. P. cleared another five-figure Festival pay day.

At the end of the Thursday afternoon of that meeting there was a large gathering and a convivial atmosphere in J. P.'s box at the top of the stand. It included friends and family, leading Irish racehorse owners and racing personalities, somebody's grandmother and a couple of Catholic Nationalist politicians. McManus stood quietly in the centre of the room, drinking tea and looking on with a kind of detached, unemotional satisfaction as his wife Noreen directed the catering staff and attended to the needs of his guests. In the corridor outside a sadly diminished celebrity from another sporting world was ranting drunkenly up and down, demanding admittance yet being firmly excluded by the McManus minders. The door to the box opened once to admit a famous high-rolling, though by no means professional, punter who had conducted a little business with McManus the bookie on the three-day encounter. The two men went out onto the balcony together, the minders shutting the sliding door behind them. J. P. carried on quietly drinking his tea and contemplating the racetrack and Cleeve Hill beyond. The punter, continually flicking his fringe back out of his eyes and sawing the air with his hands, explained and discussed the sum total of his losses and his plans for repayment. The Limerick man continued to listen and the Londoner carried on talking, the two of them creating a picture as old as racing itself. The bookie and the punter. Winner and loser. Fox and drake.

For more than seventeen years the most uplifting and life-enhancing story of gamblers so nearly clearing out the bookmakers has been the so-called Gay Future Affair, the notorious betting coup that was executed – almost – by a group of McManus's aforesaid friends in 1974. At the centre of the Gay Future story was a charming and irresistible Cork building contractor by the name of Tony Murphy. Murphy, who had built up a fortune by dint of his own efforts and who drove a silver Rolls-Royce to demonstrate it, was a passionate betting and racing enthusiast and a good companion of assorted members of that so-called Cork Mafia. Among them were Eddie O'Grady himself, Mouse Morris, John Horgan,

Brian Darrer, Patrick O'Leary and Cork Garda superintendent J. J. McMahon.

Murphy's Stroke, as Frank Cvitanovich's beautifully made and superbly acted 1981 film of the story was to be called, began properly in the July of 1974 when O'Grady paid £5,000, less commission, to buy a four-year-old chestnut gelding by the name of Gay Future from the Kildare owner–breeder–trainer John Harrington. The horse had won once and been placed four times on the flat in Ireland that season. A couple of days later, O'Grady sold on Gay Future for a nominal price of £1 to Mr Tony Collins, a permit holder and stockbroker from Troon in Scotland. A permit holder, like the notional gambling farmer at Bangor, is essentially an amateur trainer who can only train and race horses owned by himself or his wife. Both a fully licensed and a permit trainer has to have had a horse in their care for a minimum of twenty-eight days before it can race. The contest that was being planned for Gay Future was the Ulverston Novices Hurdle which was to be run at tiny but scenic Cartmel racecourse in Cumbria on 26 August, August bank holiday Monday, 1974. For Gay Future to be listed on the Cartmel racecard as owned and trained by Tony Collins it had to have been in his stable for at least twenty-eight days prior to 26 August. At the time Collins hadn't trained a winner for more than a season and he feared that if he didn't train one in 1974–5 he would lose his permit. By contrast, O'Grady was already the rising star of Irish jump racing who had saddled his first Cheltenham Festival winner, Mr Midland, ridden by Mouse Morris, that March.

On 30 July Collins took delivery of a chestnut gelding shipped over from Ireland, supposedly Gay Future. In fact, this horse was another four-year-old chestnut gelding, an unnamed and unraced son of the little-known stallion, Arctic Chevalier. Collins's head lad, Ian McAllan, was allowed in on the developing scam and told to go through the motions of schooling the new arrival whenever the stable girls were around. Meanwhile, the real Gay Future, for whom the Arctic Chevalier gelding was a virtual dead ringer, who had never raced over hurdles before, was being schooled over 'timber' at O'Grady's yard back in Tipperary and generally trained up to the standard of a serious Cheltenham aspirant.

Among the other horses that Collins owned were a pair of animals called Ankerwyke and Opera Cloak. In July 1974 these two were grazing happily on a farm thirty miles away from Troon, both totally unfit to race. But acting on instructions from Ireland the trainer entered them in two other races being run on 26 August, one at Southwell and one at Plumpton, two more of the eleven race meetings taking place on August Bank Holiday Monday, traditionally one of the busiest betting and racing days of the year.

On Friday 23 August Ian McAllan set off for Cartmel racecourse stables taking with him another of Collins's horses called Racionzer, who had some quite decent form to his name and who had been entered in the same Ulverston Hurdle race as Gay Future. On the night of 23 August a horse box belonging to Eddie O'Grady was shipped over by B & I line from Dublin to Liverpool. It contained the real Gay Future. On the Saturday morning McAllan drove his empty horse box to a lay-by off the M6 near Kendal. Around 10.30 a.m. the Irish horse box drew up. Contact was made between McAllan and the driver of the other horse box, who was Eddie O'Grady's experienced stable lad, Tim Finn. McAllan had already opened the back of his horse box. Gay Future was taken out of O'Grady's box and loaded into Collins's box, Finn joined McAllan in the driver's cab and they set off for Cartmel. The other passenger from Ireland, Christopher Hall, drove the now empty Irish box up to Troon. By Saturday lunch-time Gay Future was safely settled in at Cartmel racecourse stables where he now remained under the watchful eye of Tim Finn. Finn was actually walking around Cartmel with a security badge in his pocket (one that had been applied for on his behalf by Collins and which described him as Collins's employee) proclaiming him to be not Tim but 'Micky' Finn. This pseudonym was only the beginning of his disguise.

On the evening of 25 August seven members of the Cork Mafia, five of them shareholders in the real Gay Future, checked into London's Tara Hotel just off Kensington High Street. Among the party were Murphy himself, John Horgan, O'Leary and McMahon. Next morning, these seven punters, each carrying several thousand pounds in cash, set off to prearranged districts of London to place their money in a series of small bets, not simply on Gay Future itself but also in doubles and trebles linking him with Opera Cloak and Ankerwyke. The doubles and trebles were a crucial part of the coup. If the Irishmen's money had all gone on immediately on the one horse, the off-course betting-shop chains would have seen the extent of their possible liabilities much sooner and realised that something was afoot. They would then have attempted to take offensive action to depress the starting price. The doubles and trebles were a way of keeping the odds as high as possible. That, however, was only the beginning of the plot. Ankerwyke and Opera Cloak were not really intended to run at Southwell and Plumpton at all. Their entries were merely a smokescreen to fool the bookmakers.

On the day of the race Tony Collins didn't go to Cartmel to supervise the running of Gay Future in person. To make it look as if the horse wasn't fancied, its 'trainer' went to Southwell instead where he feigned surprise that his horse box containing Ankerwyke had apparently broken down on the way with the result that Ankerwyke had never arrived at the course. What's more, Opera Cloak's horse box had broken down, too, and he had never arrived at Plumpton. Of course, neither horse had ever set out but as a result of their 'accidental' non-participation all of the money that had been invested in the doubles and trebles was now riding on Gay Future's back alone.

At 6 a.m. on the Monday morning McAllan and Finn led Gay Future out into the rain for a workout on Cartmel racecourse. Finn was now wearing dark glasses as a precautionary measure. Gay Future was down in the morning papers to be ridden by Collins's teenage stable boy Jimmy McNeil, who had never had a ride in public before. But waiting for McAllan and Finn at the entrance to the racecourse was a smart white motor bearing a smart hard jockey. This wasn't Jimmy McNeil. This was the champion Irish amateur rider Timmy Jones and he was going to take McNeil's place in the saddle. Jones gave Gay Future a brief workout, schooled him over a hurdle and then said to Finn that he was confident that as long as he was, 'five lengths in front at the bottom turn they'll never catch us. Even if it was Cheltenham I'd fancy him.'

The events at the racetrack worked to perfection. The Cartmel clerk of the scales (the official responsible for checking that the jockeys are all carrying the correct allotted weight) didn't seem to think that there was anything odd about Jones replacing McNeil and swallowed whole his explanation that he was, 'just over in England for my holidays'. In the run-up to the race, Brian Darrer, who had travelled up to Cumbria with Jones, placed a string of bets on Racionzer, who was being ridden by David 'Gypsy Boy' Goulding, to shorten his odds and force Gay Future's odds out. To discourage further betting on the Collins–O'Grady horse and further extend his price 'Micky' Finn, now wearing a blond wig as well as his dark shades, took Gay Future into a saddling-up box and washed him down with a soapy paste made out of Lux flakes, making the horse look as if it was sweating and unwell.

When it came to the race, Jones never had a moment's worry. Wearing Collins's second colours the Irish bred jumped like an old hand and romped home by fifteen lengths at odds of 10–1. Tim 'Micky' Finn led Gay Future into the unsaddling enclosure afterwards where he was greeted by Darrer but nobody made any overt or public gestures of celebration. Later Darrer, Finn and Timmy Jones drove off together for London to join up with the rest of the 'firm' while McAllan drove Gay Future and Racionzer back to Troon. The following morning Chris Hall loaded the Arctic Chevalier gelding, who had been doubling as Gay Future, into O'Grady's horse box and drove to Liverpool to take the B & I ferry back to Dublin where the ringer appears to have vanished for ever into the Irish mists.

It had not been until the early afternoon of 26 August that the William Hill Organisation became the first large betting-shop chain to realise that a coup was under way and refused any more bets on Gay Future. It was when they tried to lay off their liabilities that the big boys suddenly realised the extent of Murphy's Stroke. In 1974 there was no telephone or blower connection between humble Cartmel and the betting-shop chains' off-course offices, and companies like Hills and Ladbrokes had no representatives on the rails there to whom they could telephone instructions to back Gay Future heavily on-course and shorten up the starting price. Fleets of fast cars were commissioned in Manchester and men with trenchcoats and blow-dried hair were sent up the motorway with all the funds they could raise – which wasn't a lot on a bank holiday Monday seventeen years ago. They arrived forty minutes too late.

It was said that more that £300,000 in 1974 money had been won off the bookmakers, some of it in Ireland but most of it on the British mainland. Not surprisingly, on the Sunday night there was a major hooley in the Tara Hotel. Tony Collins, who had never met Tony Murphy or any of the other co-conspirators before, arrived with a pair of binoculars over his left shoulder, this being the prearranged sign that would indicate his identity to the others. He found the gathering in ripping form but brought with him the first intimations of alarm. He had heard that there had been phone calls to his stable from inquisitive journalists as early as 5 p.m. and by mid-evening the wires were humming.

The story now took a comical turn due to the behaviour of the Garda man J.J. McMahon. He decided that while he was in London he might as well call up a friendly detective in Southampton whom he had met on a previous working visit. It was to be a purely social contact but his telephone call, utilising an ex-directory number for the use of police personnel only, aroused the curiosity of the Southampton force, especially as the only address that McMahon would give was the Tara. The London authorities were contacted and a detective sergeant from Kensington police station went round to the hotel to check him out. Initially alarmed to encounter a large group of Irishmen – this was, after all, only a few months before the Guildford and Birmingham pub bombings and the security situation was already tense – this CID man not only ended up joining in the party but the following afternoon he and two of his colleagues chauffeured Tony Murphy around the West End in an unmarked police car for Murphy to collect his winnings without, he said, any fear of being robbed. Unhappily for Murphy he found that only a small number of the offices were prepared to pay out. Most of them were objecting to Opera Cloak and Ankerwyke having been withdrawn from the doubles and trebles and were demanding an enquiry. Off-stage, Lord George Wigg, who was the harumphing president of the Betting Offices Licensees Association at the time, was orchestrating this concern into a hysterical demand for a full-blown police investigation.

Meanwhile, Tony Collins was beginning to feel the strain. On the Tuesday afternoon he volunteered a statement to Racecourse Security Services, which he later agreed was untrue but which he hoped at the time would prevent the full story coming out. He also got Murphy to sign two letters, one to the Scottish Stock Exchange and one to the Jockey Club, in each of which the Corkman accepted full responsibility for the coup. On the Tuesday night, Murphy and the boys flew out of London for Cork on a flight via Dublin. Twelve days later two senior Scotland Yard officers, Detective Chief Superintendent Terence O'Connell and Detective Inspector George Dent of the Serious Crime Squad, arrived in Cork City. They announced very solemnly that they were looking for a man named Murphy and the locals laughed until they cried.

O'Connell's visit to the Republic was more enjoyable than Jack Slipper's abortive trip to Brazil in search of Ronnie Biggs but it had many of the same elements of frustration, obfuscation and farce.

The two senior policemen enjoyed agreeable outings to Listowel races, to O'Grady's stable in Tipp and to Cork City dog stadium, but everyone they met simply passed them on very charmingly to someone else and nobody would tell them anything or even agree absolutely that Cartmel was a racetrack in north-west England. The Irish off-course bookmakers, who had also been hit by the coup, accepted that if the stroke had gone down the layers would have kept all the money with no demand for an enquiry and 90 per cent of the bets placed in Ireland were paid out. A few of the English bookmaking firms like Heathorns paid out, too, but most BOLA members were firmly behind Wigg. They wanted some kind of retribution to encourage the others.

When O'Connell and Dent returned from Ireland in the autumn of 1974, their investigation seemed to have gone cold. But the climactic moves were still to come. The following March most of the Cork Mafia were over in Cheltenham for the 1975 National Hunt Festival. In the early hours of 11 March, the first day of the meeting, police raided the Queen's Hotel and in scenes that were as risible as they were dramatic and which one guest compared to a raid on an illegal betting office or an Edwardian brothel they rounded up Murphy, O'Grady, John Horgan and Brian Darrer. Timmy Jones and one or two others got away. The four were held at Cheltenham police station until O'Connell arrived from London and then the Yard man had his catch driven up to Kendal where they were formally charged with conspiracy to defraud. The next day a miserable Tony Collins was arrested in Troon and charged with the same offence. Bail for the Irishmen was set at £60,000.

The case eventually came to trial at Preston Crown Court in February of 1976 and began with charges being dropped against O'Grady, Horgan and Darrer, itself an eloquent comment on the difficulties that O'Connell had experienced in his search for witnesses who would talk. The proceedings were heard by Mr Justice Caulfield, later to preside over the Jeffrey Archer–Monica Coughlan libel case, and were remarkable for the sympathy that the judge displayed to the defendants throughout. He praised Murphy warmly for having the courage to take his chances in an English court room and at one point made a telling reference to the public's continuing low estimation of the bookies. 'You might think the popular image of a bookmaker shows him well dressed with a fancy waistcoat, gold chain, Havana cigar, with a bag stuffed with money, which has written on it in large capitals DANNY

ALWAYS PAYS and the punter adding cynically, "Most reluctantly". Perhaps if there were popularity stakes bookmakers might perhaps, with lawyers, be figuring towards the bottom. But don't let any feelings of that sort affect your judgement.' The jury, a pretty dour collection of non-gambling burghers of the town, took Caulfield's advice to heart and found both Murphy and Collins guilty, although only on majority verdicts. Caulfield, continuing to see the funny side, fined them a derisory £1,000 each. The Jockey Club, who never see the funny side of anything, warned off Tony Murphy and Tony Collins from all British racecourses for the next ten years.

Murphy, whose ban didn't extend to Ireland, accepted his reversal philosophically. He and his friends were now the toast of the Irish racing community and their fame even penetrated to the tourist and leisure industries. In December 1981 Murphy was present when a cocktail bar named after Gay Future was opened in Cork's New Victoria Hotel. Ten months later he died suddenly of a heart attack. Collins survived his wretched period of 'expulsion from the school' as he put it and although he doesn't train horses any more he is still a stock-broker of sorts and was at Cheltenham in 1990 enjoying the best caviare and champagne in his friend Michael Buckley's box.

As any Irish man or woman will be the first to tell you, the Gay Future story was a peculiarly Irish triumph in that its protagonists were never actually paid. Or at least nothing like the full pay-off on their investment. BOLA later declared all bets on Gay Future void but their clients never refunded a single penny of the punters' stake money. In a sense the Cork Mafia were the losers – but what a way to lose. Wherever racing is talked about in Northern and Southern Ireland today the coup is still discussed with almost as much reverence as if it were the achievements of Arkle and Dawn Run that were being remembered. But there's an edge to that emotion which is not quite so cosy or sentimental. 'We were convicted by the Preston jury not for committing a crime but because we were Irish,' said Tony Murphy in 1981. 'Our real crime was that the Paddies, as they like to call us, fooled them by proving too clever for their big bookmakers and worse still, to their mind, was that we didn't look like Paddies. That's why they did not let us get away with it.'

In March 1991 the Irish seemed to have the English bookies by the throat once again. This time the main player in the drama was not from Cork or Tipperary but an amply proportioned carpet dealer from Dublin. His name was Noel Furlong and he had been gambling on racehorses for years. His style in the betting ring was of a piece with his character and physique: overreaching and generous.

The agency of Furlong's Cheltenham bets were two horses called Destriero and The Illiad, both of them belonging to his attractive Rubenesque wife Elizabeth, herself a distinguished equine physiotherapist. The name Destriero – and what a stylish and evocative name for a gambled-on racehorse at Cheltenham – first came to the attention of those shrewd enough to notice it in January 1990. At the time it was owned and trained by Mick O'Toole, a man who has broken and been broken by the bookmakers on many occasions. Making his racecourse début in an amateur riders' flat race at Leopardstown the then four-year-old gelding, a son of the stallion Ile de Bourbon, landed an enormous gamble, winning in a canter at even money and delivering at least one bet of IR £110,000 to IR £100,000 in the process. Micko's horses are usually for sale these days, if the price is right, and shortly after that first coup Destriero was sold on to Elizabeth Furlong for IR £55,000. The racing world heard no more of the horse until Leopardstown's Christmas meeting at the end of 1990, nearly two and a half months away from the Cheltenham Festival. This time Destriero made his début over hurdles in a small race which he won, as the Irish commentator said, 'with his head in his chest.'

Destriero would not run again before Cheltenham, a fact used by some naïve columnists to conclude that the horse might have a problem or not be quite good enough and should be overlooked accordingly. The truth was that Destriero's trainer, Andy Geraghty, who had prepared a horse called Hindsight for Tony Murphy in a trial run for the Gay Future coup at Easter 1974, was determined to keep the odds as high as he could by rationing Destriero's racecourse appearances to a minimum. From the quality of the big-bodied gelding's home gallops he knew exactly what kind of talent he possessed.

Back at Leopardstown on 10 January, Furlong stunned the ring with a breathtaking IR £2 million starting-price coup on The Illiad in no less a race than the ultra-competitive Ladbroke Hurdle, the identity of the sponsors understandably making the successful stroke that bit sweeter for the perpetrators. The Illiad had begun his racing career with another notorious Irish gambling trainer

Homer Scott who had landed some touches with the horse himself in 1986/87. The Illiad's 1991 Cheltenham target was to be the Champion Hurdle, a race he had no right to win on form as he would be stepping up from winning a handicap off a weight of ten stone three to taking on the best hurdlers around at level weights. Destriero's target was the Festival's opening race, the two-mile novice hurdle, where he would be competing at level weights too but against the rising stars of the hurdling division.

Those punters and form book specialists who pride themselves on studying past Cheltenham results with care were convinced that Destriero was going to be the business at the '91 Festival. But there were one or two confusing signs. Some Irish racing figures, including no lesser a man than J. P. McManus himself, appeared to prefer another Irish-trained runner in the two mile novice race, Dermot Weld's and Michael Smurfit's General Idea. Then there was the puzzle about Destriero's on-course odds. Opening at 5–1 he went out to 7's and then came back in a point to 6–1 and stayed there: surely not the price you'd have expected if Noel Furlong was backing it off the boards. The truth was that the gambler's money had gone on earlier off-course and for once the off-course chains, deciding that Furlong was no McManus, had decided to stand the bets instead of sending money back to the track to shorten the starting price.

For the off-course bookies the race was a horror story. For backers of Destriero it was three minutes and fifty-eight seconds of purest joy. The handsome five year old, belying his inexperience, jumped smoothly and was given a perfect ride by his young jockey Pat McWilliams. Always on the heels of the leading group the combination took it up on the turn into the home straight and came up that hill irresistibly to win by four lengths from the champion English trainer, Martin Pipe's, top novice Granville Again. General Idea finished fifth. The rails bookmakers were delighted by the result because Cheltenham being Cheltenham they had taken over £100,000 on Granville Again and General Idea alone.

Furlong greeted his winner in the grand manner in the unsaddling enclosure and he and Geraghty, both men wreathed in smiles, bowed repeatedly to their admirers. Furlong confessed that he wouldn't have been able to attend the meeting at all had he not been able to discharge the small matter of a £500,000 bill to the British VAT inspectors that morning, this being an unavoidable payment to cover alleged irregularities in his business affairs.

Destriero's victory, had he believed, cleared him in excess of £1 million in winning bets so he was already ahead on the day. But what really petrified the off-course layers were the further implications of his success. Furlong had not simply backed Destriero to win. He had put him in an assortment of each way doubles with The Illiad, Destriero having been taken at 6–1 and The Illiad at 18–1, with the result that Furlong was looking at a possible total pay out of as much as £10 million if the second leg came up.

What followed over the next hour, the time remaining between the first race and the Champion Hurdle, were scenes of madness and high drama even by Festival standards. This was the moment when the off-course betting industry, gripped with utter panic at the thought of their possible losses, utilised all of their off-track turnover and financial power to shovel back money on to The Illiad on-course to try and slash his price. And given once again that this was not Brighton on a half dead Monday but Cheltenham in March with already huge pools of money circulating, they had to dig deep into their pockets to achieve it. The Illiad, who had been available at 25–1 and 20–1 earlier that morning, opened up on-course at 12–1 and ended up at 11–2 at the off as Ladbrokes and Coral in particular frantically off-loaded their potential liabilities.

For those uncommitted punters watching from the sidelines this was a cathartic and visceral experience when all thought of the bookmakers as basically decent fellows just trying to make a living and operating within a free betting market and so on flew hopelessly out of the window. Especially as this wasn't Victor Chandler and Stephen Little or Webster, Pegley and Roberts who were shortening up the price. It was the men with blow-dried hair: the despised on-course representatives of the Big Three. And watching them run for cover was like watching a pack of frantic rats trapped in a burning barn. Except that this breed of rat managed to escape. Naturally.

The Illiad really did have no business winning the Champion Hurdle and a jumping mistake at the top of the hill saw him drop back quickly from a prominent position to eventually finish twenty-first of the twenty-four runners. The Big Double, a betting coup to eclipse even Hackler's Pride's Cambridgeshire, may have gone down but for the rest of that Tuesday afternoon and for the rest of that Cheltenham meeting you kept coming across groups of stunned and enthralled punters, British and Irish, discussing Furlong's historic gamble in awed tones and wherever you went the amounts of money that were said to have been involved got bigger and bigger each time. How many other high-rolling punters must have been created or inspired by Noel Furlong's example that March day? And how can you ever imagine such a romantic if ultimately losing stroke being planned or carried off against the Tote?

Noel Furlong has taken over the training of Destriero himself and at the time of writing was hoping to run his horse in the 1992 Champion Hurdle. Fellow Irish gambler Barney Curley has been training as well as betting on his own horses for the best part of seven years now in Britain and for ten more in Ireland before that. Any similarity between Noel and Barney ends there. Furlong is talkative, outgoing and expansive. His conversation, like his personality, leaves you in no doubt that he bets because he loves the excitement and the fun it engenders and he will never be able to resist the sheer crack of a gamble. You would find it much harder to ever plumb the depths of Barney Curley's mind.

The monkish Fermanagh man, who trained as a Jesuit novitiary at St Mungret's College in McManus's County Limerick until a bout of tuberculosis convinced him that the Good Lord had other plans for him, uses words slowly and sparely as if they come with a six-figure reserve tag, as if the person he's talking to might have a tape recorder hidden in their pocket. Watching him stealthily patrolling the rails at the big meetings you know that as with J.P. there isn't the remotest semblance of impulsive punting, of the heart controlling the crafty, shaven head. Curley's big wins, like the quarter of a million he collected on Reference Point's Derby in 1987 and the notorious £300,000 Yellow Sam coup he pulled off at tiny Bellewstown in Ireland in 1975 have all been the result of patience, shrewdness and no little self-discipline. Allied to intimate knowledge of the formbook plus, crucially for the big-time gambler, a healthy dose of luck and that instinctive sense of when to go in for the kill, of when to double your stakes and bid for the pot.

These touches have not been lacking in either personality or style. One of the main features of the Yellow Sam affair was the discovery by the off-course bookmakers that their blower connections to the track were continually 'engaged' thus preventing them from sending back money to shorten up Yellow Sam's odds. No telephone cables had been cut. No Irish Telecom officials had been hijacked or held up and therefore no criminal charges could be preferred but the continually blocked phone lines were a coincidence of remarkable good fortune.

But if the British racing public (and the Jockey Club and the bookmakers) have become increasingly familiar with Curley these past few years it's been as much with his role as an uncompromising advocate of punters rights and as a polemical scourge of the bookies as with his primary occupation as a gambler. One of his most trenchant criticisms has been of the power and influence of SIS or Satellite Information Services and of that company's independence or the lack of it.

From 1961 to 1987 the starting prices sent back to Britain's betting offices were compiled by SP reporters working for the Exchange Telegraph Company who supplied the shops with their full voice over, commentary and results service. Nobody would really want to go back to depending on a purely audio service of racing and betting information but the one advantage that Extel had over SIS is that they were completely independent of the big bookmaking firms. Nobody ever questioned the integrity of their SP reporters any more than they question the integrity of David Smalley or Doug Newton, SP reporter of the *Sporting Life* and Neal Wilkins who does the same job for the Press Association. Yet in the last few years there have been a number of incidents involving SIS shows and SP prices which have given thoughtful observers cause for concern.

Bob Terrett, a Bristol-based bookmaker's clerk with a lifetime's experience of the racing business, is one of many on-course regulars to have expressed bafflement over the way in which the SIS studio commentary will frequently declare 'nothing doing' (i.e. no betting market yet been formed) when the horses are actually at the post. 'I have worked on the racecourse for the past 40 years and betting always starts at least five to ten minutes before the off.' Terrett cited a race at Wincanton on 30 March 1990 where 'some of my colleagues got 6–1 and 4–1 about Wessex Warrior . . .' (winner of the last) '. . . but the first show in the betting shops was 5–2.'

Even the ultra-conservative Anthony Fairburn, the former Jockey Club employee who is chairman of the strictly non-controversial Racegoers Club, has conceded that there are bound to be 'niggling fears' about the integrity of SIS transmissions as long as the communication link between the courses and the betting shops is not in independent hands. For their part the SIS management have consistently dismissed criticisms of their impartiality in a blunt and unapologetic manner. At a press conference they called to air the subject on 25 April 1990 their then chief executive Christopher Stoddart declared that while they were trying their best 'to satisfy two opposing factions, the punter and the bookmaker' it was important for everyone to remember that they were primarily running a service for betting shops and that 'the bookmaker does pay for the service.' His racing director Terry Ellis insisted that the prices sent back to the shops have 'to be steady to give the shop operator the opportunity to assess his liabilities.' A reasonable defence, you might think. But the retort of some punters would be that SIS shows are really designed to give the shop operators the time and opportunity to minimise their liabilities.

However confident the SIS men may have seemed when rebutting the allegations of the ordinary bits and pieces punters they do appear to have revealed an Achilles heel over their dealings with Barney Curley. On at least one occasion in 1990 there was a suspicion that bookmaker inspired paranoia about Curley's intentions had resulted in the SIS starting price reporters effectively, if not intentionally, misleading betting shop customers as to on-course betting movements concerning a Curley runner.

On 29 March 1990 a seven-year-old Irish bred gelding called Ardbrin, owned and trained by Curley, won the West Monckton Handicap Hurdle at Taunton. SIS sent back shows fluctuating between 11–8 and 6–4 about the winner. After a complaint by the Irishman the company conducted its own internal enquiry and decided its transmissions accurately reflected the market. Yet Neal Wilkins the PA's senior starting price reporter, with twenty years' experience of the ring noted the winner opening at 7–4 drifting to 9–4 and even touching 5–2 in a place before being backed down to 11–8. In particular Wilkins recorded a bet of £10,000 to £5,000 at 2–1 with Stephen Little whose prices at the 'gaff' tracks are known to follow the odds available on the Tatts' bookmakers boards.

Curley had planned to run Ardbrin again at Ascot two days later but in the event he withdrew his horse at the start as a personal protest against SIS betting shows. The Ascot Stewards fined him £1,000 but he subsequently claimed to have been inundated by offers from other punters to pay the fine for him.

At the next Ascot meeting on 11 April the second division of the 'bumper' or National Hunt flat race was won by a horse called Piper's Son trained near Lambourn by John Oaksey's son-in-law Mark Bradstock hardly renowned as the terror of Las Vegas. Neal

Wilkins recorded the four year old at 10–1 generally and even 12–1 in a place. Piper's Son then touched 8–1 and 6–1 before 5–1 was laid, eventually closing at 4's. SIS sent out a first show of 5–1. PA Extel Sport, a company formed out of the old Extel operation, who provide a betting and commentary service for some of the premium phone lines, sent over an initial show for Piper's Son of 10–1 and in Ardbrin's Taunton race their shows for Barney Curley's horse were 7–4 at 4.36 p.m., 13–8 at 4.40 p.m. and 6–4 at 4.43 p.m. The initial show sent out by SIS was 6–4. The race started at 4.45 p.m.

Barney Curley's view is that the Big Three bookmakers through their SIS shareholding are systematically milking the average punter. 'No other system in the world would, or does, stand for it,' he says. His criticisms of the big companies are not confined to his experiences with his own horses either. He firmly believes that the off-course chains are suffocating the life out of the British Turf like some massive boa-constrictor wrapped around its middle. He wants to see a widespread Government enquiry into the way betting is run and at the very least the establishment of some kind of independent overseeing authority such as that which controls betting in casinos, 'because in racing no one is in charge.'

In the spring of 1991 Curley responded to this vacuum by setting up a pressure group of his own entitled the Independent Racing Organisation. So far the maestro's rather delphic utterances and plans for such unlikely events as an owners strike (to deprive the bookmakers of any racing to make a book on and thus supposedly to hit them in their wallets) have made it difficult to foresee the IRO ever playing a leading role in compelling Cyril Stein into sudden Khieu Sampanh style exile and flight. But then however inspiring Barney Curley may seem as a symbol of consumer resistance he is first and foremost a professional punter. And one who is unlikely to ever feel obliged to inform every optimist or face or even those subscribers to his IRO every time he's out to engineer a betting coup. On 17 July 1991 he pulled off a very respectable touch in an evening race at Sandown Park. His horse, Threshfield, was down in the morning papers to be ridden by the unknown and inexperienced apprentice jockey Tony D'Arcy. But unbeknown to off-course punters (because the betting shops had closed by that time) the professional rider John Reid was substituted at the last minute. Threshfield was backed from 9–1 to 3–1 favourite and landed the odds by one and a half lengths.

The great triumphs of men like Curley and McManus, even though they may often have been gained at the expense of the ordinary punters as much as the bookmakers, still seem like a beacon of hope and inspiration to the rest of us. We choose to forget just how very small the numbers of successful professional gamblers are and we prefer not to think at all about the thousands of losers for whom that beacon of inspiration became a signpost to ruin and loss.

CHAPTER SIXTEEN

A Game of Chance

THE MOST spectacular recent casualty of the betting ring has been the former commodity broker and high-flying Glen International boss, Terry Ramsden. The diminutive 'Tel-Boy' (as *Private Eye* used to call him) was the classic eighties chancer. The Cockney fast-mover whose paper wealth, like his betting turnover, ran into millions. For a few short but colourful years Ramsden, whose love of racing and gambling was never in doubt, strutted and fretted his brief hour upon the stage – flicking his long hair off his forehead before television interviews, wagering a reported £300,000 each way on his own horse Mr Snugfit in the 1986 Grand National and, rather touchingly, trying to buy his way into the closed, conservative world of horse-racing with assorted charitable donations and race sponsorships.

Ramsden was aware of, and understandably sensitive about, what he felt was the Turf's snobbish resentment of his success but even the 'good guys' were never quite sure what to make of him. Was he a humorous, sexy, Jack the Lad? A life-enhancing cheeky chappie without whom racing would be infinitely the poorer? Or was he something altogether less charming?

One of the main problems about the Ramsden phenomenon, and therefore a stumbling block to any fair assessment of his character and achievements, was that no one ever seemed able to explain precisely what it was that he was doing or why it was making him so much money. Even the financial correspondents for the respectable papers used to write about his activities with a kind of polite incredulity. 'He does something in the Japanese commodity market that no one else had thought of doing – and it works,' was all that Paul Haigh could report when he interviewed Ramsden for *Pacemaker* magazine in 1986.

Between 1979 and 1985, Ramsden was employed as a stockbroker by the firm T.C. Coombs (who were declared in default by the Stock Exchange in 1991) for whom he is said to have generated a turnover of as much as £3 billion in Japanese warrants. He left Coombs to set up Glen as his own personal investment vehicle or, as he liked to describe it, as a 'private investment consultancy'. For the financial year 1986–7, Glen was supposed to have shown a profit of over £50 million. 'I've always believed that you can do anything if you set your mind to it and so far I've been proved right,' claimed Ramsden. 'It might have been easier if I'd been based in Bermuda but it wouldn't have been anything like as much fun.' But Ramsden was heavily exposed, through his involvement in the Japanese warrants' market, to the 1987 stock-market crash and in 1988 Glen International collapsed with accumulated losses of more than £142 million.

It was at this moment, just as the Serious Fraud Office began a probe into Glen's affairs, that the trader was warned off all racetracks by the Jockey Club for non-payment of gambling debts. He tried to carry on in commodity dealing, operating principally out of Canada and Switzerland, but also found himself vigorously pursued by personal creditor Bill Collins, former senior partner of disbanded stockbroker Guy Puckle. In April 1991 the Midland Bank started repossession proceedings on Ramsden's Blackheath 'mansion' which had been charged to the bank as security since 1988. On 13 September 1991, the fallen millionaire was arrested by US Customs officers in Los Angeles and held on a warrant issued by magistrates in the City of London. There was no application for bail. A detective chief inspector and an accountant from the SFO confirmed before flying out to California to interview Ramsden that his arrest was on charges relating to Glen International. Extradition applications, they said, would be pursued 'in due course'. A detailed explanation of Glen International's activities may yet be furnished at some future date in a British court but some sides of Ramsden's racing and gambling life look set to remain a mystery.

In May 1988, Ramsden was cleared from charges of VAT evasion at Southwark Crown Court, amid persistent rumours that he had offered the authorities information about certain non-tax-paying illicit bookmakers who had supposedly taken him for a hefty sum long before the Big Three got a piece of his action. In the end it was, inevitably, Ladbrokes who brought about his exclusion from the racecourse by reporting him to Tattersalls' Committee for non-payment of a debt to them of £1 million. Informed sources said that Ramsden had gambled away more than £100 million in total and that he owed money to numerous other rails layers, although he has always insisted that his debts were of a lesser magnitude and that his non-payment to Ladbrokes was over a point of principle and did not reflect any serious difficulties with cash flow.

Whether he was the aggrieved party or not, few would dispute that Tel-Boy was in the grip of an obsession. 'It means nothing to me to be the biggest punter in Britain,' he said once. 'It's a game. I just do it for the crack. There wouldn't be much point in me putting £200 each way on something, would there? I have to put enough on to get a bit of a buzz.' He also said that he was 'not quite sure' whether he was in front or not. 'Not quite sure.' Can you imagine J. P. McManus being 'not quite sure' whether or not he was ahead at the Cheltenham Festival?

The buzz and crack of betting wasn't Terry's only obsession. He also appeared paranoically fearful for his own safety and well-being which led him to go around with a team of over-weight minders who seemed to have stepped straight out of the world of George Cornell and Jack 'The Hat' McVitie, those one-time associates and later victims of the Kray Twins.

At the 1987 Cheltenham Festival, over a year before the VAT trial, Ramsden virtually barricaded himself into a poky upstairs box in the old toffs part of the Cheltenham stand while the minders dealt briskly with any suspicious types – be they in bowlers, Robin Hood or brown trilby hats – who tried to make their way up and down the corridor outside.

The private company running helicopter flights to the course to beat the traffic had laid on a minibus service that year to take their clients from the grandstand back to the in-field landing strip at the end of each day. As Ramsden and his chief bodyguard, a twenty-seven-stone flesh-and-muscle mountain called Wayne, were riding out to their chopper at the end of one afternoon, a breathless, red-faced punter in a velvet-collared coat tried to board the bus at the last minute. Just as he had managed to scramble inside, the mighty Wayne, who had already informed him, 'Not this one, squire', picked him up by the lapels and flung him out on to his back on the grass. A private charge of assault with intent to cause actual bodily

harm was brought against Wayne by the punter but at the subsequent trial at Gloucester the court was told of death threats
against Ramsden that week and that one of the other passengers in
the bus, supposedly another suave high-rolling racegoer, was, in
fact, an armed plain-clothes detective. Wayne was acquitted.

As of December 1991 Ramsden had still not settled his accounts
with the bookmakers and has not been seen on a British racecourse
for over three years – although one Saturday afternoon in 1988, the
manager of a small neighbourhood betting office in north London
was astonished to look up from his cash register and see the once-
mighty high-roller scrabbling around in a corner of the shop with
the optimists and mugs. Ramsden had a £15 win bet on Mtoto in
the King George VI and Queen Elizabeth Diamond Stakes and
coupled him with two other horses in a £10 treble. Mtoto won but
the treble went down. The punter never came back to collect his
winnings.

The truth about Ramsden's alleged connections with some of
the dodgier sides of the racing milieu may never be established any
more than whether he was genuinely an honest trader, cruelly
undermined by the distressingly English habit of knocking a good
man when he's up, or just another compulsive mug punter and
wide-boy with an exaggerated sense of his own importance. What
his story does illustrate is, that the question of just how ethical it is
for a big bookmaking firm to continue extending credit to a man
who is patently hanging himself by degrees is no less relevant in
the 1990s than it was in the era of Howard Padwick and the
Marquis of Hastings.

Terry Ramsden's feigned indifference as to whether he won or
lost reminded some observers of the outwardly devil-may-care
attitude of the old-fashioned casino high-roller – the *soigné* roulette
and chemin-de-fer player for whom winning is never quite as
important as actually playing the game.

Casino gambling can be no less stimulating or enjoyable than
playing the horses but there are one or two important differences.
The sense of affirmation, the gratification and inflated virility
that comes from being a big winner are the same, but most professional horse-race gamblers are a different breed from high-
stakes' players of blackjack and roulette. Some racecourse big
hitters enjoy gracing the tables regularly but, although J. P.
McManus may relax away from the racetrack by sitting down at a
backgammon board, most disciplined professionals wouldn't

dream of staking large sums of money in a casino because they regard it, pejoratively, as a game of pure chance. Plenty of race-course optimists and mugs enjoy playing roulette for fun, and no shortage of Timeform shrewdies relish a game of poker, backgammon or bridge, all activities demanding a high degree of observation, concentration, patience and skill. But piling the chips on to red or black isn't Barney Curley's scene at all, although he would readily admit that, compared with the long hours of study and the relentless application of knowledge, contacts and experience that goes into trying to decipher the Derby winner three months in advance, a casino game of purest chance provides a much more immediate thrill.

The most extravagant casino gamblers, men like Kerry Packer and Adnan Kashoggi, both of whom have often won or lost more than £1 million in a single night, experience their thrills in an atmosphere far removed from the betting ring at Kempton Park or even a box at Cheltenham. They are the men, and very occasionally the women, who have access to the private lifts leading up to the exclusive salons and top-floor rooms of the most famous gaming houses. The feeling inside those rooms is of immense comfort, sleek, plush, velvety expense. And, despite the repetitive whir of the roulette wheel, it is infinitely quieter and more discreet than the bearpit conditions of the racetrack. A top-drawer casino feels more like an environment for the rich, the elderly, the conventional and, in the case of the late Robert Maxwell, the unwell, than for a hyperactive hustler like Mickey Fletcher. They can be seductive places, too. If it is possible to become addicted to gambling just from the trappings and the paraphernalia, a casino is the place for it to happen. It is a world of deep-pile carpets and soft lights, of green baize and low voices. The chips and plaques and the crisp, clean shoes of virginal playing cards have a cold but sensuous feel to them. The jewellery, the scent (the evening dress in Monte Carlo) and the amazing speed and dexterity with which the croupiers rake away the losing throws create an ambience of quality, luxury and money, which seems to flatter you even as you lose.

One of the best, most atmospheric descriptions of casino luxury came in Ian Fleming's first Bond novel *Casino Royale*. Who can fail to be engrossed by the clash of egos and systems that takes place over the grass-green baize battlefield of the baccarat table at Royale-les-Eaux? Or be gripped by the less exotic but much more realistic descriptions of the nauseating 'scent and smoke and sweat' of a casino at three in the morning when 'the soul erosion produced by high gambling – a compost of greed and fear and nervous tension – becomes unbearable and the senses awake and revolt from it'?

Fleming would have loved the old Aspinall's Club in London's Curzon Street, particularly in the days before its founder John Aspinall sold the business to Peter de Savary's Landleisure group in 1987. The restaurant at 'Aspers' served nursery food of a high order. The top-floor lounge enabled one to watch and bet on horse-racing in surroundings of ease and comfort equal to those in the gaming rooms next door and downstairs. And the veteran resident barman, an expert with the cocktail shaker, used to refer to the more distinguished club members such as Charles Benson, Robert Sangster, James Goldsmith and for that matter John Aspinall himself as Mr Charles, Mr Robert, Mr Jimmy and Mr John.

Mr Ian – or Mr James – might have felt less at ease in one of the proliferating numbers of modern casinos that have grown up around the country in the past five years. At the Tiberius Club, which adjoins and is a part of the Royal Bath Hotel in Bournemouth, the colour scheme of the carpets and curtains may not quite be Las Vegas but it is still more eighties function suite than Royale-les-Eaux. The waiters, who wear tight, striped waist-coats and matching bow-ties, look like teenagers on a youth oppor-tunity scheme and an aroma of overcooked roast beef, stronger than any combination of scent, sweat and cigarette smoke, wafts through from the hotel kitchens. Parties of single, rich, elderly ladies from Canford Cliffs sit around the roulette wheel with Marino the Italian restaurant owner, Albert the ex-bookmaker from Swanage, and a trio of rather impoverished looking Iranian exiles. Glamorous or dangerous it isn't.

Since the introduction of the Gaming Act in 1970 and the result-ant creation of the Gaming Board (the body that continues to regulate the casino industry today), all casino operators have had to stick rigidly to the law requiring that gambling facilities should be sufficient only to meet unstimulated demand. It was Ladbrokes' alleged infringement of that law that cost them their licences in 1979: they were accused of taking down the registration numbers of cars parked outside rival West End casinos, of gaining access to the national police computer to track down the owners of those cars who subsequently received unsolicited invitations to gamble on Ladbrokes' premises in future. Contemporary casino proprietors

like Max Kingsley, chairman of London Clubs which owns the
Casanova, Palm Beach and Ritz Clubs, know that they cannot
afford that kind of aggressive marketing. But, just like the big
betting-shop chains, they keep an eagle eye on their employees to
ensure that there are no instances of fraud, embezzlement or
skimming off the top. 'The greatest protection a casino has is its
system,' says Kingsley. 'If you watch a blackjack game in any of
our casinos in London, Cairo or Cannes, you will see the cards
dealt in exactly the same way, the chips collected in exactly the
same way, and the pay-outs made in the same way. They do it as if
by second nature. If an inspector sees a dealer paying with the
wrong hand he will want to know why.'

Kingsley's staff are taught to be 'excessively pleasant' so that the
punters 'come back even when they have lost'. The croupiers and
dealers know that they must not only be clever with their fingers in
handling chips but that they must also understand how to relate to
people. It is no good showing resentment or displeasure if the
house is losing and equally it is vital to continue to be charming
and attentive when the punter is losing, and, as Chris Gore-Booth,
who trains croupiers for London Clubs, continually reminds them,
they must always keep things moving on. 'We make money by
keeping the game going. If the game slows down the punter has
time to think: "I've won £2,000. I'll stop." A punter isn't my
favourite person if he wins and then stops playing. We want them
to win and put the money back on the table.'

The ordinary, losing casino punter – not the comfortably uphol-
stered tycoon but the roulette chaser in an open-necked shirt to be
found sweating it out at the Golden Nugget in Piccadilly Circus
from opening time until 2 a.m. – is just like the ordinary loser at the
racetrack. Like all optimists and mugs, casino losers refuse to
accept that if they go on and on gambling, the house will always
win in the end and they cannot get around this by raising the
stakes or rethinking their staking methods. Casino losers genuinely believe that they can somehow influence the spin of the
wheel by their own actions or manner of playing, or that by
monitoring developments carefully enough they will be able to
foretell what colours and numbers to bet on and when. Casinos
encourage the illusion that winning numbers can somehow be
anticipated in advance by providing roulette players with special
cards to record and analyse trends. But each spin of the wheel is
different and independent and there is no way a win can be

predicted. The fair odds are one in thirty-seven that the ball will land on a particular number or zero but the house only pays 35–1 when the punter scores. In blackjack by assiduously counting cards it is possible to beat the house in the long run, although anyone spotted counting or taking notes at the table will be asked to stop or, in some cases, to leave.

Dozens of roulette and blackjack players base their approach on cherished systems that they may have spent days and nights perfecting, but the systems are no more likely to yield them a profit than scattering their chips at random while standing on the top table wearing a blindfold. 'The more systems people invent the better we like it because they have no validity,' confirms Chris Gore-Booth. 'It's the old story, isn't it? Remember the telegram: "System perfected. Send more money."'

The more impetuous casino punters may not bother with systems and accept that they cannot influence the spin of the wheel or the fall of the cards because these things are all a matter of chance. But they believe passionately in luck and for them luck and chance are not the same thing at all. They regard luck as a kind of metaphysical or elemental force. You cannot compel it to come but when it does you must not only use it but use it well. When it has self-evidently run out, you must not abuse it by trying to keep it going or you may jeopardise everything that it has brought you previously. To hit a lucky streak in a casino and to be seen doing so is not only intensely, even sexually, pleasurable but, like backing six winners at the racetrack, makes it seem as if you are one of those very fortunate and special individuals who are equally blessed in all areas of life.

But when you have dispensed with systems and finished talking about luck there remains that exhilarating burst of adrenalin triggered by the action. And for an addictive roulette player, the turn of the wheel is every bit as intense a sensation as that which the horse player experiences during the running of the four o'clock race at Yarmouth. Dr Iain Brown, a psychologist at Glasgow University, found that a group of casino gamblers he surveyed regularly experienced a rapid increase in their pulse when they were playing roulette and blackjack.

'Gamblers become highly aroused while they are playing,' he says. 'The gambler's heart rate may increase by as much as fifty beats per minute, giving a pulse of about a hundred and twenty. This is the sort of increase that would occur when an athlete is sprinting a hundred yards. The excitement releases noradrenalin, a hormone which is associated in the extreme with manic states.' Brown believes that compulsive casino gamblers are addicted to their own adrenalin.

In the late-seventies and the early to mid-eighties, London's casino owners could depend for business on a steady stream of international high-rollers and plungers. London was and still is the only capital city in Europe or the Western world with a casino presence and has traditionally drawn wealthy players not only from the Middle East but also from Malaysia, Japan and Hong Kong. The rising tide of Arab fundamentalism in the mid-eighties, however, made it impolitic for so many Saudis and other Gulf potentates to be seen splashing their fortunes around at the gaming tables. The falling oil price and the Iran–Iraq war contributed to the declining numbers of Middle Eastern punters and with turnover dropping accordingly casino owners started to sell. Between 1986 and 1990 all except one of London's twenty-one licensed gaming clubs changed hands at least once. Max Kingsley believes that some of those *arriviste* owners like Mecca Leisure, who paid £750 million to purchase five casinos from Pleasurama in 1988 and then had to sell the Clermont for £30 million two years later, lost money on their investments because they didn't understand the casino business. 'The amount of money exchanged for chips in London in 1990 was £1,186 million but at the top end of the business a casino could be seven figures down at the end of one day if one or two big players happened to get lucky. You have to have the financial guts to take that in your stride. You have to bite your lip, sit back and wait for the percentage to work for you.'

Walking away a big winner from the Palm Beach or the Ritz Club is every bit as exhilarating as receiving a five-figure cheque from Ladbrokes, or more probably Victor Chandler. The classiest casinos also have the advantage of at least offering you a swanky and well-equipped environment in which to lose. They are terrific places in which to bite your lip, thumb or hand silently as the bitter draught of ruin spreads through your veins, or in which to drink yourself under the table or, better still, in which to loosen your black tie and tip the doorman your final £100 chip before walking out with affected nonchalance into the Mayfair dawn. Losing your entire roll at a dog track has few of those compensatory attractions. Indeed, some cynics would sneeringly say that an outing to the dogs is rarely uplifting even if you win.

Back in the 1940s and 1950s a night at the dogs was almost as popular a gambling experience as a trip to the Derby or the Grand National. With no legalised off-course cash-betting offices, working-class punters turned instinctively to greyhound racing as an opportunity for a harmless flutter. It took place in the evenings after work, there were easily accessible stadia in most large towns and cities, and admission prices were modest.

Contemporary professional horse-race players would no sooner patronise a dog track than they would be seen hanging around a crap game. But some racecourse mugs profess to derive almost as much pleasure from dog racing as from the ponies and retain fond and not so fond memories of going on to White City after an afternoon at Newbury or Sandown Park and backing ten more consecutive losers to add to the six that they had picked out at the racecourse earlier in the day. Alas, White City is no more, the entire stadium having been razed to the ground in 1984. The essence of the old White City experience used to be the foggy winter nights, the floodlights in the dark, the shouting bookies and tic-tac men, the neon and hissing electricity, the animated punters and the fag smoke and the triple vodkas.

Successful dog stadia in the eighties and nineties tend to be cleaned-up, anaesthetised and yuppified environments where the grasses and touts are heavily outnumbered by slick young city types in the kind of red braces that you thought had all perished with Filofaxes and personal organisers. At Wimbledon the City boys and middle-class family outings take in the racing as a back-drop while munching happily away in the tiered restaurant where the waitresses place your bets for you and a female announcer warns primly in clipped tones that staff are 'forbidden to have betting transactions with persons under the age of eighteen'. There is no earthly reason why respectable citizens from SW19 shouldn't be allowed to have a birthday party or a meal out at a dog track, but it's not quite the Andy Capp spirit of yesteryear. Trying to engi-neer a touch on the three dog (meaning the greyhound running out of trap three), perhaps by paying the kennelmaid of the favour-ite to give it a large bucket of water, or even unkindly to squeeze its genitalia just before the off, doesn't have quite the same *frisson* of villainy when half the punters standing or sitting around next to you seem to be jolly middle-class mums all chatting anxiously about nannies and school fees.

This is not to say that venues like Wimbledon aren't popular (attendances were booming before the recession) and the management would avow that the appeal is directly connected to the nice, clean, safe and respectable new look – the bright, cheerful air of Toyland acceptability right down to the red and yellow paint, the carpeted foyer, the spotlessly clean lavatories and the highly polished lino on the stairs. You scarcely notice the difference between the front side of the stadium and the understandably scrubbed and antiseptic kennel and tack area at the back of the paddock bar. Strip lighting illuminates a stern 'No Smoking' sign above the kennel girls' lockers and, if they wish, punters can see for themselves the unimpeachable integrity of the pre- and post-race proceedings and watch through the window of the paddock bar as the greyhounds produce their obligatory post-race urine sample, which they do by watering a small bunch of twigs which have to do service for a lamp-post on Merton High Street.

For a taste of the old sleaze-pit, nicotine-coated dog-racing ambience of the forties you have to take a journey down the Waterden Road in East London. Past Tibbett and Britten plc, past the boarded-up gates of Senola Banqueting and on to Hackney Stadium which is a grand name for a venue not much bigger or smarter than a poorly endowed comprehensive-school soccer pitch. Some parts of the windows and roofing are cracked and dilapidated and the slatted wooden seats that cover the concrete terracing cannot conceal the carpet of fag ends and losing betting tickets at your feet. In the bar at the top of the stand you watch the SIS racing coverage in between races while eating a lethal cheeseburger composed of very pink 'meat' topped off with a thin strip of cold unmelted processed cheese, piled high with evil-smelling onions. And you look around you at the Stratford environs, the clouds, flats and flyovers, and the pylons in the distance, and know that you are a long way from the restaurant at Wimbledon, let alone Ascot Heath.

The muddy-looking sand track, which is raked by a tractor-pulled roller after every race, is narrow and tight though not so narrow as at Crayford where they seem to have a first bend pile-up in every other heat. Before each event, the dogs, a wistful-looking collection on the whole, are brought out by their kennelmaids and taken up a wooden ramp leading over the course and out into the 'infield' where they briefly loosen up before being loaded into the traps. The races themselves last about as long as an Epsom five-furlong sprint. Hackney has a surprisingly strong market, the strongest of surprisingly strong market, the strongest of the daytime grey-hound stadia and no shortage of excitement and noise stirs the crowd as the contestants round the final bend. But once they have passed the winning post it quickly dies down again, replaced by the usual mixture of speculation, recrimination and chat.

There are rarely more than 300 punters present at Hackney and 90 per cent of them will be male. Some are sharp, cocky lads who wear shades and shorts in summer. One or two are elderly Max Wall lookalikes in faded suits and carpet slippers. There are old fat men and young hard men and white-faced plain-clothes police-men running an eye over the usual attendance of small-time off-duty spivs. The flash-looking character in the Italian suit with the white shirt, red-patterned tie, brogues, dark glasses and cordless phone is not a dogs' high-roller. He's an agent for an off-course betting-shop chain, staking money at the track, exactly as at a racetrack, to protect his employers' profit margins and ensure that those starting prices don't get too far out of line with off-course trends.

Usually the only other people wearing a jacket and tie at Hackney are the bookies or at least one or two of them. There are sometimes no more than five boards bookmakers present and the current star turn is always the resplendent John Jenkins who trades as John Power and who at present is regrettably, though only temporarily, banned from his rails pitch at the horse-race meetings as a result of a fracas in the bar at Huntingdon one day in 1988. The John Power firm have been long-term sponsors and supporters of greyhound racing at both the gaff tracks and the prestige venues though given the dribble of money and customers most Tuesdays, Thursdays and Saturdays in the Waterden Road they must some-times wonder why they bother. With his permanent suntan, long blond hair, sideburns, moustache and accompanying medallion, watch and signet ring, John brings a welcome touch of panache to wherever he bets, and his company and conversation are in-variably a major attraction of any gathering in the Waterden Road.

In one sense the punter's experience at the dogs is rather like the experience of the dogs themselves. You start off barking with excitement as the hare appears. You feel that great surge of adrena-lin and elation when the dog you've backed makes a challenge for the lead down the far side, but then, so often, your dog is knocked back at the final turn and you end up feeling as disillusioned and cheated as the greyhounds when they get to the winning post and discover that the fat juicy hare that they thought they were chasing is nothing but a bedraggled toy rabbit on wheels.

The owners of Hackney Stadium, Brent Walker Ltd, parent company of William Hill, are unmoved by such philosophical reflections. Neither are they much bothered about whether or not John Power makes a profit. This is because Hackney is a BAGS track, which means that it is one of the stadia that participate in the Bookmakers' Afternoon Greyhound Service. This is an arrangement whereby the big off-course bookmaking firms pay certain greyhound tracks to open up for racing on weekday afternoons when they couldn't possibly expect to make a profit on such fixtures from punters coming in through the turnstiles. This way the big chains are guaranteed a regular supply of dogs' action (or cannon fodder?) for their betting-office clientele between, and before the daily diet of horse-racing. Hackney also stages Saturday morning fixtures which are a kind of extension of the BAGS principle to another little corner of the gambling week. Incorrigible shop regulars turning up at opening time to scrutinise the afternoon's television racing form in the *Life* and the *Post* can hopefully be tempted into frittering away some money on incomprehensible greyhound racing long before the horses are under orders.

The kindest, most benign thing you can say about your local betting office at 10 a.m. on a Saturday morning, or at 2 p.m. and 5 p.m. on a Monday, Tuesday and Wednesday afternoon, is that it provides you with a clubby and apparently sympathetic milieu, populated by familiar faces and hardened fellow travellers. This is equally true of a racetrack, a dog track and even, after a fashion, a casino. To the ex-gambler, the compulsive punter now reformed or the punter who may have foreseen their impending ruin and somehow managed to turn back at the edge, those gatherings may be a club but only of the most clueless, wretched and compulsive losers. And nobody is better or more merciless at detecting the desperation that may exist beneath the punter's façade than a former addict who has changed his ways.

Gamblers Anonymous have approximately 150 registered groups in Britain and many others in Europe and America. But GA spokesmen and women believe that their official British membership of between 5,000 and 10,000 is only the tip of an enormous iceberg. 'We only get people when they're at the end of the line,' explained a member of the Gamblers Anonymous Croydon group, which is fairly typical of countless small GA groups around the country. 'People who've stolen. People who've been to jail. People who've literally tried to murder their family to get the money to gamble with. Then we get a lot of other punters who may come two or three times but then disappear again, presumably because the message has not yet sunk in. But in ten years' time they'll be back.'

GA is not a vast, monolithic organisation staffed by impersonal experts or psychologists. It is made up of individual ex-gamblers meeting in small local groups, along the lines of Alcoholics Anonymous, and giving or trying to give fellowship and support to other gamblers who are trying to beat the habit. The Croydon group, which meets every Monday night, has twenty to thirty regular members. The addicts and the ex-punters meet in the gambling room while the wives, husbands, families and friends meet in another room next door, before the two groups get together at the end of the evening. These Samaritans of the betting world are continually trying to get across the point that you can never wholly, truly or permanently win at gambling and that to carry on, no matter the cost, in the hope of eventually doing so is not only futile but an assured way of losing everything. But in the eyes of GA, a compulsive gambler is someone who gambles to lose and who, whether knowingly or otherwise, is only satisfied when they do lose. Trying to break that obsession, if the punters are not prepared to recognise it, is nearly impossible.

The Croydon GA members included a man, now in his early thirties, who began playing the slot machines in amusement arcades in his teens and first borrowed, then stole money from his family and friends to continue gambling. They had a once-married man, now divorced and living in a hostel, who started betting on horse-racing while he was still at school and was renowned for his diligent study of the form book and controlled and disciplined approach. When he was fifty-two his wife suddenly discovered he had run up debts of over three times the value of their twice-mortgaged house and had been gambling away his, her own and their children's future for the best part of twenty-five years. Another Croydon GA member was once an archetypal racecourse face and insider dealer, a high-roller who had paid informants in a string of Newmarket stables and liked to stroll around the yearling sales rings of England and Ireland chatting to prominent racing figures on first-name terms. This face broke his own rules about value betting just once and invested three times more than his usual maximum bet on a runner in the 2,000 Guineas at Newmarket. The horse finished second. The punter started to chase his losses and break his rules with abandon. Ten months later he was living in a caravan parked in a lay-by off the A4. All these punters started out with successful, exciting and winning gambling experiences.

Sometimes these stories have an upbeat ending. GA publishes a monthly magazine entitled *New Life* and each issue contains about twenty personal accounts written by ex-gamblers and chronic losers who managed to clean themselves up and rebuild their lives away from the horses, dogs and poker chips. Despite these often harrowing accounts, GA is not censorious of betting, racing, roulette or gambling of any kind. They understand its appeal even if they seem to know before you do that your fondness for the high life and fast times at Cheltenham, Epsom and the Ritz Club, the occasional hedonism that you think you have safely under control, is the first, if not already the advanced, stage of an addiction that may easily lead you onto the rocks. The element of free will and the punter's right to choose is not in dispute. 'We don't condemn gambling,' says a Cheltenham GA member, 'but we do deplore the extent to which the odds are stacked in the bookies' favour. The punter always pays.' Depending on the outcome of the arguments currently raging between the off-course bookmakers and the racing authorities, the punters, though not necessarily the betting-shop owners, could end up paying still more.

CHAPTER SEVENTEEN

The Punter Always Pays

ONE OF the most contentious subjects in modern British racing is the vexed issue of prize money. Numerous concerned sections of the industry feel that the average prize-money levels on the British turf are steadily sinking so far behind those of rival countries such as France and Italy that the sport in this country is rapidly heading for second-division status at best. Middle- and lower-tier owners, it is said, even if they win two or three races a year, can no longer cover their training costs, let alone show a profit on their investment. And where will the future employment of breeders, trainers, jockeys and stable lads be if owners can no longer see any financial incentive for getting involved? The usual corollary to this argument is that if only British racing, like the French and American models, could get its hands on that portion of the profits generated by off-track betting that currently pass through the offices of private bookmaking companies then this situation could be reversed. Prize money could be raised and new owners could be attracted. The Derby would no longer be only the thirty-third most valuable race in the world and trainers' futures would be secure.

So how about a massive increase in the Betting Levy? Not possible, say the off-course bookmakers. You simply don't understand the betting industry. It could never absorb a dramatic increase in the levy without continuing to pass on the cost to its customers as increased deductions, which would depress turnover and threaten an even greater decline in prosperity. We don't believe you, say the bookies' critics. We'll ask the Home Office for a statutory mechanism to prevent you passing the bill onto the punters. Or, better still, let's have an off-course Tote Monopoly as they do in Australia, even a total Pari Mutuel based system like France. Then we might have an income in excess of £200 million a year from betting instead of the present paltry £37.7 million.

Ever since they hosted a one-day conference on the future of the racing industry at Sandown Park racecourse in April 1990, the Jockey Club, who in the past have displayed no more interest in the bookies than they have in their punters, have attempted to put themselves at the head of a campaign to wrest more money for the Turf from off-course betting, to remedy what they and others now perceive to be the grave financial crisis threatening the very survival of the sport.

In 1990 roughly 60 per cent of the £250 million a year that the Club say it costs to run racing was paid by racehorse owners in the entry fees they have to pay, often months in advance for the biggest races, to have a chance of their horses participating. A further 20 per cent came from race-goers coming in through the turnstiles, 4 per cent from sponsorship and 16 per cent from off-track punters via the Betting Levy, that percentage yielding, in practice, the sum of £37.7 million. The Jockey Club and its supporters believe that this is a wholly inadequate figure and that betting-shop owners and not just their customers should be forced to contribute more in return for the use that they make of racing's 'product'.

The Jockey Club justify their position by pointing to the numbers of training establishments in Lambourn and Newmarket currently on the market but where their owners cannot find a buyer. They talk of racing stables where less than half the boxes are filled and continue the damaging comparison between the value of Britain's most prestigious races and overseas events such as France's sumptuously well-endowed and CIGA-sponsored Arc de Triomphe weekend in Paris in October. That two-day Longchamp fixture with its ten Group races, five of them with Group One status, posting a pool of £1.2 million in win prize money alone, is now established as the premier flat-racing occasion of the European year and a truly star-studded event equal to the $10 million Breeders' Cup meetings in America.

Other sincere, committed racing enthusiasts who may share some of the Jockey Club's general concerns are less bothered about the fate of the wealthier race-horse owners and feel that any increases in prize money should be directed initially at the basement level, which is where most owners and trainers have to chance their arm. They point out that while the Derby may be worth less on paper than big races abroad the winning owner still annually lines up for a potential bonanza in stud fees. Given that, of the last eleven runnings of the Derby, three have been won by indecently rich Arab princes, three by the Aga Khan and one by Robert Sangster they can see little point in adding yet more noughts to the bank balances of these enviably well-heeled gentlemen. This school of criticism is far more concerned with the plight of racing's workforce: the amalgam of stable lads (meaning men, women, young boys and teenage girls), work riders and apprentices, who have been systematically underpaid and, in some cases, abused and exploited for generations. There is absolutely no firm evidence to back up the old contention that paying more money to the owners at the top will result in this cash progressively filtering its way down to the workers at the bottom and it is rightly argued that unless racing shows itself willing to address this imbalance first it will forfeit any claim to wider public funding and support.

Every bit as important as the pay and conditions of racing's indispensable labour force is the issue of how much it costs to conduct an only normally expensive day out at a British racetrack. Punters visiting Longchamp in October are not only treated to a superb programme of racing they also have to pay only £5 a head to walk in through the gate. Race-goers attending Britain's nearest equivalent event, the King George VI and Queen Elizabeth Diamond Stakes at Ascot in July, have to find £20 if they wish to subscribe to the Club or Members' Enclosure. They will pay £10 each to go into the Members' at god-forsaken Nottingham or Leicester on a rainswept Monday afternoon. Supporters of a total or off-course Tote Monopoly invariably step in here with what is undoubtedly their strongest argument: the admirably cheap admission prices at Longchamp and the generous levels of prize money are a direct consequence of France's integrated system of betting and racing. The PMU has a monopoly on horse-race betting and, although it has to pay for its overheads, running costs and make an annual payment to the French government, it has no risk-taking private shareholders to please and no private companies with which to compete. This is why in 1990 French racing's share of betting turnover was nearly 5 per cent of the whole resulting in a contribution of £164 million out of a total take of £3.38 billion. In the same period the amount passed on by bookmakers to British racing was less than 1 per cent.

The need to improve on the quality of service that the customer enjoys at the racetrack is indisputable, yet not all the arguments are as simple or as one-sided or as obviously balanced in the Jockey Club's favour. There are those within the racing industry who believe that anyone who goes into racehorse ownership with the idea that they should be able automatically to count on a commercial return needs instant psychiatric attention.

Others would go even further and say that any subsidy of what has traditionally been a rich man's hobby, particularly if that subsidy comes from the pockets of modest betting-shop punters, is morally offensive. When the House of Lords debated the financial well-being of British racing in February 1991, a series of Jockey Club members got up to talk about the grave economic difficulties facing the sport, caused primarily, they said, by the main proceeds of off-track betting going to off-track betting-shop owners and not to racing's competing constituencies to spend as they would like. Countless deserving trainers were being forced out of the game, yards were on the market with an absence of prospective purchasers and bank managers were closing in. No Jockey Club member or supporter referred to anything as vulgar as a business plan for the future of the industry but well-heeled racing toffs like Lord Vestey of Stowell, the fox-hunting 'Master Butcher', whose family businesses include the Dewhurst meat chain and whose family trusts enjoy all the advantages of one of the biggest tax loopholes in revenue history, got up to speak about the near unimprovable perfection of the Jockey Club, of its members' remarkable and unstinting devotion to their autocratic role and their unique suitability to continue in it unchanged and unopposed for decades to come.

However, one or two discordant notes were struck. One of them, unfortunately for the Clubmen, by the seventy-one-year-old Duke of Devonshire, father of the current Senior Steward of the Jockey Club, the Marquis of Hartington, and himself the owner in his time of such distinguished competitors as the mare Park Top, runner-up to Levmoss in the 1969 Prix de l'Arc de Triomphe. The Duke poured scorn on the notion that racehorse owners were a species deserving of the same kind of monetary support as hospitals, schools and public transport systems. Owning thoroughbreds, he said, was a luxury like owning a yacht or having a taste for the finest Havana cigars. Nobody subsidises those activities so how can it be appropriate to subsidise owning a novice chaser or two-year-old colt? He and his father had never expected such benevolence and others should have to live without it too.

A similar theme was propounded by the then Trade and Industry Minister, Lord Hesketh, who implied that racing would have to sort out its own problems and if its income was insufficient to meet its needs then its needs would have to be pruned. Good trainers would survive, though some mediocre ones might fall by the wayside; racing could not expect to be immune to market forces any more than any other commercial enterprise. And there was no likelihood of a Conservative government awarding the Tote any monopoly, either on- or off-course.

Five days before the debate in the Lords the Jockey Club had been presented with a golden opportunity to put their case on an even more influential stage. They appeared before the Commons Home Affairs Select Committee, who were conducting their own wide-ranging enquiry into the workings of the Betting Levy to determine whether it was still an appropriate charge on betting and still serving the interests of punters and horse-racing.

On-course bookmakers began to pay the Racecourse Association a voluntary contribution from their Amenities Fund 'to aid and improve horse-racing' as early as the late 1950s. The formal levy principle was first established in the Betting and Gaming Act of 1961 and originally intended to compensate racecourses for any loss of revenue they might suffer from potential customers deciding to patronise a betting shop instead. The present levy rate of 0.89 per cent is in no sense a payment made directly to racing by the bookmakers out of their own profits. Shop owners pay income tax, corporation tax and VAT on those profits but they take the 8 per cent betting duty that they are required to pay to the Government and the 0.89 per cent of turnover that they are currently obliged to pay racing, throw in an extra 1.1 per cent for themselves to cover their handling charges and their non-recoverable VAT payments and call the whole 10 per cent sum the 'tax' on off-course betting. Therefore, it is their customers who pay these bills and their customers who partly subsidise owners' prize money levels at Cheltenham, Royal Ascot and elsewhere. The punters can pay this 10 per cent deduction either when they place their stake money or when they collect their winnings (that being the more expensive course), if they are lucky enough to have any. The bookies insist that their handling charges, such as paying for copies of racing's two trade papers to be displayed on the walls of their shops each day, are no different from the commission charged to an investor by his stockbroker or any other speculative trader. They prefer not to explain why they also make a full 10 per cent deduction on greyhound bets as well as sports and political bets even though no levy arrangement exists in favour of those activities.

Bookmakers' representatives and members of the Levy Board meet annually to try and agree on a levy figure. The bookies only have one seat on the Levy Board: the other seven are split between three Home Office nominees, three Jockey Club members and the chairman of the Tote Board. A Bookmakers Committee deputation negotiates on their industry's behalf and the Levy Board negotiates for racing. The figure arrived at is invariably a compromise between what the bookies say that 'they' can afford and what the Levy Board say that racing needs. If the two parties cannot agree, the Home Secretary intervenes and sets a rate. Successive Home Office ministers have made no secret of their intense irritation at being asked to resolve what they regard as a purely racing matter.

Leading the joint Jockey Club and Horseracing Advisory Council (an umbrella group of differing racing interests) submission to the Home Affairs Committee were the Senior Steward Lord Peregrine 'Stoker' Hartington, who deserves some credit for approaching his role in a considerably more enlightened fashion than his predecessors. Accompaying him was his pink-faced chief executive, the first such paid employee in the Jockey Club's history, Mr Christopher Haines. Mr Haines is a former executive of the British Sugar Corporation and is remembered by one of his erstwhile fellow board members as 'the last person you'd notice in a crowded room'. Quite what it was about him that persuaded his current employers that he was the ideal man to front a horse-racing business is not entirely clear.

Arrayed before Haines, Stoker and their supporters when they trooped into Westminster's Grand Committee Room on 13 February 1991 were a disparate group of parliamentarians ranging from the soberly respectable Tory chairman Sir John Wheeler to the redoubtable Dame Janet Fookes, the robust free marketeer David Ashby, the former police officer John Greenway and the Kinnockite socialists Alan Meale, Joe Ashton and Keith Vaz. The generally shared view of these mostly, though not entirely, non-gambling backbench MPs, relatively tactfully expressed in their eventual report but put more bluntly off the record, was that the

248

Haines–Hartington double act was by turns inept, confusing and naïve and quite the poorest performance of any of the witnesses they had talked to in the course of their investigations.

Lord Hartington was the first to make waves when he began his evidence by demanding that the levy system should be scrapped altogether and replaced by a 2½ per cent 'royalty' payment from off-course bookmakers in return for them being allowed to bet on horse-racing. Asked whether this figure had been 'plucked out of the air' Christopher Haines's response was that it was 'the ball-park figure' equivalent to awards in other comparable industries. David Ashby wanted to know 'what other industries' and suggested that the Jockey Club were effectively 'making a takeover bid' for the levy and seeking 'a monopoly position for Horse-racing Industry Inc'. Haines insisted that one advantage of introducing a royalty payment was that it would remove the need for the Home Secretary to arbitrate in future disputes. He also did his best to refute the suggestions of several MPs that the Club were neither 'competent' nor 'professional' enough to take on the bookmakers in direct negotiations. His protestations failed to convince.

The following day David Ashby informed some members of the racing press that he felt the Jockey Club had been 'trying to cover up their ineptitude with a veneer of efficiency which is only skin deep. As the proceedings went on the more amused I became at their naïvety. I felt sad, really, because they missed a good opportunity of putting forward their case.' Alan Meale echoed these sentiments, observing that the Jockey Club team had been so unimpressive that there had seemed 'little point rubbing their noses in it'. Referring to the supposed coaching in presentation skills that Haines and Hartington were believed to have received in advance he added that the result 'just goes to show that you can't teach an old dog new tricks'.

The main off-course bookmakers were inevitably scornful of the Jockey Club's proposals and mocked them for demonstrating once again their ignorance – as they saw it – of the real profitability of the off-course betting industry. They were adamant that an increased levy could only be sustained by increasing the deductions they make from punters' winnings, which would depress turnover and lead to a reduced yield for everyone.

When it came to their turn the bookies' representatives led by Tom Kelly and the smoothly professional Peter George were every bit as silky and long-suffering as the Al Pacino and Robert Duvall characters when they appear before the Kefauver Senate Committee on organised crime in *The Godfather, Part Two*. When the Select Committee came to publish their report in May 1991 they had clearly been impressed by the bookmakers' arguments – up to a point – and, as far as the ambitions of the Jockey Club are concerned, seemed to feel that Stoker and Chris are marginally less qualified to conduct direct commercial negotiations with the bookies than Gussie Fink-Nottle and Catismeat Potter-Pirbright. The committee's recommendation was that the current Levy system should remain in place for the present as 'the racing industry does not have the commercial skills or unity and clarity of purpose to take on the big bookmakers in the open market. They would be ill-advised to seek to abandon the current system and we would be fearful of the consequences for the racing industry of a market free-for-all.' The committee also suggested that if racing was ever to be able to take advantage of some replacement of the levy in future, it would have to modernise its power structure, become more efficient and more aware of the need to look after its customers at *every* level. It should wake up to the imperative to promote itself actively in both the domestic and international markets. 'We believe that the racing industry will do itself a grave disservice if it does not unite behind a leadership with business acumen.' Racing's proliferation of overlapping ruling bodies, the committee went on, should be merged into one new *de facto* British Horseracing Authority, which would mean if not the effective abolition of the Jockey Club then a considerable dilution of its powers.

As far as the bookmakers were concerned the committee reaffirmed that their liability to duty and levy is *their* liability and not that of the punters. 'To call bookmakers' deductions "tax" is at the least disingenuous, at worst less than honest.' The MPs declared that they 'would apply a large pinch of salt before swallowing the proposition that large bookmakers are in any sense hard up'. The committee had been able to compel the Big Three to disclose to them, confidentially, the precise figures relating to their take and profit margins from betting on horse-racing, which they will not reveal to anybody else. It was therefore particularly intriguing that they should propose that for the next levy agreement the bookmakers' contribution should comprise a 'modest increase' to take it up to a total sum of £50 million. They were prepared to put in writing that the Home Secretary, if called in again to arbitrate, should determine the scheme to this effect, but regrettably did not recommend that legislation should be introduced – some unavoidable leverage or legal stick – to prevent the bookies from simply passing on this extra cost to their customers.

The initial reaction to the report by most ordinary race-goers and punters was one of almost unrestrained delight. Two deeply unpopular power bases, the Jockey Club and the Big Three betting-shop chains, had been roundly criticised and on top of that the committee had actively endorsed the campaign for Sunday racing in Britain, even if it had to happen with betting shops closed (due to the continuing absence of a consensus over the issue of Sunday trading). The MPs came in for considerable criticism over this last point due to their apparent failure to realise that such a move would result in only a marginal increase in the levy and would be bound to encourage some upsurge in illegal betting – hardly on a scale to bother most relaxed and tolerant citizens but definitely enough to alert the niggardly officers of HM Customs and Excise.

Yet for all the disagreements about gambling on Sundays which already takes place on credit accounts and with Switch cards, it would still be hard to overestimate the crushing sense of anticlimax that could be detected in every area of the racing community when Kenneth Baker subsequently rejected almost every one of his committee's recommendations. He would not intervene to set a statutory next levy rate of £50 million. He would not take measures to prevent the bookies from passing on their levy deductions to the punters. There would be no Home Office pressure to create a British Horse-racing Authority to replace the Jockey Club, no racing on Sundays unless betting shops could be legally opened first and no punters' representatives on the Levy Board. Indeed, the ease with which a Cabinet minister and his civil servants felt able to dismiss any suggestion of punter representation was a further reflection of the contempt and derision with which the betting-shop community has traditionally been held by the non-gambling sections of the population.

What Baker's veto made abundantly clear was that the one government department to take any real interest in racing was not the Home Office but the Treasury. They currently rake in some £467 million a year in betting duty and if anyone has been given a licence to print money since the legalisation of off-course betting shops thirty-one years ago then it is as much they as the bookies. Treasury civil servants regard the big off-course bookmakers as effective tax collectors and are not prepared to tolerate any changes to the present levy arrangements that might either depress turn-over or result in responsibility for that tax collection passing into other less-experienced hands. Until British racing can put up credible representatives with the financial expertise and political influence to challenge those assumptions inside Whitehall, little is going to change.

For the time being the Baker ruling has simply forced the Jockey Club and the off-course betting industry back into their respective corners. It has been belatedly pointed out to the Jockey Club that racing – and betting – cannot expect to escape the consequences of the recession any more than any other branch of the leisure industry. It was grim news when Lynda and Jack Ramsden announced in July 1991 that they had decided that, as a result of bookmaker sharp practice and declining prize money, they could no longer make their business pay and were putting their yard on the market (a decision they have since reversed). But when you've taken out the Ramsdens, the Easterbys, Barry Hills, Jimmy FitzGerald and the likes of Henry Cecil, Michael Stoute, Luca Cumani and Martin Pipe, many struggling and unfortunate individuals remain who may just not be very good at training racehorses. Trainers as a breed are probably one of the most overrated and undeservedly exalted groups in sport. Nine times out of ten the stable staff and the jockeys do all the work and quite a few trainers in Newmarket alone hardly deserve to be let loose in the local Waitrose with £100-worth of housekeeping money, let alone entrusted with thousands of their owners' pounds and dollars to spend at yearling sales in Britain and America. And despite the recession the 1991 edition of *Horses in Training*, an acknowledged and reliable guide, listed over 16,000 registered racehorses in Britain, a drop of only 400 on the previous year.

Crisis or no crisis, horse-racing is the only sport to be favoured with its own private levy and has received more than £200 million from that source over the past thirty years. It continues to enjoy the attentions of two daily trade papers, to receive vastly more television coverage than it gets in either France or America and to benefit from a vulnerable but not inconsiderable degree of sponsorship. And, when not just the racing but the atmosphere and the managerial touch are right, as at York's fabulous three-day Ebor meeting in August, the public gladly pays £25 a head to go into the Members' Enclosure and continues to turn up in ever-increasing numbers each year.

This is also the moment to remember that for all the cheap admission prices and lavish prize-money levels at Longchamp numerous disadvantages are inherent for the punter in the PMU's monopoly position. When the PMU, its management and staff are faced with a serious demand for their services as on Arc Sunday they are pathetically incapable of satisfying it as the long queues of irate customers annually testify. In Britain the Tote deduct 16 per cent from the on-course win pool, their equivalent of the book-makers' percentage profit over-round. In France the PMU take a fat 28 per cent from the pool. This accounts for their administrative expenses, the share that they pay to the French government and the share that goes back to French racing leaving a miserly 72 per cent to be paid out to punters as winnings. No serious gambler would dream of betting to such percentages, which ought to make the point yet again that introducing a similar monopoly in this country would be the quickest way to create an upsurge in illegal betting and further empty the racetracks.

From time to time the argument is still put forward that even if we cannot or would not want to abolish on-course bookmaking we should still establish a British off-course Tote monopoly. Informed and well-intentioned advocates of this view remain convinced that, from a purely racing perspective, such a move would have been the best way forward back in 1961. One of its leading proponents has been the Marquis of Zetland, the dynamic chairman of Redcar racecourse who gives the impression of being one of the few thinking members of the Jockey Club and who ironically, or per-haps understandably, is also a major shareholder in Ladbrokes. Yet it is surely a fantastical notion to imagine that either of the two main political parties are going to fly in the face of ten years' economic wisdom and find £6 billion to compensate private bookmaking companies for taking their businesses away and handing them over to a less than dynamic public monopoly. Since the establishment of the jackpot in the 1960s the Tote's management have come forward with no new national pool bet, with the exception of the poorly promoted Trio, that could capture the public's imagination and offer a possible big pay-out for only a small stake. 'Can't be done, old boy,' seems to be the Tote's prevailing line. 'Demand unproven and, besides, we'd have to get the bookmakers to allow us to install Tote terminals in their shops to handle the bets.' Well, the book-makers could surely be persuaded to co-operate if the deal was made financially attractive enough and if the Tote make no new initiative soon, someone might eventually come forward with a National Lottery scheme, which could be both to racing's and the bookies' disadvantage.

In a separate report that followed their enquiry into the Betting Levy, the Home Affairs Select Committee were critical of the Tote's management structure and past record and recommended (for what it's worth which may not be much given Baker's outright rejection of most of their views on the Levy) that in future the Tote should be 'given' to horse-racing for racing's benefit. Since the Tote's chairman is still that remarkable music-hall performer and friend of the former Prime Minister, Lord Wyatt of Weeford, it is profoundly to be hoped that racing is never given to the Tote – at least not while Lord Wyatt is still in the chair. That's the sort of nightmare scenario that would have many gamblers waking up in a cold sweat and turning to clutch their bedside portraits of Cyril Stein gratefully to their bosom.

In February 1991 the Levy Board chairman, Sir John Sparrow, had more bad news for the Jockey Club when he announced that, as a result of levy yields from betting turnover falling £6.5 million below 1990 forecasts, the Levy Board would have to make a 10 per cent cut in prize-money grants in 1992. Attributing the shortfall to the consequences of the recession with punters having less dispos-able income to play with, he also called for a reduction in the number of fixtures that the board would support from 1,136 to 1,000. By May he was revising that figure downwards to 836 and unveiling total Levy Board cutbacks of £8.7 million. He suggested one possible way forward for racing. The Jockey Club should devise a new levy-friendly fixture list, cutting down on the overall number of meetings but switching more meetings to the end of the week when most punters like to bet, and moving the big betting-centred races such as the Derby, the Cheltenham Gold Cup and the Ebor Handicap away from their historic mid-week dates to more accessible slots on Saturday afternoons. The Jockey Club, sensing that such a move would do as much for the off-course bookmakers as it would for racing, were unwilling to consider any such changes unless they had a guarantee in advance that the bookies would in turn increase their contributions to the Levy (and by 'their' one hopes that the Club mean the bookies' contributions and not just those of their punters).

In the autumn of 1991 the Jockey Club submitted to the Levy Board a demand for £100 million from betting income in 1992. The first £50 million would be the straightforward levy agreement (the figure of £50 million having clearly been borrowed from the Home Affairs Committee's recommendation), an extra £15 million, it was said, could be provided by the evening opening of betting shops and a further £35 million from the removal of the so-called tax-on-tax anomaly, whereby the Government continue to extract 8 per cent betting duty from bets on which the punter may already have paid a 10 per cent deduction at the time of placing the wager.

The National Association for the Protection of Punters regarded the Jockey Club's proposals as completely unrealistic. Why would the Treasury return any betting duty in the middle of a recession? Why would the bookmakers willingly pay more in the middle of the same recession without instantly passing the cost on to their punters? And how could there be evening opening of betting shops before a general election – effectively postponing such a move until 1993 at the earliest? But the NAPP's cautious line was not shared by Desert Orchid's owner, Mr Richard Burridge, who apparently once worked in a betting shop. Addressing a racing lunch in Newcastle on 3 October he condemned the bookmakers for, as he saw it, not taking the same 'risks' as other members of the racing industry. 'They even try to put the punter against the owner by portraying the image of an owner with a string of horses and a Rolls-Royce whereas in reality the owners and punters are the same people. It's the owner who puts the show on the road and it's the punter who keeps it there.'

But in the same week the Jockey Club's – and by implication Richard Burridge's – arguments were torn to shreds by the Timeform Organisation, who joined the NAPP in describing the Jockey Club's Levy Board proposals as unrealistic and unacceptable and labelled the tenor of their submission 'brass-necked and presumptuous'. Timeform were particularly harsh about the attempt to 'present owners in the role of altruistic providers of a product for the "betting industry"'. Owning a racehorse, they said, was a luxury. 'Owners are in it for pleasure and have shown they are quite prepared to pay for the pleasure. Collectively they paid £150 million for their fun last year.' They added: 'There is no justice in seeking to obtain more money from punters to subsidise owners. It is a specious argument in the first place that punters in the betting shop should contribute to the viability of race meetings on which they bet.'

The Jockey Club's problem is that the publicity they have

encouraged to try to highlight their case against the bookies has thrown more light than ever on to their own and their arguments' shortcomings.

Racing's current and future prosperity *is* connected by an umbilical cord to the financial well-being of the betting industry. Yet due to its inherent snobbery and disdain for self-made money, the Jockey Club cannot bring itself to accept the logic of its position and try to work *with* the bookies rather than setting up in glorious isolation against them. When you listen to some owners, trainers and racehorse breeders, many of them enthusiastic supporters of bloodsports, you feel that they are possessed of the same irrational loathing of bookmakers that they themselves are frequently subjected to by ardent critics of fox-hunting. They talk about the bookies as if they are the weasels and stoats who have disgracefully taken over Toad Hall. Forgetting their own lamentable custodianship of the property, they keep looking round for a benign badger to kick these upstarts back into the Wild Wood. They overlook the fact that Britain is a bookmaking culture, that bookies – on- and off-course – are as integral a part of our tradition as Cheltenham and Royal Ascot. They seem to believe that they should be allowed to make up for decades of their own blinkered mismanagement by helping themselves to more punters' money or by being given a government mandate to denude an entrepreneurial company like Ladbrokes of the profits that it has shrewdly and ruthlessly accumulated by exploiting every opportunity available to it. Racing has difficulties, all right. It is self-evidently under-funded. It would benefit from a more equitable financial arrangement with off-course betting. Yet to talk about a 'crisis' on the Turf as if it is on a par with a crisis in the health service, education or the beleaguered public transport system and then to lay all the blame at the door of the bookies is to display an insularity that is almost beyond redemption.

At the end of 1991, Lord Hartington was making encouraging noises about the possibility of a Jockey-Club-supported racing authority that would include representatives of the Horse-racing Advisory Council and the Racehorse Owners' Association. (There were plans, too, for a Sunday race meeting without bookies or cash bettings.) His lordship was congratulated for his reformist tendencies, although some suspected a ruse to preserve most of the Club's old powers under a new name. Hartington proposed that four of the ten seats on the new board should be held by the Jockey

Club but gave the unmistakable impression that the bookmakers, the people who really know how to run a commercial betting and racing enterprise, will still be cast as adversaries. Could a bookie ever be elected to the Jockey Club? Graham Sharpe is bound to have drawn up a list of prices about it though on the evidence of the past thirty (let alone the past 250) years, don't expect it to happen much before a successful British space shot to Mars.

CHAPTER EIGHTEEN

The Sting

You CAN say all you like about the desirability of punters being represented on the Levy Board, about the need for them to be protected in betting shops by signs warning them about book-makers' deductions and hedging activities and about the import-ance of prudence, restraint, knowledgeability and guile. Yet when all these splendid injunctions have been heard and digested there remains the crucial, inescapable fact that for many of us the point of gambling, the essential requirement, if it is to be a truly satisfy-ing and nerve-tingling experience, is that we should be able to get thoroughly and enjoyably out of our depth. Gaze into the abyss. Inspect the flames. Travel to the limit of our credit and beyond.

It was partly to construct that kind of jeopardy, but also with every hope and expectation of getting out of it again, that we embarked on another train journey on the Friday morning of Royal Ascot week, four days after our trip to Brighton. The party this time included the splendid Major Tom as well as A.J. Kincaid and John Moynahan. And waiting for us up the line in Leeds and then at Redcar racecourse were Cheltenham Tony, Maurice and various other crafty co-conspirators, all hoping that collectively we would successfully execute a contrived but authentic betting coup. A stroke. A touch. With a horse who was about to show a major improvement in form. An apparently dramatic and unexpected turnaround which, of course, had been wholly anticipated by his wily connections. You've read the book. You've heard the stories. This was to be the real thing.

An air of understandable intensity, therefore, hung about this expedition and one of an altogether greater magnitude than had pertained to our eve-of-Ascot quest for three winners on the humid south coast.It was not only essential to the success of our future relationship with Tony and his associates that we should not cock up our respective parts in the venture. It was not simply the prospect of the real pecuniary profit that might accrue from the bets Tony would place on our behalf. After a disastrous first three days at Ascot we were all in desperate need of any relief that might come galloping over the horizon, but for one of us this Redcar coup was to be the getting-out stakes of positively life-saving importance.

It had been just after the first race at Ascot the previous afternoon, as we were descending the steps into that horrid Stygian tunnel that conducts the low-life from the paddock to the ring underneath, rather than in sight of, the Royal Lawn, that A.J. Kincaid had finally revealed the full scale of his liabilities. The moment that had tipped him over the edge had been when his Ascot first-day 'banker', a much-touted Luca Cumani-trained three-year-old colt, had gone down quite as comprehensively as General Custer's mount at the Battle of the Little Big Horn. He said that he now owed money all along the rails and that two firms in particular were threatening to take him to Tattersalls' Committee. It seemed that these two watchful layers had pounced on him after hearing the disastrous news that the famous family whisky firm had been ambushed on the stockmarket on the very day that we had been careering drunkenly around Brighton. Dissatisfied banks and institutional investors were suddenly taking over. Kincaid senior was out. Kincaid's brother was out. No more lavish expense account. No more year-round salary for four months' work. No more grouse shooting, free booze and Continental travel under the heading of corporate entertainment. No more fun. Only woe, penury and even the distinct possibility of durance vile, this last being due, naturally, to Kincaid's bank manager (or, at least, the main one of many). He, typically alive to events in the City, had made use of the news of this company crisis to inform A.J. that unless his personal overdraft was dramatically reduced by the end of June, now only eight days' away, he would have 'no alternative' other than to demand repayment in full.

And yet none of these things had Kincaid worried at all. Well, not much. What was upsetting him was the impact of it on his relationship with his wife-to-be, a tall ash-blonde and extremely voluptuous forty-two-year-old restaurant-owner from Marlow, herself a cleaned-up ex-gambler and veteran of an unsuccessful marriage to an Irish cattle dealer. This wonderful, compassionate woman had offered to stick by her man providing he agreed to undertake a course of 'detoxification' at the same quiet, secluded, residential premises near Eastbourne that she had booked into several years previously.

Kincaid wasn't bothered about doing his time in 'stir' but he was worried about what would happen when he came out again if, in the intervening period, he had been warned off by Tattersalls for non-payment of debts. How could he continue to race and bet as before? he asked us sincerely. We suggested that perhaps after his 'cure' he wasn't meant to continue to race and bet as before but Kincaid couldn't see that. He was quite happy to go inside and try to learn from his past mistakes, he said, but where was the harm in also plotting for his eventual comeback not as a punter but as a newly reformed, shrewd and disciplined 'investor' like Barney, Alex and the rest? Which is why this Redcar scam was so vital to him and why he fervently hoped that it would indeed furnish him with the necessary funds to settle things with the most fractious of the layers so that he could lie low and rest up for a better day.

The race in question was a six-furlong handicap for three- and four-year-olds only and was worth a modest £3,850 to the winner. The significance of picking Redcar on 22 June was that it was a small away meeting on a day when most racing and bookmaking interest would still be focused on the final afternoon of Royal Ascot. The horse at the centre of the coup (whose identity we would not actually be permitted to know until they were being loaded into the stalls) was a four-year-old sprint-bred filly, twice a Redcar course and distance winner but down the field on her last three runs. She had been deliberately campaigned out of her depth in those races and as a result had dropped down handily in the weights. Her trainer was a shrewd, competent but avowedly second-division handler from Royston. A Newmarket-based jockey, second string to a leading yard, had been booked to ride.

The filly's owners, both friends of Tony, were two brothers, a pair of haulage contractors from Gidea Park. They were not going to be at Redcar but at Royal Ascot, watching their other trainer saddle a three-year-old handicapper in the Britannia Stakes. And we certainly weren't going to be backing the filly ourselves on-course. The gamble was in the hands of Cheltenham Tony, Maurice and a small network of agents who were going to be placing their, our and the owners' money off-course at SP in lots of small bets in different offices and in different amounts. Our job – Kincaid's, Moynahan's, the Major's and my own – was to back on-course the two most fancied runners in the race, the intention being to get enough cash on them to ensure that their odds would contract and the odds of our filly consequently drift out.

The Major was travelling up specifically to back the likely favourite, an improving three-year-old colt from Malton whose owner was a well-known actor and gambling enthusiast currently out of the country. The actor had always had an account with the Major's firm and it was known in racing and bookmaking circles that he was a good friend and confidant of the ex-Guards officer. We hoped that the sight of the Major, apparently going all the way up to Redcar on the last afternoon of Ascot to execute an on-course commission for his *compadre*, would send out a signal that the actor's horse was 'hot'. In truth, of course, the actor had instructed his trainer and jockey, in return for them all being cut in for a piece of the action, that today was not their day, that they should unluckily miss the break or experience a few irritating difficulties getting a run. In short, that they should do anything other than win.

John Moynahan and I had been entrusted with backing the probable second favourite, a tough, consistent Lancastrian sprinter who rarely finished out of the first three and whose highly professional trainer was definitely not the sort who could be tactfully invited to take a dive. Our filly had to give this gelding six pounds. Moynahan, our form book expert, reckoned that on her two- and three-year-old running (and the trainer was convinced she was back in that kind of form today) she had a stone in hand.

Due to the mad secrecy that other devotees will understand always pertains to a stroke, it had been decided by Tony that we should travel initially to Leeds, nearly seventy miles away from Redcar. Most of the off-course money was going on in the Leeds–Bradford area because that was one of the places where Tony had a network of private and unattributable commissioning agents. Tony and his team had, with intentional irony, chosen Ladbrokes' Leeds Hilton International Hotel as their headquarters. None of us had ever set foot in the place before and in spite of the potentially risqué connotations, especially given the Dublin airport story, Tony was convinced he could get away with it, and felt that success would be that much more delectable if it had been achieved using Cyril Stein's own hotel suites and phones.

And so it was that the Major and I settled down in the dining car of the Intercity 225 Yorkshire Pullman service from King's Cross to Leeds. We were ready to tackle the full grill tray but John Moynahan had inevitably eschewed breakfast in favour of intensive study of the form book with a view to trying to crack some of the other Redcar events. As for A.J. Kincaid, he was suffering from the effects of only four hours' rest after an abortive attempt to chase his losses in the Palm Beach Club and fell heavily asleep within five minutes of the train pulling out. As we would need him to be at least partially alert when we reached the other end we decided that it was best to leave him be.

The neighbouring seats were all filled with haggard, nervous-looking young business travellers, leftovers from the Thatcherite high watermark of the late eighties and still desperately attempting to keep the spirit of free enterprise alive in a bankrupt and run-down land. 'Give me a croissant and a cordless phone and the future can still be mine,' they seemed to be saying. Most were drinking decaffeinated coffee and mineral water at 8.15 a.m., which must be a miserable way to start any day.

By comparison with these unfortunate salary, mortgage and BUPA slaves, the Major, in dark-grey suit, brown suede shoes and pale blue Hermès tie, looked at his most effortlessly assured. He was Henry Cecil if he was anyone. Employing the same disarming manner that he turns on suckers to get them to open an account on the rails, he managed to persuade the 'stewardesses' to bring us second and third helpings of everything. He even managed to charm the Chief Steward, a rather humourless Fawltyesque figure with a toothbrush moustache and a braided navy-blue British Rail uniform, into not bringing us our toast until *after* the fry-up was over, thus ensuring that it wouldn't be stone cold by the time we were ready for it.

The brand-new train, with its pale grey seats and red and grey fleck carpet on the walls and floors, shot forward through the suburbs like a bullet. Outside the smoked-glass windows was another abject apology for a midsummer's day. Mainly overcast, misty and damp with just teasing intervals of blue sky and sun. After Hitchin, Stevenage and Peterborough, the Pullman screeched suddenly and noisily to a halt amid the eerie flatness of the East Midlands plain. The nauseating stench of asbestos brake pads overwhelmed the previously agreeable, if no doubt equally life-threatening, aroma of sausage, bacon and eggs. Undeterred by the delay the Major sat back in his seat, lit up his first cigarette of the day and over a third cup of coffee expounded his views on Kincaid, gamblers and debt.

'I've always felt that when a punter gets in that deep it's our fault. The bookmakers' fault. You have to try and choke them back early on. For everybody's benefit. But there you are.' He shrugged his shoulders. 'He's a compulsive gambler. Always charging around everywhere and betting on anything. They're not amenable to logic.'

'So, is it immoral for us to encourage him? Or for Tony to keep on laying him bets?'

'These are real-life situations. If you want to play you have to pay. Tony laid him bets because he was waiting to make use of him. And today's the day. A.J. knows that and accepts it. And, mark my words, Tony'll have him backing our prospective winner not just the decoys. Kincaid's got a name as a loser. A Big Loser. When he asks to back a horse up at Redcar, any horse, the market will instantly conclude that it hasn't got a chance.'

'And that's his best hope of winning? To make use of his reputation as a mug?'

'That's his only hope of winning. But you're not encouraging him. If he wasn't doing it with us he'd be gambling somewhere else. In a casino. In a card game. At Hackney dogs. I'm just glad I'm not the bookie who's saddled with his debts any more.'

'He's not a good client? He loses enough money.'

'He's not an ideal client.'

'Who is an ideal client?'

'Well, we don't want any dross and we don't want anyone who knows more than we do. I know that sounds mean but it's the way it has to be. We like the kind of punter who's not afraid to drop five or ten grand on a single bet. Former Big Three credit-account clients who have got fed up with the Ladbrokes style and want a change. We look after them well. They like that.' He looked across wistfully at the executives, phoning, dictating and personally computing in the seats opposite. 'Back around the time of Big Bang, 1985–6, that's when it was possible for everyone to score. We already had our older, more traditional, City clients. They tended to be owners or part owners of horses. The new boys were something different. We sucked them in on financial bets and then moved them on to racing. They couldn't get enough of it. I used to go down to the viewing gallery in the Futures Exchange in

Threadneedle Street and keep reminding myself that it was just like Tattersalls' at Kempton on Easter Bank Holiday Monday. They were our ticket.'

One of the traders who had perhaps helped to write the Major's ticket had recently been involved in a costly litigation against the company in which he had attempted to claim that he should be no more legally liable for a financial debt he had incurred with the firm than he would be if it were a bet on the horses. The court's ruling, which had come on the day of our trip to Brighton and which had been responsible for the Major being unable to join us there, had been that the two were quite different and separate 'investments' and that the trader would have to face up to paying his share-dealing bills in full. I put it to the Major that it was a rotten sort of business to have to chase after a debtor who clearly couldn't pay.

'It's the gambler's prerogative to see things in a romantic light,' he informed me very grandly. 'Which is wonderful and lovely and I wish that I could be like that myself. But any bookmaker who ran his affairs on similar lines would soon end up in Queer Street.'

'So who's the most successful big-time punter?'

'J. P. McManus. A charming man. But don't let that altar-boy face and image fool you for a moment. He's as hard as a professional assassin.'

'And the greatest modern bookie?'

'Victor Chandler. Stephen Little's absolutely fearless and brilliant with figures but he's too colourless for me. Victor loves horses and racing. It's in his blood. Like his father and grandfather before him. You know about that picture in his Portland Street office of the horse that the old man backed to win him a fortune on the Cambridgeshire in 1948. He was a real bookie and Victor's the same. He'd lay virtually any bet to anyone even if he barely knew them. I could never be that brave.'

He's an intriguing man, our Major. All louche and throwaway on the outside, as at Cheltenham the previous March, but underneath I suspect that he's not much softer than McManus. He wears it well, though. And in an age when everyone seems to have an increasingly homogenised look about them, when the upper classes have been squeezed down and what used to be the working classes have been squeezed up, it's good to be reminded that there are still some upper-class spivs with style.

Fortunately the train's loss of power turned out to be only a brief interruption, and soon back on schedule again, we actually arrived in Leeds a few minutes ahead of time. When we got to the hotel, a standard multi-storey concrete and glass block, our cab door was opened by a morose-looking doorman in full Sam Weller gear, complete with blue-and-grey top hat with a little tufted brush in the hatband. The first-floor foyer looked as if it had been designed by someone who had been frightened by a Club Med holiday to Samoa. There were lots of lurid black flowered chairs and black, yellow and pink coloured curtains on a jungle green background. A trio of bland-looking receptionists in red and blue uniforms that wouldn't have looked out of place on the cashiers in a Ladbrokes' betting office stood behind a desk dishing out the usual phoney politesse to newly arriving business guests. 'Good morning, sir. Thank you for choosing the Hilton International. Would you like to show me a major credit card?' A noticeboard gave directions to the meetings taking place in various function rooms and from the adjoining open-plan Blue Notes bar came the sounds of a hard-working pianist doing his mid-morning best with 'Maria' and the theme music from *Dr Zhivago*.

Tony's top-floor executive suite was in pale brown, as opposed to William Hill dark brown, vinyl library panelling with black and brown and rust-coloured bedspreads and carpet. The heavy white floor-length curtains had been pulled back to reveal beyond the windows a rainy vista of high-rise flats and coal-fired power stations and railway lines stretching away to the horizon. Dominating one wall was a yellow and brown print of Ancient Rome complete with men in togas, gladiators and baths. A clue perhaps to the imperial pretensions of the Ladbrokes' chairman. In all honesty, though, it was difficult to focus on the print, the curtains or the view beyond the window. This was because as soon as you walked into the room your attention was riveted by the two open suitcases laid out on the top of the double bed. Each one appeared to be filled to the brim with bank notes. Standing beside the bed was Cheltenham Tony himself, the beaming Mr Tony Siravo, punter, fixer, unlicensed bookie and face. Maurice, the same taciturn and curly-haired accomplice, was positioned on the other side of the room by the obligatory 'Robo-bar'.

'Good morning, gentlemen,' said Tony. 'Welcome to Leeds.'

'I always wondered what happened to the proceeds of the Brinks-Mat robbery,' said John Moynahan.

'You'll all get yours in a moment,' laughed Tony. 'This is for the betting shops. Only small denominations. The agents'll be in to pick it up in half an hour.' He closed both the cases as a precaution.

'What if a chambermaid gets curious?' asked Kincaid nervously. 'Or a porter or the man who comes to restock the fridge?'

'I've told them that we're interviewing applicants for a new sales agency,' said Tony. 'Door-to-door skills and all that stuff. It never fails. Now, how about a drink on Cyril? Maurice?' Maurice offered us all a choice of Bloody Marys or half bottles of champagne from the Robo-bar. Kincaid noticeably and unusually abstained. 'You know how much they charge for a gin and tonic and a packet of nuts in this place?' asked Tony. 'Eight quid. Eight bleeding nicker for one Gordon's and a couple of cashews. No wonder Ladbrokes were so keen to get into the hotel business.' After our drinks we all accompanied Tony into the bathroom one by one where we were each given our personal stash for the course. Each packet of readies was neatly clipped together along with a note naming which bookmaker's pitch we were to place them with. We were to commit the on-course money at 3.35 p.m. ten minutes before the off. The betting-office money would go on in lots of small amounts at SP throughout the late morning and early afternoon and at the last minute Tony would ring through half a dozen or so credit account bets for the decoy horses to back up our wagers at the track. The off-course firms might still shave a point or two off the filly's odds in the closing exchanges but if everything else worked out we should still get our winner at a competitive price.

Major Tom left first giving us all a debonair farewell salute as if he was an RAF ace about to embark on the Dambusters raid. The Major, to conform with the idea of him being on the actor's business, had been hired a car in which to make a solo journey to Redcar, but Kincaid, Moynahan and myself were to be driven up by Maurice. The prudent Tony clearly wanted to make absolutely sure that there was no opportunity for us to undertake a private investment or, in Michael Caine's immortal words, 'to scarper with the ackers'.

We headed north up the A1 past Wetherby and Boroughbridge and then began to swing away to the right north east towards Middlesbrough. Maurice was no more talkative in the car than he had been in the hotel or during our previous encounter in Brighton.

'Do you like racing, Maurice?' Moynahan asked him as the Cleveland Hills loomed up ahead on the horizon. The driver allowed himself a smile.

'Do you like to bet?' asked Kincaid.

'Racing's for mugs,' said Maurice, catching Kincaid's eye in his rear view mirror. 'I stick to the City pages. Securities. Gilts. That's the smart boy's gamble.'

'I should have met this man ten years ago,' muttered A.J. Kincaid.

After Middlesbrough the clouds grew dark and almost as threatening as the old black industrial architecture of the British Steel works at Grangetown with its heavy iron plant, its smelters, converters and tall Orwellian smokestacks silhouetted against the sky. Human beings have had to toil in these mills in long shifts of pulverising physical labour to earn much less in a year than we were going to gamble in one afternoon. How can you justify it? How on earth can you explain to the painfully employed or the painfully unemployed that your 'work' involves frittering around at a racecourse? 'What are we doing up in Grangetown? Well, we're up for the races actually. To back a horse. To get a bet on. That sort of thing.' Very impressive.

The further you go down that road along the Teesside estuary the more you begin to feel that you are riding towards the end of the line, that very soon the land will give way and be swallowed up by the sea. Redcar town and Redcar racecourse, situated at the outer edge of this flat, industrialised landscape, seem a world away from the madness of Cheltenham, the top hats of Ascot and the cosy prosperity of the Sussex coast. As you stand on the terracing of the club enclosure you can see the smoking chimneys of the steelworks standing out above the rooftops of row upon row of detached and semi-detached post-war housing. With grey skies and a chilly wind blowing in off the sea, on a bad day it is a sight that can easily sink the spirits.

Not that everything about Redcar conforms to some black-and-white *A Kind of Loving* cliché of the benighted industrial north: if you look down the course towards the six-furlong start you can see the north Yorkshire moors tumbling right down to the coast at Saltburn and Staithes. And just because there are no Pimms' tents or corporate marquees it doesn't follow that there are no enthusiastic punters or managements in the north east. Lord Zetland's enterprising efforts to look after both his paying customers and his visiting stable staff put the contrasting 'amenities' of some big southern racecourses to shame.

That said, there was an undeniably desolate atmosphere about the place half an hour before the first on this cold, grey late-June afternoon. Half a dozen signs were up along the rails, including one each for the ubiquitous representatives of Ladbrokes and William Hills. Yet none of these rails layers were standing outside to bet yet and only three boards bookmakers were betting in the ring, all huddled beneath their large red, black, green and yellow golfing umbrellas.

Those spectators present (and there weren't many whether due to the recession, the weather or the competing attraction of Ascot on television) were mainly sticking to the warmth and comfort of the bars. There wasn't the same outgoing atmosphere as at Brighton five days earlier and there were fewer of the brassy and ebullient punters that you meet at the bigger northern meetings at York or Haydock in winter and at Doncaster for St Leger week. Other than that, though, the types and styles were pretty much the same as the ones you will find at any gaff track on any mid-week afternoon throughout the year. The odd face in his customary velvet-collar coat. Small gatherings of lads in trenchcoats and white shoes standing with their feet apart and their toes pointing out. And a couple of owners in chalk-stripe suits, the inevitable lady-friends in tow with handbags on chains, black, patterned tights and a lot of make-up.

We found Major Tom ensconced in the champagne bar which was at one end of the luncheon room on the second floor. Moynahan, who was pretending to be covering the meeting for his newspaper, greeted the Major as if in surprise and they engaged in an enthusiastic, public and audible discussion of the Major's Malton fancy. Moynahan then carried news of this supposed 'good thing' down to the weighing room with its, 'Racing is fun at Redcar' hoarding posted over the door.

'Good afternoon, ladies and gentlemen, and welcome to Redcar,' declared a public-address announcement continuing the same consumer-friendly approach. 'I'd particularly like to welcome Mr Mal Bridges, commercial director of Gosforth Engineering who are sponsoring our principal race here today.' The principal race. Which was also our race. The 3.45. Fourth on the card. The six-furlong handicap. The coup. The gamble.

For once none of us felt really able to concentrate on the first few events and we mainly watched them out of the window of the bar while keeping an eye on the first two at Ascot on satellite TV. Just before half past three, Kincaid, Moynahan and myself each went into a separate cubicle in the men's room to count out our betting money for the umpteenth time and to check once again which pitches we were supposed to stake it with.

When we walked outside into the ring a ray of sunshine lit up the racecourse for the first time all afternoon. This, surely, was to be our day. The Tattersalls' crowd must have amounted to barely half the number of punters that had been down at Brighton on Monday but it is only a small ring at Redcar and with no more than eighteen or twenty boards bookies present and all the action compressed into a space about thirty feet by twenty-five the atmosphere seemed pressurised enough.

We saw Major Tom in his distinctive cream felt fedora with the brown hatband. He was standing over by the rails, conferring with Ladbrokes' northern representative, Tom Munt. We later discovered that the Major placed two credit wagers on the Malton 'good thing' – one of five thousand to two with rails layer Francis Habbershawe and another of two and a half thousand to one with Ladbrokes themselves. The 'good thing' – all the real names must be secret so let's just call him Shack – opened up at 9–4 first show on the boards and just after 3.35 p.m. we saw the Major going down the front line to back him again with cash. Moynahan and myself had each been allotted six pitches in two different rows and at 3.37 p.m. after a final, quick, nervous look at one another we moved in. It takes little more than a minute to rid yourself of a wallet full of money at a racetrack and by 3.38 p.m. and thirty seconds the business was done. Our target had been the Lancastrian sprinter, let's call him Glenside Delaware, who had opened up at 7–2 and 4–1 in places first show. Our bets of £50, £100 and in one case £200 a time appeared to strike no fear in the hearts and faces of Ralph Harris, Tom Webster, Morry Peter, Cyril Lynch and others but by 3.41 p.m. they had trimmed Glenside to 5–2 while Shack had dropped to 2–1 and 11–8 in places.

During these two or three minutes of earnest trading we had lost sight of A. J. Kincaid. I was certain that the Major was right and that Kincaid would have been briefed to back the intended winner and not the decoys. Standing at the back of the crowd on the bottom tier of the terracing I suddenly picked out his crumpled suit, his glasses and his distinctive heavy weight's frame turning away from the Ladbrokes pitch and heading down the rails to Francis Habbershawe. It was 3.42 p.m. I saw him talking to Habbershawe and presumably striking a bet but it was impossible to know who the bet was for. Then I saw him move across to the boards to the pitch of 'Captain George' of Harrogate. The Captain leaned forward to accept his commission. Fortunately the punter next to me had a pair of bins around his neck which he wasn't using. Hastily training them on the Captain's board I was in time to see him point enquiringly at one of the horse's names. I saw Kincaid nodding. I saw the Captain taking a handful of cash and returning a ticket. He made no effort to reduce the odds. I looked down at my racecard. The horse, naturally, was a four-year-old sprint-bred filly – let's call her Hyacinth Lady – twice a Redcar course and distance winner who had finished down the field on her previous two runs. She was to be ridden by a Newmarket-based jockey, a second string to a leading yard. And her current price? 7–1. It was 3.43 p.m.

I charged frantically out of the ring through the underpass and around to the on-course cash betting shop at the back of Tatts. This bleak and airless little office was packed with smoking, sweat-shirted punters. Until that point I had never really believed that the coup would come off. I had heard and seen it all too many times before. It seemed plain daft to take any of it seriously. And yet, now that we were actually here with the crucial action only minutes away, it would have been equally foolish not to try to get the maximum excitement out of it all. So why not double up the filly with another horse in another race?

The 3.45 at Ascot was about to start. It, too, was a six-furlong handicap, the £35,000 Wokingham Stakes for three-year-olds and up. There were twenty-eight runners and a plethora of tempting big-priced bets. But never mind the horses for once. Which jockey would you back if your life depended on it? If you had to choose one rider above all others, one jockey with the skill, the strength, the determination and the sheer ruthless will to win? No, you wouldn't pick Willie Carson. He's got the strength but he rides into too many holes. You wouldn't pick Steve Cauthen either. He's an artist not a street fighter. You'd pick Pat Eddery. One hundred per cent dead behind the eyes but the consummate driven pro-fessional. He's almost as lost off a racehorse as Lester Piggott.

Eddery's mount in the Wokingham was a former Ascot course-winner, a southern sprinting specialist from a well-known gam-bling yard. And yet his price was an unbelievable 14–1. With the betting-shop clock showing less than a minute before 3.45 p.m. I scribbled down the names of Pat's horse and the filly in a double,

nominating almost the last pound I had in my possession, fought
my way up to the windows, pushed the money and the betting slip
into the hands of the cashier, received my counterfoil and then
pushed and elbowed my way back out of the shop, ran back
through the underpass, across the ring, back into Members' and
then stumbled half-way up the terracing to join Moynahan and
A.J. Kincaid.

'They're under starters' orders. And they're off,' declared the
Redcar course commentator.

'It's Hyacinth Lady,' whispered Moynahan, enigmatically.

'I know,' I said.

'How did you know?' asked Kincaid.

'I guessed,' I replied.

A few feet above me and fractionally to my left I could see the
Wokingham Stakes on the television set in the bar. Directly ahead
of me the runners in the six-furlong Redcar handicap were coming
up the straight. This was racing and gambling with both barrels.
Left and right. In stereophonic sound and Panavision. And yet
there is something about a race in which you, personally, have
everything to lose that is the very opposite of a whip-cracking,
heroically struggling, death-or-glory Dick Francis finale. When the
money is really down, the horses seem to move as if in slow
motion. They seem cut off and cocooned from the world as if the
whole thing were happening in a dream with the sound turned
down – until that sudden awful or jubilant moment when the
volume is turned back up again and you hear either the crash of the
trapdoor opening or you see the horse, your horse, coming out of
the pack on its own.

The Redcar result was decided within the first half furlong.
Shack broke slowly and seemed to be hampered just after the start.
The incident cost him valuable lengths and although he started to
make the ground up rapidly once he was switched to the outside,
he always had too much to do. You had to admire the skill and
aplomb with which his jockey had managed to lose the race on
purpose. Pat Eddery had other ideas. The Ascot handicap was run
at a blinding pace and they had scarcely gone three furlongs at
Redcar before I picked up out of the corner of my left eye the sight
of Eddery bursting free of a wall of horses inside the final furlong.
And going clear. Pat the Knife in full flow. In yellow silks on a
chestnut gelding. The power and the glory. At Ascot on a midsummer afternoon. And as Eddery left the winning post behind him I

swung back round again live, on-course, to the joyous, unbelievable and never-expected sight of Hyacinth Lady and the
Newmarket second string taking it up from Glenside Delaware at
the distance. And coming up the standside rail on their own. All
the way to the wire. To the line. A big winner at Redcar. In the
watery sunshine after the rain. 'Go on, you Hyacinth. Go on, you
lady. Go on, you beautiful girl.'

So what does it feel like? Winning? Well, it's the moment of
fission. The moment when something just explodes in your head
and in front of your eyes. When the third bomb of the final plane
bounces and bounces and bounces again and then lifts up majesti-
cally out of the water and scores a direct hit on the Mohne Dam,
scattering the pieces up high into the air and spreading with it a
warm and sensual glow from the tip of your toes to your scalp.

We didn't go down to the unsaddling enclosure. We hung on
nervously by the line waiting for the official SP to come through.
Would Ladbrokes have fallen for all the decoy wagers or would
they have backed the filly at the last minute and depressed the
odds? After a pale and deathly two or three minutes our fears were
allayed. Hyacinth Lady was officially returned at 7–1 the same
price at which Captain George had unconcernedly laid her to
A. J. Kincaid.

The relief was overwhelming. We all felt suddenly and totally
exhausted. The terracing had virtually emptied now but there,
standing just in front of us on his own, was the still debonair figure
of the Major. He doffed his hat and smiled.

Maurice was waiting in the champagne bar, still as unemotional
as ever. He had just been on the phone to Tony in Leeds and he
informed us all that Tony's verdict on the coup was that 'the eagle
has landed'. Those were his words precisely, according to Maurice.
John Moynahan looked as if he was about to die laughing. 'Tony
would like you all to have this on him,' said Maurice. He snapped
his fingers at the waitress behind the bar, who in turn cued a
young waiter, who came over to our table in what looked like a
Ladbrokes Hilton bellboy costume. The waiter was carrying a tray
with five glasses on it and two bottles of Louis Roederer Cristal
Vintage champagne. On ice. Later we were joined by the winning
trainer and jockey (though not by Shack's jockey, which would
have been pushing it a bit) and more bottles were ordered and the
celebratory spirit flowed all round.

Betting on horse-racing is no way for any but the very smartest

or craziest individuals to make a living. But while we were definitely not in the first category and while we had nothing like as much
to come as the haulage contractors or their unlicensed bookmaker-
cum-commissioning agent we had, on this occasion, managed to
end up with a medal. The Major later advised me that he suspected
that the whole coup had amounted to well over £100,000. Still not
in the McManus league maybe, but more than just an outing for
tourists. I had no idea precisely how much Kincaid or the Major
had won but Moynahan and I would certainly be able to afford to
renew our form book subscriptions for the next few months. John
Moynahan was as transported with delight as he had been after the
last back at Cheltenham in March. He and the Major began talking
in a warm and animated fashion, not only with the trainer but also
with a blonde personality girl in a white PVC mac who was
wearing a sort of plastic bandolier made up of green writing on a
white background and advertising Gymcrack Thoroughbred
Racing plc. Yet Kincaid, A. J. Kincaid, our man at the centre of the
getting-out stakes, was uncharacteristically quiet and subdued.

'Is this the most you've ever won on a single race?' I asked him.

'Well, I haven't actually won anything,' he replied.

'But, surely? You were on with Tony like the rest of us? And we
all get a "drink" for successfully discharging our role.' Kincaid
shook his head.

'Officially, I don't receive a penny. That wasn't part of the deal.'

'Then what was the deal?'

'In return for acting as the mug . . .'

'The Big Loser?' He nodded.

'In return for acting as the Big Loser . . . Tony has paid off my
debts along the rails. Which is great. It means I won't be warned
off. And it means that I can start back again . . . with a clean slate.'

'After the cure?'

He hesitated. 'After the cure.'

'Although after the cure . . . you might not want to bet again.
Might you?'

'There is that possibility.'

'Then what shall we drink to?' I asked him. 'Only two-hundred-
and-sixty-three betting days to the National Hunt Festival?'

'I know,' he said. He poured more champagne for us both. 'To
an almost winning day.'

I picked up my glass and looked him in the eye.

'To an almost winning day.'

Down on the beach in the industrial town the big waves were coming in from the North Sea. A tanker edged its way along the horizon while a man walked his dog by the water's edge and a middle-aged couple lay hugging and kissing in the sand. The smell of ozone and chip fat drifted up the half-empty high street past Santino's Easy Diner, a Coral Racing office and the premises of Harry Brough: Fishing Tackle and Guns For Sale.

In the local evening paper they reported that the Hungarian State Circus was about to begin its summer season at Whitby, that the weather forecast was for more rain spreading in from the east and that a major betting coup had been pulled off at Redcar races that day.

Tony was going to pay us all our shares at his club down in Epsom on the Monday night. Maurice drove away back to Leeds and we drove to Darlington station with the Major where he turned in his hired car.

The other first-class passengers in the train on the way back from Darlington to London looked tired, sullen, ugly and unwell. Perhaps they were spies for the Inland Revenue or Racecourse Security Services but we hardly noticed them. We travelled home in a different world. They had a restaurant car on the train, so to pass the time we sampled our final British Rail meal of the week. About an hour before reaching King's Cross the steward came round to settle up. A. J. Kincaid picked up the cheque, looked at it and then looked at us.

'Let's cut cards for the bill,' he said.

'I haven't got any cards,' said Moynahan.

'I have,' said Kincaid, and he pulled out a deck from his right jacket pocket. He shuffled them suddenly and impressively in front of our eyes.

'Who's in? Is everybody in?'

Can I take much more of this? I wondered.

Oh, yes. Much more.

Glossary

Accumulator An accumulative bet such as a double or a treble consisting of two or more selections. The winnings and stake money from each successive leg are automatically restaked on the next leg. If there is a losing leg, the wager fails.

Ante-post Bets struck before the day of the event, hopefully at odds which will turn out to be bigger than the horse's eventual starting price.

BAGS Bookmakers Afternoon Greyhound Services Ltd, a book-makers' organisation which negotiates contracts with greyhound stadia to provide a daytime dog-racing service to betting shops.

Big Three The big three off-course betting shop chains: Ladbrokes, Coral and Hills.

Boards On-course cash-only bookmakers who mark up their prices on a board.

BOLA Betting Offices Licensees Association, a trade association representing the interests of betting-shop owners.

Each way A win-and-place bet. If the selection wins, both win and place bets pay a return. If it is placed the win bet fails and the win stake is lost but the place bet pays a return and the place stake is returned to the punter. There is no each way betting on either horse- or greyhound-racing where there are only 2 to 4 runners. In races of 5 to 7 runners, one-quarter the odds are paid on the first two and in races of 8 runners or over one-fifth the odds a place on the first three. In horse-racing handicaps of 12 to 15 runners, one quarter the odds a place is paid on the first three and in handicaps of 16 or more runners, such as the Grand National, one-quarter the odds a place on the first four.

Evens or **even money** A wager in which the bookmaker and the punter stake equal amounts, that is, a £10 bet on an evens favourite means that the punter gives the bookie £10 and vice versa plus his or her £10 stake if the horse wins.

Face A bookie's and punter's term for a usually well-informed regular gambler and racecourse insider.

Favourite The runner in a race at the lowest odds.

First show The first set of odds on a contest chalked up by the on-course bookmakers. In a betting shop, the first show is the first set of odds transmitted from the racetrack.

Forecast A bet in which you must nominate in correct order the runners to finish first and second in a race. A reverse forecast means you nominate the runners in either order but must therefore put down two stakes.

Jackpot A pool bet operated by the Tote. It is a win accumulator on the first six races and unwon pools are carried forward to the next day.

Job See **Stroke** and **Touch**.

Jockey Club The ruling body of British racing responsible for the rules, discipline and administration of the sport. Founded in 1750 and incorporated by royal charter in 1970.

Joint The equipment erected by a racecourse bookmaker with which to ply his trade from his pitch in the betting ring.

Layer A colloquial expression for a bookmaker, meaning somebody who 'lays' or offers the odds.

Levy A payment made to help finance horse-racing, raised from off-course horse-racing bets. Off-course punters in betting shops pay a 10 per cent 'tax' on their bets. Of this sum 8 per cent is the betting duty payable to the Government while a portion of the remaining 2 per cent, currently 0.89 per cent, goes to racing.

Levy Board The Horserace Betting Levy Board. The body that negotiates the levy annually with the bookmaking industry and administers the distribution of that income for the benefit of racing.

Members The Members' Enclosure at a racecourse. The most expensive area of the track to which the public can gain admittance on a daily basis and technically that part of the course offering the best view and facilities.

NAB The National Association of Bookmakers. A trade association comprising mainly, though not exclusively, on-course book-makers.

NAPP The National Association for the Protection of Punters. A pressure group formed in 1991 to lobby on behalf of punters' interests and to seek punter representation on the Levy Board.

Non-trier A runner that is not 'off' or not intended to win by its connections.

Odds The price offered by a bookmaker about a particular runner. The odds describe the terms of a bet. On the left is the stake put up by the bookie, on the right the stake put up by the punter. If the odds are 2–1 then the punter puts up one unit (be it £1, £10, £100 or whatever) and the bookmaker two. If the horse wins at 2–1 then the bookie pays back 2 x 1 unit be it £2, £20, £200 plus the punter's stake money. If the bet is placed off-course the punter will have to pay their 10 per cent tax which can be paid when they place their bet, which is the cheaper way, or deducted from their winnings.

Odds against A bet where the stake put up by the bookmaker is greater than the stake put up by the punter.

Odds on A bet where the bookmaker stakes less than the punter. If a horse's odds are 2–1 on, they are written up as 1–2 which means the punter only gets back one unit for every two they put up.

Off-course Betting away from the racetrack, be it in a betting shop or with a telephone credit account.

On-course Betting at the racetrack or greyhound stadium.

Over broke A set of bookies odds in which a punter can theoretically back all the runners and whichever one wins be sure of a profit.

Over-round A set of odds based on a percentage chance table but constructed to ensure that whichever horse wins a percentage of potential profit should accrue to the bookmaker.

Photo A print of the finish of a race taken on the line by a photo finish camera and sometimes called for by the judge to help him adjudicate a close result.

Pitch That allotted place in the betting ring at a racecourse where a course bookmaker sets up his joint.

PMU The initials of the Pari-Mutuel Urbain, the organisation that runs France's monopoly pool-betting system, analogous to the British Tote. The Pari-Mutuel, meaning literally a mutual wager, is also the system of racecourse betting in the USA where, as in France, there are no on-course bookmakers.

Punter A client of a bookmaker either at a racetrack or in a betting shop. The term was originally used to describe someone betting against the bank in a casino.

RCA The Racecourse Association, the body that attempts collectively to represent Britain's fifty-nine racecourses and their owners.

Rails The railings on a racecourse that separate the Members' Enclosure from the adjoining but cheaper Tattersalls next door. Bookmakers are not allowed to set up their pitches in the Members' but the élite credit and high-stakes rails bookies have pitches along the railings and do most of their business with the supposedly better-off punters in Members'. The on-course representatives of the big off-course betting-shop chains have their racecourse bookmaking pitches on the rails.

Return The sum due from a bookmaker on a winning bet.

Ring As in Betting Ring. The main betting ring at a racetrack is in Tattersalls and the term covers all the bookmakers, rails and board, who work there. Bookmakers are also allowed pitches in the still cheaper Silver Ring next door to Tatts.

Ringer A horse substituted for another for which it may bear a close physical resemblance. Ringers are usually only employed during an attempt to execute some kind of betting coup.

RSS Racecourse Security Services, horse-racing's internal police force.

SIS Satellite Information Services, the company that transmits betting shows, results and live satellite television coverage of horse and greyhound racing to betting shops.

Starting price The starting price, or SP, of a horse is the offcial odds of each runner in a race returned by special press representatives in attendance in the betting ring at all race meetings. The SP is based on the final betting show available on the racecourse before the 'off'. Unless agreed otherwise the starting prices are the odds at which all off-course bets are settled.

Stewards Jockey Club members or individuals appointed by the Jockey Club to act as officials responsible for the conduct of a race meeting and charged with upholding the rules.

Stroke A colloquial expression popular in Ireland and used in racing company to describe a 'job' or betting coup.

Tatts' Race-goers shorthand for Tattersalls, the Tattersalls Enclosure, the location of the main betting ring at a racetrack and a less expensive, if also less well-appointed, viewing area than

Members'. Tattersalls Committee is the body that regulates all horse-race betting disputes.

Tax The Betting Tax, which is currently only payable on off-course bets. The tax is presently at a level of 10 per cent although only 8 per cent of that sum is collected by the Government (see **Levy**).

Tissue A betting forecast, compiled by a form expert, and used by the bookmakers as the basis of their 'first show'.

Tote A pool-betting system operated at horse and greyhound tracks. In Tote betting all the money staked enters a pool and, after permitted deductions for the operators' overheads and profit, the remainder is shared out equitably among the holders of winning tickets. French and American betting pools are known as *parimutuels* (see **PMU**). The Horserace Totalisator Board, or Tote Board, is a public body responsible for managing this system and generating money for horse-racing.

Touch Another colloquial word for a coup or a stroke.

Traps The numbered boxes, listed on the racecard, from which the runner start in a greyhound race.

Under orders Under Starters Orders. The warning that the start of a race is imminent.

Yankee A multiple bet covering four selections in different races and consisting of six doubles, four trebles and one four-timer, making eleven bets at eleven times the stake money in all. A £1 Yankee costs £11 to place.

Index

281